Hidden History of the Kovno Ghetto

Hidden History
of the Kovno Ghetto

United States Holocaust Memorial Museum

A Project of the United States Holocaust Memorial Council, Washington, D.C.

A Bulfinch Press Book

Little, Brown and Company

Boston • New York • Toronto • London

Published on the occasion of the exhibition *Hidden History of the Kovno Ghetto,*
held at the United States Holocaust Memorial Museum, Washington, D.C.,
November 21, 1997–October 3, 1999.

The exhibition and this publication were made possible with the generous support
of Lorraine and Jack N. Friedman.

First Edition
Library of Congress Catalog Card Number 97-73686
ISBN 0-8212-2457-3 (hardcover edition)
ISBN 0-8212-2530-8 (Museum paperback edition)

Bulfinch Press is an imprint and trademark of Little, Brown and Company (Inc.)
Published simultaneously in Canada by Little, Brown & Company (Canada) Limited

Project Director: Stephen Goodell

General Editor: Dennis B. Klein

Assistant Editor: Edward Phillips

Editorial and Research Assistance: Elizabeth Kessin Berman, Linda Bixby, Andrew Campana,
Judith Cohen, Tina Lunson, Jürgen Matthäus, Loreta Mizariene (Lithuania), Paul Rose,
Beth Rubin, Nava Schreiber (Israel)

Design: Marc Zaref Design, Inc., Norwalk, CT

Object Photography: Edward Owen, Bruce Katz (USA), Yair Peleg (Israel), Arunas Baltenas,
Kestutis Stoškus (Lithuania)

Printing: Herlin Press, West Haven, CT

PRINTED IN THE UNITED STATES OF AMERICA

Cover and frontispiece: Jacob Lifschitz (1903–45), untitled scene of the Kovno Ghetto in the
evening, 1943 (watercolor, $8^{1}/_{8}$ x $12^{1}/_{4}$ in.). From the collection of Pepa Sharon, Israel.

CONTENTS

ACKNOWLEDGMENTS

Miles Lerman, Chairperson, and Ruth B. Mandel, Vice-Chairperson
United States Holocaust Memorial Council

An exhibition and publication of this magnitude depend upon the assistance of many dedicated people working in several languages and countries over a span of several years. These projects were inspired by the abundance and richness of ghetto artifacts and documentation gathered together by Avraham Tory, author of a ghetto diary of major historical significance. The Museum owes an enormous debt of gratitude to Dr. Joel Elkes, son of the prominent physician Elkhanan Elkes, chairman of the Kovno Ghetto Jewish Council, and Dr. Jack Brauns, son of the late Moses Brauns, director of the ghetto's Sanitation Service. Their generous assistance enabled Avraham Tory and his wife, Pnina, also a ghetto survivor, to visit the Museum in 1991. That visit provided the impetus to mount a comprehensive exhibition on the Kovno Ghetto.

The Museum expresses its warmest thanks to all individuals and institutions whose assistance made these projects possible. The Museum regrets in advance any inadvertent oversights or omissions, and wishes to call particular attention to the assistance received from survivors of the Kovno Ghetto, listed below in italics.

Austria—Dokumentationsarchiv des österreichischen Widerstandes, Vienna: Elisabeth Klamper

Belarus—National Archive of the Republic of Belarus, Minsk: Vyacheslav D. Selemenov

Canada—*Sara Ginaite; Michael Wosczyna; Helen Yermus* Christopher A. Amerasinghe, Department of Justice, Toronto; Sol Littman, Simon Wiesenthal Center, Toronto; Anthony Von Mandel, Vancouver

Czech Republic—Jan Parik; Arno Parnik, Jewish Museum in Prague

France—Eve Line Blum, Gerard Sylvain

Germany—Wolfgang Klaue; Maria Keipert, German Foreign Office, Bonn; Ernst Klee; Cilly Kugleman, Jüdisches Museum, Frankfurt am Main

Bilderdienst Süddeutscher Verlag, Munich; Bundesarchiv; Ullstein Bilderdienst, Berlin; Zentrale Stelle der Landesjustizverwaltungen, Ludwigsburg: Willi Dressen, director

Israel—*Moisej Aronson; Ahron Barak; Shmuel & Rivka Ben Menachem; Zeev & Trudi Birger; Shalom Eilati; Shmuel Elhanan; Alex Faitelson; Solly Ganor; Yitzhak Gibraltar; Haim Gurwich; Danny Hanoch; Uri Hanoch; Chiyena Jacobsen; Grigorius Kanovich; Israel Kaplan; Sara Koper; Rivka Discant Krakanowski; Hanni Krispin; Dov Levin; Azriel Levy; Esther Lurie; Avraham Melamed; Joseph Melamed; Sarah Miloh; Pola & Moses Musel; Moshe Prusak; Shulamith Rabinowitz*; Carmela Rosen; Dvora Rosenholz; Tamara Lazerson Rostovsky; Judith Segal; Arieh Segalson; Shlomo & Mina Shafir; Pepa Sharon; Raya Shoshan; Dita Sperling; Avraham & Pnina Tory; Masha Vinik; Shraga Weiner; Meir Yelin; Eliezer Zilber*

Sara Benjamin; Ruth Ben David; Zussia Efron; Estelle Finkel, Sir Isaac Wolfson Museum, Jerusalem; Rabbi Ahron Graz; Bill Gross; Mordecai Paldiel, Yad Vashem, Jerusalem; Yair Peleg; Dina Porat, Tel Aviv University; Shalom Sabar, Hebrew University of Jerusalem; Moshe Sicron; Sora Rivka Zoltan

Association of Lithuanian Jews in Israel, Tel Aviv: *Rachel Levin;* Beth Hatefutsoth, Tel Aviv: Ruth Porter; Central Archives for the History of Jewish People, Jerusalem; Central Zionist Archives, Jerusalem; Dimona Public Library, Dimona; Ein Herod Art Museum, Ein Herod; Ghetto Fighters' House, Kibbutz Lohamei Haghetaot: Yossi Shavit, director of archives; Jabotinsky Institute, Tel Aviv; Jewish National and University Library, Jerusalem; Lavon Institute for Labor Archives, Tel Aviv; Massuah, The New Holocaust Educational Museum, Tel Yitzhak; Moreshet Archives, Givat Haviva; Yad Vashem, Jerusalem: Jacob Lozovick, director, Yehudit Klineman, Yehudit Inbar, and Bella Shomer-Zaichik

Japan—Hiroki Sugihara; Yukiko Sugihara

Latvia—Latvian State Historical Archives, Riga: Nikolajs Rizovs, director

Lithuania—*Gita Bargman; Shulamis Lermanaite-Gelperniene; Dimitrijus Gelpernas; Feiga Fridman Guterman; Jocheved Inčiuniene; Simon Kaplansky; David Leibzon; Jakov Lopianskis; Judelis Ronderis; Gregoris Smoliakis; Geršon Šusteris; Irena Veisaite; Miriam Shafir Zaborskiene; Paulina Zingeriene*

Arunas Baltenas; Chaim Bargman; Arunas Beksta, Pr. Gudynas Restoration Centre, Lithuanian Art Museum, Vilnius; Saulius Beržinis; Evgeny Ceitlin; Simonas Davidavičius, Kaunas Jewish Community; Asia Guterman, Kaunas Jewish Community; Rimkus Juozas, Kaunas Archives; Alginiantas Liekis, Lithuanian Genocide & Resistance Research Institute, Vilnius; Vytautas Skuodas, Lithuanian Genocide & Resistance Research Center, Vilnius; Antanas Lukšena; Kestutis Stoškus; The Honorable James Swihart, U.S. Ambassador to Lithuania; Yosef Tatz, Kaunas Jewish Community; His Excellency Dainius Trinkunas, Minister of Culture, Vilnius; Markas Zingeris

M. K. Čiurlionis National Museum of Art, Kaunas: Osvaldas Daugelis, director; Jewish State Museum of Lithuania, Vilnius: Emanuelis Zingeris, director, and Rachel Kostanian; Kaunas 9th Fort Museum: Zita Nekrošyte, former director, and Julija Menciuniene, director; Lithuanian Archives Department, Vilnius: Gediminas Ilgunas, former director, and Viktoras Domarkas, chief archivist; Lithuanian Central State Archives, Vilnius: Alfonsas Piliponis, director, and Stase Marcinkoniene, former deputy director; Lithuanian Museum of Genocide Victims, Vilnius; Lithuanian National Museum, Vilnius: Birute Kulnyte, director; Lithuanian Photographic and Video Archives, Vilnius; National Library of Lithuania, Vilnius: Vladas Bulavas, director, Ona Taluntyte, deputy director, and *Esfira Bramson-Alperniene*

Poland—Janina Grabowska-Chalka, Stutthof Museum Archives, Sztutowo; Jerzy Tomaszewski

    Main Commission for the Investigation of Nazi Crimes in Poland, Warsaw

Russia—Vladimir Malyshev, Russian State Film Foundation, Moscow; Mansur Mukhamedzhanov, Center for the Preservation of Historical Documentary Collections, Moscow

    Novosti Press, Moscow

United Kingdom—*Waldemar Ginsberg*

    John Delaney, Imperial War Museum, London; Sir Martin Gilbert, Merton College, Oxford University; Robin O'Neil

United States—*Assistance to Lithuanian Jews: Josef Griliches, Sonja Karpus; Marsha Wolpe Baras; George Birman; Jack Brauns; Enrique Hershel Don; Sy Frumpkin; Renee Gadiel; Harry Gordon; Anna Gure; Jay Ipson; Ralph Jaffe; Jewish Lithuanian Organization of Los Angeles; George Kadish*; Margaret Kagan; Esther Mishelski Kagen; Freda Karpul; Henry Kellen; Boris Kot*; Moshe Krakinowski; David Levine; Henia Lewin; Nathan Lewin; Abe Malnik; Judith Meisel; Leo Melamed; Pola Mishell; Esther Rubin Mishkin; Rabbi Ephraim Oshry; Theodore Pais; Goldie Rassen; Mira Reibstein; Abe Resnick; Abe Rodstein; Abe Roth; Sidney Schachow; Ivar Segalowitz; Alex Shtromas; Gita Taitz; Ben Woods*; Berl Zisman*

    Ilya Bereznikas; Shulamith Berger; Judith Birger; Peter Black, U.S. Department of Justice; Susan Braunstein, The Jewish Museum, New York; Rabbi Paul Caplan; Irene Burnham Chambers, Library of Congress; Nathan F. Cogan, Portland State University; Corrine Collett; Aaron Dabbah; His Excellency Alfonsas Eidintas, Lithuanian Ambassador to the U.S.; Yaffa Eliach, Brooklyn College; Joel Elkes; Nina Ellis; David Engel, New York University; Eugene W. Feldman; Shelly Fletcher, National Gallery of Art, Washington; Henry Friedlander, Brooklyn College; Karen Friedman; Seymour Fromer, Judah Magnes Museum, Berkeley; Aaron Goldberg; Randi Goldman; Grace Cohen Grossman, Skirball Cultural Center, Los Angeles; Michael Grunberger, Library of Congress; Noah Hartman; Sylvia Herskowitz, Yeshiva University Museum, New York; Aviva Kempner; Rabbi Abe Klausner; Adaire J. Klein, Simon Wiesenthal Center, Los Angeles; Linda Kohn; Moshe Kolodny, Agudas Israel of America, New York; Ramunas Kondratas, National Museum of American History, Washington; Danas Lapkus, Balzekas Museum of Lithuanian Culture, Chicago; Judy Lucas; Vivian Mann, The Jewish Museum, New York; Peter Martz; Jack Michaelson; Alfred Moldovan; Harold Oshry; Peggy Pearlstein, Library of Congress; Morris Rosen; Rodney A. Ross; Eric Saul; Romas Sakadolskis, Voice of America, Washington; Stephen Schrier; Rabbi Jerry Schwartzbard, Jewish Theological Seminary of America, New York; Henrietta Shapiro; Myra Sklarew; Marlene Stern; Jonathan Sunshine, Yiddish of Greater Washington; Max Titchen; Robert Waite, U.S. Department of Justice; Robert Wolf, National Archives, Washington; Dennis Zembala, Baltimore Museum of Industry; Jan Zwartendyk

    AP/Wide World Photos; Buffalo and Erie County Public Library; Library of Congress; National Archives, Washington; Mordecai M. Kaplan Library, Reconstructionist Rabbinical College, Wyncote, Pa.; George A. Smathers Libraries, University of Florida, Gainesville; St. Petersburg [Florida] Times; University of Massachusetts, Amherst; YIVO Institute for Jewish Research, New York

Historical and Exhibition Advisers

Solon Beinfeld, Washington University in St. Louis; Michael Berenbaum, Survivors of the Shoah Visual History Foundation; Arunas Bubnys, KGB Archives, Vilnius; Zvi Gitelman, University of Michigan; Gershon Greenberg, American University; Alice Greenwald; Raul Hilberg, University of Vermont; Barbara Kirshenblatt-Gimblett, New York University; David Kranzler; Dov Levin, Hebrew University of Jerusalem; Hillel Levine, Boston University; Michael McQueen, U.S. Department of Justice; Sybil Milton; Susan Morgenstein; Samuel Norich; Yulyan Rafes; Jeshajahu Weinberg, Israel

Translators

Solon Beinfeld; Linda Bixby; Judith Cohen; Moshe Dor; Andrew Eitavicius; Mendy Fliegler; Lillian Israeli; Alfred Katz; Ida Leivick; Gerald Liebenau; Tina Lunson; Mark Mazerovski, Cybertrans, Washington; Thomas Michalskis, Embassy of Lithuania, Washington; *Fira Paulauskas;* Phyllis Rhode; Ruth Salton; Aliza Schneck; Yiddish of Greater Washington; Bernie Wassertzug; Martha Wexler

* Deceased

FOREWORD

Walter Reich, Director
United States Holocaust Memorial Museum

For some who haven't learned much about it, the Holocaust may seem like a statistical black hole. In this simplistic image, the Germans started the Second World War in 1939, were defeated in 1945, and during that time six million Jews disappeared, as if drawn, instantaneously and silently, into a cosmic void.

Six million Jews did indeed disappear in those years. But they weren't just drawn into a void, and they didn't go silently. They were systematically murdered by the Germans. And, in the weeks, months, or years between the time they were rounded up and the time they were killed, they lived remarkable lives that illuminate the possibilities and extremities of human endurance.

The simplistic image of the Holocaust as a black hole into which Jews simply disappeared ignores, first of all, the infinite variety and protracted agony of Holocaust suffering. It ignores the reality of watching your parents shot; your children ripped away to be machine-gunned in a ditch; your brothers, sisters, aunts, uncles, cousins, and friends "deported" to killing centers. It ignores the loss of your dignity, decency, home, possessions, sustenance, strength, self-respect. It ignores the pain of hanging on to life as you witness these mounting losses, and as you wait, every day, for your own death. It ignores, in short, the pummeling reality of *Holocaust time*.

This image ignores, too, manifestations of life that seem, under those circumstances, utterly incomprehensible: creativity, spirituality, endurance, defiance, resistance, and even, sometimes, hope.

It also ignores the psychological manipulations used by the perpetrators designed to make the Holocaust run smoothly. In the ghettos, where the Jews were stored and forced to work until they could be killed, the Germans took advantage of the profoundly human inclination on the part of the victims to want to believe that the terror would surely end, that no power could be so cruel forever, that no human beings could possibly want to murder an entire people. Understanding that inclination, and wanting those Jews to continue working, the Germans would promise that there would be no more "actions" of mass murder. They recognized that providing even the flimsiest pretext for hope could make it easier for them to control a desperate population.

And this limited image of the Holocaust ignores the determination by many of the victims, even though they knew they would almost surely be killed, to record their experiences. They wanted others to know that they and their fellow Jews had once lived, that they were killed, who killed them, how they were killed, and how they resisted, against all odds, and in every possible way, their almost inevitable deaths.

This book, based on an exhibit at the United States Holocaust Memorial Museum, "Hidden History of the Kovno Ghetto," is an antidote to that simple image. The story it tells illuminates a significant dimension of the Holocaust experience. It records the details of Holocaust time. The Kovno Ghetto was a place in which Jews were confined, fed starvation rations, and forced to do slave labor until they would be killed. It was a place in which, from time to time, hundreds or thousands of Jews were rounded up for execution by the Germans and their Lithuanian collaborators. It was a place in which impossible choices were foisted on a leadership that sought to protect a community from what turned out to be a lethal fate. It was a place that became, ultimately, a concentration camp. It was a place in which Jews did all they could to endure, sustain their dignity despite inhuman assaults, hold on to their traditions, defy their oppressors through creativity and community, and resist them by finding ways, in the face of impossible realities, to physically fight the Germans.

This book can document that story because, at the risk of immediate death, the Jews of the Kovno Ghetto systematically recorded their experiences. They did so in writing, photographs, artistic images, music, memoirs, statistical graphs, and religious treatises. They recorded German orders; the murderous actions of both the Germans and their Lithuanian collaborators; the community's inexorable destruction; the day-to-dayness of the terror; and the vicissitudes of despair, hope, defiance, and resistance. They hid these records and, after the Holocaust, a few of the survivors retrieved them and made them known. In this book, these once-hidden materials tell the story of this remarkable community's life. But they also illustrate the experience of the Holocaust itself, as well as the possibilities in the world for evil, good, death, life, tragedy, nobility, and, even in desperate circumstances, resistance.

Two centuries before the Kovno Ghetto was created and destroyed, the Ba'al Shem Tov, the founder of Hasidism, wrote that "Forgetfulness leads to exile, while remembrance is the secret of redemption." This book displays the triumph of remembrance over forgetfulness, and the triumph by the ghetto to record its history over the efforts by the Germans to keep that history unknown. In this triumph it is the murderers who are documented in infamy, and it is the victims of the Kovno Ghetto who achieve the immortality of abiding memory. May their memory be a blessing for us all.

INTRODUCTION

Elizabeth Kessin Berman, Guest Curator
United States Holocaust Memorial Museum

Only days after the German *Wehrmacht*'s invasion of the Soviet Union on June 22, 1941, Lithuania was transformed into a vast open-air theater for experimental mass-murder. It was to become the first laboratory toward implementing a Nazi master plan for the annihilation of the Jews of Europe. According to the so-called Stahlecker and Jäger reports, two of the most compelling German administrative records to survive the Holocaust, by February 1942, German-organized mobile killing units in conjunction with Lithuanian collaborators had killed 136,421 Jews in Lithuania. The majority of those left alive survived in the major ghettos at Vilna, Shavli, and Kovno, where they existed purely as a slave labor pool. Clearly a major tactical achievement for the Germans, the murders were given high regard in reports illustrated with elaborate charts and graphics.

These early reports, submitted by the prosecution at war crimes trials after the war, provided the key evidence of Nazi Germany's clear intention to destroy Jewish life and culture in Lithuania.[1] Uncensored reports from the field were almost never prepared with as much detail as the war progressed. In October 1943, in a speech to his subordinates, SS chief Heinrich Himmler minimized the role of record-keeping: "This is an unwritten and never-to-be-written page of glory in our history."[2]

These reports were not, however, the only secret record of crimes committed in Lithuania to have survived. From within the confines of the Kovno Ghetto, the inmates prepared their own record of this assault. An extraordinary cache of documentary evidence was collected. This accounting, compiled by the victims in their own way and each according to their own talents, was done at great risk: the Germans had decreed that collecting evidence of the crime was forbidden. Nonetheless, the vast and disparate materials compiled by ghetto inmates in Kovno stand in clear defiance of this order. These records, brought together for the first time for a special exhibition at the United States Holocaust Memorial Museum, offer a view of a community's collective and individual struggles to assemble evidence of the crimes committed against them.

Although Kovno Ghetto survivors lived in hope that the documents they prepared would be viewed by the world at large, the hidden history of the Kovno Ghetto has been seen only in fragments. Immediately after the war, an exhibition of George Kadish's ghetto photographs was arranged in the displaced persons camp of Landsberg, Germany, in August 1945. The prolific ghetto artist Esther Lurie held an exhibition of her drawings for the Jewish Soldiers' Home in Rome in May 1945, only a few months after her liberation from the Leibisch labor camp, a subcamp of Stutthof. Avraham Tory's diary of daily events in the ghetto has been presented in recent decades at the deportation trials of Germans and Lithuanian collaborators brought by the governments of Germany, Canada, and the United States. Only with the opening of archives

in Lithuania, Russia, and other former Soviet republics has the full story of the Kovno Ghetto been revealed. Thousands of documents, virtually inaccessible in the West for decades, shed light on the fact that the entire community—young and aged, official and unofficial—gathered evidence, each from their own perspective.

From the moment the Germans issued decrees establishing the Kovno Ghetto, Dr. Elkhanan Elkes, the chairman of the Jewish council, the *Ältestenrat*, charged Kovno's Jews to take up the task of writing their own history. Within the enclosed ghetto, this challenge was met with a multiplicity of responses: clandestine photography, artists' illustrations, miniaturized albums containing charts and graphs, protocol books, meeting minutes, and official and personal diaries. Even *responsa,* the traditional rabbinical form of answering queries based on centuries of rabbinical codes, were carefully saved as a record of transgressions against Jewish law and traditions. The ghetto's chief scholar, the linguist and educator Chaim Nachman Shapiro, spearheaded the writing of internal histories to capture every detail of survival and resistance. During three years of imprisonment, a stream of documentation was amassed, including a detailed history of Kovno's Jewish Ghetto Police and shorter treatises detailing the implications of German orders for nearly every one of the ghetto's administrative departments. Poets and historians of the ghetto were also commissioned for this documentary endeavor. Although their material culture, institutions, and synagogues had been plundered, Kovno's Jews set out to write a new chapter of their communal history.

Elkes, in his call for record-keeping, was not necessarily acting outside of a historical context. Jewish communities across Europe wrote communal histories. The most intensive historical and ethnographic studies were carried out at the Yiddish Scientific Institute (YIVO), founded in Vilna in 1925.[3] That archival projects continued in the ghettos of Warsaw, Lodz, Vilna, and Bialystok testifies to the importance with which they were regarded. In Kovno, however, one may discern that this communal undertaking provided hope and courage to survive the day-to-day oppression witnessed within the ghetto.

The summation of the ghetto's history came to be written down in three miniature and metaphorical chronicles—the compilation of decrees "And These Are the Laws—German Style," a small notebook resembling a stenographer's legal pad; the yearbook "Slobodka Ghetto 1942," similar to a child's scrapbook; and a small, paper memorial plaque "Numbers That Demand an Accounting!" All three were hidden in crates buried beneath the floors of ghetto structures. The compilation holds decrees and orders issued to the Jewish community from August 1941 to March 1943. The yearbook, conceived as an almanac, contains a description of events in the ghetto for the year 1942 and references to the anniversaries of atrocities committed the previous year. Like the illustrated Stahlecker reports, it is accompanied by maps documenting the reductions of size in the ghetto and full descriptions of the German operations. In addition, the appurtenances of the ghetto—armbands, work cards, official seals—show the facade Jews were forced to create in the ghetto. The third chronicle, the paper memorial plaque, is perhaps the most startling of the three. Resembling traditional Jewish stone memorials to honor the deceased, instead of names to be memorialized, its doors open to reveal the fate of Kovno's Jewish population with embellished graphs and charts. Using demographics compiled in the ghetto's Statistics Office, the plaque presents a stark record of the Germans' attempt to annihilate the Jews of Kovno.

The compilation of decrees is prefaced with a quotation from SA-Captain Fritz Jordan, the chief German administrator for Jewish affairs in Kovno, from August 7, 1941: "You will not expect that one communicates with you in writing." In fact, apart from the Stahlecker reports and the reports of the mobile killing units, the *Einsatzgruppen,* there is barely a trace written by the perpetrators and local collaborators that documents the monitoring of the ghetto and its exploitive goals. Almost every individual order was passed orally through the office of the *Ältestenrat*'s secretary, Avraham Tory, whose office kept copies of all communiqués, orders, and transcriptions of meetings; these provided the materials for the compilation and the yearbook. By candlelight in the evenings, with the help of Pnina Sheinzon, Tory also kept an extensive personal diary of the ordeals inside the Kovno Ghetto and news of Jews outside the ghetto: the deportations and killings of thousands of Central European Jews at Fort IX, Kovno's main killing site, and the slaughter of thousands of Jews from Vilna at Ponar. Tory also preserved careful descriptions of face-to-face dealing with German authorities. Many of his lengthiest entries are devoted to Elkes's reported encounters with German ghetto officials.

The ghetto's written record was also supported by an intensive effort to assemble a corresponding visual record. Under the direction of Peter "Fritz" Gadiel, a German-born Jew and graphic artist trained at the Bauhaus, the ghetto's graphics office, the Paint and Sign Workshop, produced thousands of certificates, passes, and forms. Templates for these forms, as well as unused examples—thousands of pieces of paper—were deposited in one of the ghetto's secret archives as part of the determination to record and preserve. In addition to the graphic record, Esther Lurie and several other artists were enlisted, in Tory's words, to "immortalize—each according to his ability and technique—every aspect of ghetto reality."[4] Their sketches provide simple records of the buildings, the gates, the people who inhabited this compressed world. George Kadish, an engineer whose work assignment in the city was as a repairer of x-ray equipment, launched his own campaign of documentation. His homemade cameras and his access to film and developing equipment enabled him to take nearly one thousand photographs from within and without the boundaries of the ghetto.

In fall 1943, as Soviet armies advanced to the borders of Lithuania, the Germans attempted to erase the physical evidence of their crimes against humanity, beginning with burning the most startling evidence—the tens of thousands of corpses of Jews from Kovno and Central Europe in mass graves at Fort IX. Jews in the ghetto continued to document their history, although with far more brevity. Elkes wrote a simple last letter to his children, safe in England, in which the startling events of the ghetto's years were succinctly recorded. Another such testament, written by ghetto prisoner Shulamith Rabinowitz, simply states: "I perceive our end. . . . It is both good and very hard to die now. It is good to have lived to see that the end is coming, and it is very hard to die just a moment before salvation."[5] Others, including prisoners at the Fort IX execution site, scrawled their testaments on the plaster walls.

For more than three years, the Kovno Ghetto lived in uncertainty, documenting how history had turned on them, their optimistic plans of resistance, and their courageous day-to-day struggle to survive. On July 2, 1944, with the Soviets only miles away, the Germans set fire to the ghetto. Nearly 6,100 men and women were transported to the Dachau and Stutthof concentration camps. In these camps, survivors of the Kovno Ghetto faced further horrors.

With the liquidation of the Kovno Ghetto in July 1944, a large corpus of books, art, and other remnants of Kovno was destroyed. What survived—buried records and the few possessions deported inmates and survivors managed to conceal—give remarkable voice to Kovno's hidden history.

Notes

1. See Ronald Headland, *Messages of Murder. A Study of the Reports of the Einsatzgruppen of the Security Police and the Security Service* (Rutherford, N.J., 1992), 152ff. See also International Military Tribunal, *Trial of the Major War Criminals,* 42 vols. (Nuremberg: International Military Tribunal, 1947–49), vol. 37, doc. L180; and "United States of America v. Otto Ohlendorf et al. (Case 9: 'Einsatzgruppen Case')," *Trials of War Criminals Before the Nuernberg Military Tribunals under Control Council Law No. 10,* 15 vols. (Washington, D.C., [1950]), vol. 4.

2. *Trial of Major War Criminals* 29:145–46 (doc. PS 1919), and excerpted in *Documents on the Holocaust: Selected Sources on the Destruction of the Jews of Germany and Austria, Poland, and the Soviet Union,* ed. Yitzhak Arad, Yisrael Gutman, and Abraham Margaliot (Jerusalem, 1981), 344–45.

3. David E. Fishman, *Embers Plucked from the Fire: The Rescue of Jewish Cultural Treasures in Vilna* (New York, 1996), 1–4 .

4. Avraham Tory, *Surviving the Holocaust: The Kovno Ghetto Diary,* ed. Martin Gilbert (Cambridge, Mass., 1990), 438.

5. Letter from Shulamith Rabinowitz to her children, June 27, 1944, Shmuel Elhanan, Israel.

NOTE TO THE READER

Geographical Terms

In the 1930s, the then-capital of Lithuania bore several names in several languages: "Kovno," the internationally known Russian name, the result of Lithuania's place in the tsars' empire for more than a century before World War I; "Kaunas," the native Lithuanian; "Kovne" in Yiddish and "Kovna" in Hebrew to its large Jewish population; "Kowno," the Polish, rooted to times when the two nations were one; and "Kauen," used by the Germans to the west. The ghetto's survivors call the city Kovno, the usage generally adopted for this book.

The district within Kovno's city limits in which the Kovno Ghetto was located also bore two names: the formal Lithuanian name "Vilijampole," and the traditional Jewish name "Slobodka." Those imprisoned in the ghetto generally used Slobodka; those who created and controlled the ghetto usually referred to the district as Vilijampole. Both terms appear throughout this book.

Other historically common names have now been supplanted by modern Lithuanian: Vilna/Vilnius and Shavli/Šiauliai were also the sites of Jewish ghettos during the Nazi German occupation; the Augustow/Augustavas Forest and the Rudniki/Rudninkai Forest were both places of anti-Nazi partisan activity. Holocaust historiography has generally adopted the more common names, a practice continued here.

Translations

All translations of original manuscripts and documents are new for this volume. Source, language, and translation credit for these are cited in the Notes, beginning on page 238.

Credits

This book presents a wide range of original photographs, documents, and historical objects contemporary to the Kovno Ghetto (1941–44). Photographs taken by George Kadish inside the Kovno Ghetto are identified with his name. The individual or institution from whose collection each artifact comes is credited alongside its appearance in the text; abbreviations used are listed in full below.

Abbreviation

ALJI	Association of the Lithuanian Jews in Israel, Tel Aviv, Israel
Bundesarchiv	Bundesarchiv, Germany
BH	Beth Hatefutsoth, Tel Aviv, Israel
CAHJP	The Central Archives for the History of the Jewish People, Jerusalem, Israel
CPHDC	Center for the Preservation of Historical-Documentary Collections, Moscow, Russia
Ghetto Fighters' House	Ghetto Fighter's House, Kibbutz Lohamei Haghetaot, Oshrat, Israel
GK	George Kadish, Florida
JSM	Jewish State Museum of Lithuania, Vilnius, Lithuania
LCSA	Lithuanian Central State Archives, Vilnius, Lithuania
LVVA	Latvian State Historical Archives (LVVA), Riga, Latvia
LPVA	Lithuanian Photographic and Video Archives, Vilnius, Lithuania
NARA	National Archives and Records Administration, Washington, D.C.
Oshry Collection	Rabbi Ephraim Oshry, formerly Kovno Ghetto, now New York City
Rostovsky Collection	Courtesy of Tamara Lazerson Rostovsky in memory of her family who perished in the Holocaust
Tory Collection	Avraham and Pnina Tory, Israel
USHMM	United States Holocaust Memorial Museum, Washington, D.C.
Yad Vashem	Yad Vashem, Jerusalem, Israel
YIVO	YIVO Institute for Jewish Research, New York
ZSL	Zentrale Stelle des Landesjustizverwaltungen, Ludwigsburg, Germany

Part I

Kovno and the Holocaust

"Operation Barbarossa," the German invasion of the Soviet Union

Jürgen Matthäus

The German army's massive attack on the Soviet Union on June 22, 1941, led to the political subjugation, the economic exploitation, and by 1944 the physical destruction of vast occupied territories. Although ultimately unsuccessful, the assault nevertheless brought about the death of between 20 and 26 million Soviet citizens. Among the dead were nearly 2.9 million Jews who, from the first days of the campaign, fell victim to German as well as non-German killers. The Soviet republic of Lithuania, occupied by the German *Wehrmacht* (Armed Forces) within days after the attack and under German control for about three years, lost approximately 95 percent of its Jewish population. Out of a total of 235,000 Jews in Soviet Lithuania, only a few thousand survived the war.

Though the magnitude of the destruction is common knowledge, historians are only now beginning to develop a deeper understanding of the dynamic process that led to the annihilation of Jewish life and culture. The breakthrough in historical research occurred with the end of the Cold War. Until then, information about German-occupied Lithuania was limited to documentary fragments that somehow survived the perpetrators' campaign to destroy evidence and were made available by Soviet authorities, as well as to occasional reports by a small number of witnesses who were willing or able to testify. With the opening of archives in Eastern Europe and the uncovering of documentation, it has become possible to investigate the destruction process as it had taken place on the regional and local level. As a result, historians are realizing that the Holocaust—defined as the organized mass murder of the Jewish population—first took place in Lithuania.

For the Germans to commit mass murder as part of their fight against the Soviet Union, they needed orders from superiors as well as compliance from subordinates who would not question the legitimacy of anti-Jewish slogans and measures. Prior to the war, the Nazi policy of marginalizing Jews in order to make their life in Germany intolerable had met no active opposition from the general public. Moral indifference to anti-Jewish measures formed an ideal background for rabid Jew-haters and zealous bureaucrats to push ahead. Following the attack on Poland in September 1939, and in line with ambitious plans for the Germanization of the occupied Polish territory with its large Jewish minority, more radical measures, including large scale though still selective executions, were applied. Solving the "Jewish question" prior to the attack on the Soviet Union meant getting rid of the unwanted element by shipping it off beyond the German sphere of interest. In the meantime, the Germans made preparations to separate the Jews from the Gentiles.

During the early weeks of German rule over Poland, high-ranking bureaucrats, especially in Heinrich Himmler's SS apparatus, issued regulations regarding the marking and ghettoization of Polish Jews

LPVA

German troops en route to Kovno.
June 1941

and the creation of Jewish councils (*Judenräte* or *Ältestenräte*) for the ghettos.[1] The concept of a Jewish council commended itself to German administrators who were used to hierarchical systems, as reflected in the *"Führer*-principle": authority from the top down, responsibility from the bottom up. First, a council provided a clear-cut channel of communication; second, practical problems were left to the *Judenrat* whereas the Germans were interested only in results; and third, the ghetto inmates would view a Jewish council as responsible for measures that increased misery and despair within the community. The intricate bureaucratic apparatus established by the Jewish councils to provide important communal services and meet German demands for "useful workers" would create the illusion that the councils acted independently or were only loosely connected with the German terror apparatus.[2]

While plans were discussed in Berlin about how to proceed in regard to the "Jewish question," a macabre competition ensued among German officials within occupied Poland to be the first to report that the centuries-old links between Gentiles and Jews had been cut in their district. In Wloclawek [in German: Leslau] during the first days of occupation, Jewish men were dragged from their homes where they had been praying; five or six were shot in the streets. A day later the SS burned down the two synagogues and several private homes. The newly appointed Jewish Council faced the task of paying a ransom while male Jews were taken for forced labor, often beaten up, and in some cases killed. Requiring Jews to wear a yellow star of David was introduced by Wloclawek's German mayor, SA-Colonel Hans Cramer, in October 1939—earlier than in the General Government (November 1939) or in the Reich proper (September 1941).[3] Cramer acted on the basis of experiences acquired during his previous service as mayor of the German city of Dachau, where prisoners of the local concentration camp wore similar badges. In July 1941, Cramer was transferred to the Lithuanian city of Kovno, where, as *Stadtkommissar* (city commissioner), he became a key figure in deciding the fate of the city's Jews.

Given the precedents of anti-Jewish measures implemented in Poland since fall 1939, it was predictable that, following the attack on the Soviet Union, the Germans would act just as harshly in Lithuania by establishing ghettos, appointing Jewish councils, and cutting the lifelines that had connected Jews with their Gentile surroundings. It was not, however, predictable that large-scale mass murder would accompany or even precede ghettoization. Two major factors contributed to the dramatic radicalization of German anti-Jewish policy during summer 1941. First, the attack on the Soviet Union (code-named "Operation Barbarossa") had no precedents in history. It was a war aimed not only at crushing the Red Army but also at establishing a thoroughly Germanized eastern Europe to the Ural Mountains. Already during the planning stages of the attack, German military authorities discarded internationally accepted rules of warfare. Violent actions against civilians, especially Nazi Germany's arch-enemies, Communists and Jews, went hand in hand with fighting the Red Army. From 1933 on (with the exception of the two-year interval created in 1939 by the Molotov-Ribbentrop Pact), Nazi propaganda claimed that Communists and Jews were identical. The caricature of the hook-nosed, curly-haired

string-puller behind the red banner had been a familiar figure on posters and in Nazi journals. In the context of ideological warfare, the encounter in the Soviet Union with Communists and Jews meant their elimination.

Second, the so-called *Einsatzgruppen*, highly mobile task forces attached to major German army units, played a much more destructive role than they did in Poland. The *Einsatzgruppen*, deployed right behind the frontline, were special units of the German Security Police (which comprised the Gestapo) and the Security Service (*Sicherheitsdienst*—SD), an intelligence service drawn from the Nazi Party. They received their orders from Reinhard Heydrich, chief of the Reich Security Main Office (the *Reichssicherheitshauptamt*—RSHA), and his superior, Heinrich Himmler, chief of the SS.

Of the four units in the Soviet theater, the one that mattered for Lithuanian Jews was *Einsatzgruppe A*. Led by SS-Brigadier General Walther Stahlecker, it followed Army Group North into the Baltic States and parts of Belorussia. Its total strength was 990 personnel, including 172 drivers, 340 members of the *Waffen-SS* (the military arm of the SS, which also had a share in the killing of great numbers of civilians), 133 Order policemen, and 13 female employees. Local recruits improved the numerical imbalance between perpetrators and victims.[4]

The Nazi regime in Germany produced antisemitic posters in several languages for distribution to many European countries. This poster for Lithuania reads *(top)* "The Jew—Your Eternal Enemy" and *(bottom)* "Stalin and the Jews—One Evil Gang!"

Movement of *Einsatzgruppe A* into the Soviet Union

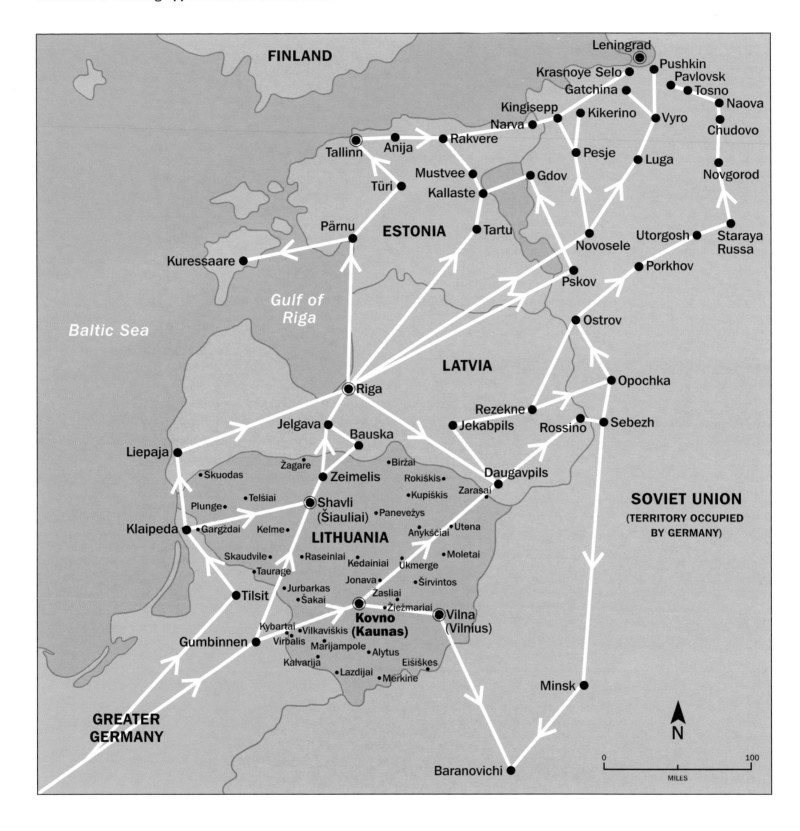

Kadish/BH

For reasons of higher mobility and effectiveness, the *Einsatzgruppen* were subdivided into operational segments—the *Sonder-* or *Einsatzkommandos* (SK, EK)—each of them between 100 and 170 men strong. In Lithuania, most of the killings were performed by *Einsatzkommando 3* headed by SS-Colonel Karl Jäger. Stahlecker and Jäger were the main perpetrators in the murder of Lithuanian Jews; they also took pride in documenting their crimes in order to impress their superiors. In addition to Stahlecker's comprehensive reports dated October 16, 1941, and again in early 1942, Jäger reported at least four times between September 1941 and February 1942 on the killings in Lithuania. More than any other contemporary documentation, these reports give a unique account of the deadly activities of *Einsatzkommando 3* and its auxiliaries in Lithuania.[5]

Before the attack on the Soviet Union, no German master plan existed for killing the Jews in the occupied area, a void that not only created extraordinary uncertainty for Lithuanian Jews (who became hostages of war on June 22, 1941), but also gave the perpetrators wide scope for local initiative. It was during the first days after the beginning of "Operation Barbarossa" that Germans in the area prepared for the physical annihilation of Lithuanian Jews. The initial killings in Lithuania took place on June 24, 25, and 27 in the western towns of Gargždai [in German: Garsden], Kretinga [Krottingen] and Palanga [Polangen]. In three "actions"—organized operations against a Jewish population—Gestapo and policemen from the nearby German city of Tilsit murdered 526 persons, mostly Jews (including two women). In a contemporary report from Tilsit, it was stressed that local German officers took the initiative for these killings. During postwar trials in West Germany, however, Gestapo officers claimed that they had acted on written orders from Berlin, opened on the first day of the German attack on the Soviet Union, to shoot Jews across the German-Lithuanian border. They also insisted that Stahlecker, the commander of *Einsatzgruppe A*, had briefed them on their mission. In point of fact, Stahlecker, Heydrich, and Himmler agreed to these first killings only after they had occurred.[6]

The specific setting of Lithuania was of crucial importance for the destruction process to take shape. The hasty retreat of the Red Army removed the symbols and strongholds of Soviet power and restored Lithuanian national aspirations for the first time since Stalin annexed the formerly independent Baltic States to his empire in summer 1940. While the initial impulse for murderous violence came from the Germans, Lithuanian nationalists simultaneously took advantage of the politically as well as emotionally charged atmosphere to settle their own scores. Lithuanian soldiers changed sides, preferring to fight their former Soviet comrades instead of Hitler's *Wehrmacht*. In Kovno and numerous smaller places, the anti-Soviet activism by parts of the population erupted in violent riots against local Jewish men even before the Germans had moved in. Lithuanian activists, supported by Germany since the Soviet takeover, felt that there was hardly a better way of placing Lithuania on the map of Nazi-dominated Europe than to demonstrate zeal and determination in settling the domestic "Jewish question."

The Jews were trapped. Overrun by the German military machine, they found themselves victimized by the occupiers as well as by their former neighbors. When the German Army conquered Kovno on June 24, 1941, several thousand Jews were already reported dead. During the next four days, Lithuanian "partisans" killed another eight hundred.[7] While the *Wehrmacht* took a benevolent attitude, *Einsatzgruppe A* was eager to foster these "self-cleansing actions and to direct them into the right channels in order to achieve the aim of this cleansing as rapidly as possible."[8]

These local actions were in line with general orders from Berlin, but quickly, before the situation got out of hand, Berlin established law and order. On June 28, the army commander in Kovno abolished the Lithuanian partisans. Self-appointed Lithuanian agencies like the Provisional Government were allowed to exist only until August 1941.[9] Simultaneously, the first five companies of German-supervised Lithuanian auxiliary police came into existence, one of which was exclusively used to guard and carry out executions at the

"Jewish concentration camp" (*Judenkonzentrationslager*) at Fort VII, one of the fortifications built during tsarist times around Kovno.[10] These units formed the core group from which was to emerge the so-called *Schutzmannschaft*—a police force of local collaborators that came to be a crucial factor in implementing the goals of ideological warfare not only in Lithuania but in all the occupied Soviet Union.

During the first days of July, 1,500 Jews were held at Fort VII and 1,869 in a prison in the center of Kovno. More people were arrested after Forts IV and IX became prisons and execution sites. Separation being the precondition for efficient mass killing, most of the Jews kept in the forts and the central prison were executed shortly after their arrest. The routine pattern of mass murder remained in place as it would throughout the occupation regardless of administrative changes in late July 1941 from military to civil authority. (The Germans began to establish a civil administration for the Baltic States and part of Belorussia, the *Reichskommissariat Ostland,* under Hinrich Lohse, with Stahlecker's *Einsatzgruppe A* as the *Ostland*'s

office of the Commanding Officer of the Security Police and the SD [*Befehlshaber der Sicherheitspolizei und des SD*—BdS] and Jäger's *Einsatzkommando 3* as Lithuania's office of the Commander of the Security Police and the SD [*Kommandeur der Sicherheitspolizei und des SD*—KdS].) Once the officers of *Einsatzgruppe A* were initiated to mass murder, and all the necessary logistics were in place, the killing of men and, after August 1941, women and children became, in Jäger's words, primarily "an organizational question."

Mass graves had to be dug, the Jews rounded up, and the pressing transportation question solved. In Rokiškis, about 110 miles northeast of Kovno, 60 of the 80 available Lithuanian collaborators were busy with bringing 3,208 persons to a pit located about three miles away from the collecting point within 24 hours. Those who tried to escape were killed on the spot; the others were lined up and shot point-blank in the backs of their heads so that they would fall into the pit. The next victims arranged the corpses to fit as many as possible into the mass grave. Compared with the problems faced

Lithuanians welcome German troops on the streets of Kovno

German soldiers and Lithuanian civilians observe the spectacle of Lithuanian nationalists bludgeoning Jews to death at the Lietukis Garage in Kovno. June 26, 1941

The following map labels appear within the image:

HELSINKI · ST. PETERSBURG · KRASNOJE SELO · PUSCHKIN · SLUZK · URITZKI · KRASNOGWARDEISK · KIKERINO · MESHNO · TOSSNO · TSCHUDOWO · NARWA · REVAL · ANZJA · ISENBERG · 963 · MUSTWIE · DAGO · E.WORMS · L.WORMS · TURGEL · JUDENFREI · ODOW · PESJE · LURA · NOWGOROD · ÖSEL · ARENSBURG · LAISTE · DORPAT · NOWOSELJE · 3600 · UTOROSCH · STARAJA RUSSA · PERNAU · OPLESKAU · PORCHOW · OSTROW · GHETTO 2500 · RIGA · MITAU · 35.238 · ROSSITTEN · ROSENOW · SERESCH · LIBAU · BAUSK · TAKOBSTADT · ZEIMEHAI · ITSCHKA · MOSKAU · MEMEL · SCHAULEN · GHETTO 4500 · DILLUST · DINABURG · GHETTO 950 · 136.421 · TILSIT · KAUEN · GHETTO 15.000 · WILNA · GUMBINNEN · 41.828 · ORTELSBURG · MINSK · GESCHÄTZTE ZAHL DER NOCH VORHANDENEN JUDEN 128.000 · BARANOWITSCHE · WARSCHAU

LVVA

by Jäger's *Einsatzkommando* in "cleansing" the countryside of Jewish inhabitants, the urban setting provided circumstances more conducive to mass executions. Jäger described the killings in and around Kovno as a *"Paradeschiessen,"* a shooting exercise reminiscent of a military parade.[11]

The prime target group of these "actions" was Jews. However, the Germans also killed Communists, the mentally insane, Russians, Gypsies, and Poles. From fall 1941 on, after the Germans established the Kovno Ghetto, Fort IX served as the main execution site for ghetto prisoners as well as for Jews deported from the Reich or other countries. Jäger's grisly statistics report 76,355 persons executed by mid-September 1941, 137,346 by early December, and 138,272 by February 1942. Of this number, 136,421 were Jews.[12] In early December 1941 Jäger wrote Berlin that "the aim to solve the Jewish problem for Lithuania" had been achieved.

Local exigencies and immediate German interests pointed toward keeping at least some Jews alive for the time being. In early July 1941, after *Einsatzgruppe A* reported (prematurely) to Berlin that further mass shootings were no longer possible, German authorities charged a "Jewish committee" with the responsibility of preparing the transfer of Kovno's Jews to Vilijampole, a district across the river. On July 10, Kovno's mayor, Kazys Palčiauskas, and its military commander, Jurgis Bobelis, both Lithuanians, ordered the Jewish popula-

tion irrespective of age and sex to wear a yellow star of David. They also ordered the relocation of the more than 29,000 Kovno Jews be completed by August 15. In his "public announcement no. 2," dated July 31, 1941, SA-Colonel Cramer, who had taken over the office of *Stadtkommissar* a couple of days before, basically repeated what had been ordered already by the mayor.[13] Ghettoization would only be a slight detour, not a major deviation, from the path of mass murder. Eventually, at any time convenient, Jews in the Kovno Ghetto —as well as Jews concentrated in Lithuania's two other largest ghettos, Shavli [Šiauliai] and Vilna [Vilnius]—would be destroyed.[14]

In the meantime, employers like the *Wehrmacht* or private companies involved in business enterprises in Lithuania could turn to the ghetto for a constant supply of workers. Other available sources of forced labor were rapidly declining: by February 1942, two million of the more than 3.3 million Soviet prisoners of war taken by the Germans had already died as a result of malnutrition, exhaustion, or outright murder.[15] Considering the prevailing racist image of "the Jews" as lazy, cunning, and unfit for physical work, it is somewhat surprising that the Germans regarded them as better laborers and artisans than Lithuanians.

In addition to the need for workers, there were other reasons for keeping Jews alive. The urban ghettos already in existence or about to be formed whetted the appetite of many an administrator not only in regard to potential exploits for the Reich but also for himself. While the "actions" offered large-scale though short-lived opportunities for looting, the ghetto served as a cornucopia for all those who were looking for furs, gold, furniture, carpets, clothing, and other valuables. In July 1944, just before the ghetto's liquidation, *Stadtkommissar* Cramer retreated from Kovno with a whole railroad car filled with valuables. His subordinates, especially those involved in "Jewish affairs," had reason to hope that, in addition to staying away from the frontline, they could at least send some boxes of expensive items back to Germany.[16]

Before taking over affairs from the military in late July 1941, civil administration officials in Lithuania had received from authorities in Berlin—Alfred Rosenberg's Reich Ministry for the Eastern Occupied Territories—deliberately vague guidelines. In regard to the Jewish question, they called for "partial preliminary measures" (*vorbereitende Teilmaßnahmen*) in anticipation of a Europe-wide solution after the war.[17] In early August 1941 *Reichskommissar* Lohse provided clarification with his "preliminary guidelines for the treatment of the Jews." This remarkable document combined a compilation of anti-Jewish measures enacted in Germany since 1935 with more rigid regulations specifically devised for eastern Europe. Lohse's guidelines for ghettos proposed that food supplies should

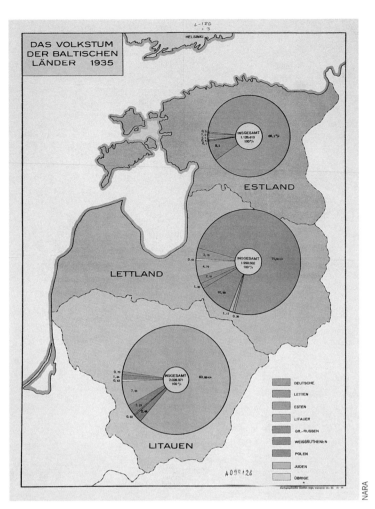

This chart, created to illustrate Stahlecker's summary report to his superiors at the Reich Security Main Office in Berlin, shows the ethnic groups in Estonia, Latvia, and Lithuania as of 1935.

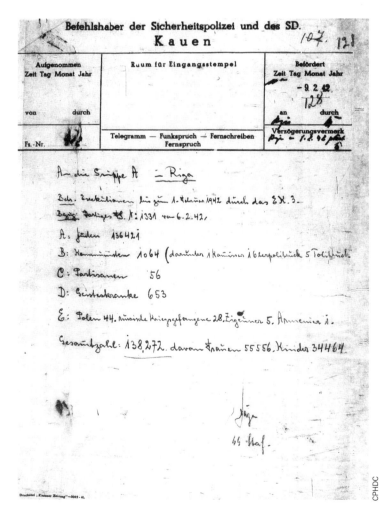

In response to a query regarding the number of people executed in Lithuania, SS-Colonel Karl Jäger, commander of the Security Police and SD for Lithuania, reports that as of February 6, 1942, a total of 138,272 people were killed, among whom were 136,421 Jews.

not exceed the level necessary for keeping the inmates alive, that internal matters—including the establishment of Jewish councils and a Jewish police armed with truncheons—were to be handled by the Jews themselves, that the ghettos had to be hermetically sealed and guarded, and that the Jews had to work either outside or inside the ghetto gates.[18]

It was Stahlecker who complained about Lohse's draft regulations: the guidelines appeared to interfere with the Security Police's ongoing killings. Lohse relented, inserting a clause stating that he merely wanted to make sure the new civil administration would adopt "minimal measures," and that he would not interfere with "further measures, especially by the Security Police."[19] He sent these revised guidelines on August 18, 1941, to the various regional commissioners in the *Reichskommissariat*, with the caveat that they be transmitted orally, not in writing, to the ghettos' Jewish councils. Reassured, Stahlecker wrote to his officers in late August that the Security Police would continue solving the Jewish question "by very different measures from the ones envisaged by the *Reichskommissar* [Lohse]."[20]

For the German authorities in Lithuania, the process of relocating Jews was only a preliminary step. Their task was to weed out those who seemed dangerous, replaceable, or unable to work. The ensuing "selection" of the ghetto population, proceeding in stages, marked a further radicalization of a process that had begun with the killing of Jewish men in the German-Lithuanian border region in late June 1941 and that encompassed, from August on, the killing of Jewish women and children. In deciding who was to live for the time being and who was to die at once, the Germans acted in a manner similar to establishing ghettos, neither exclusively on the basis of economic considerations nor purely along preconceived lines. The early history of the Kovno Ghetto is a case in point.

First, the ghetto community, even before it had a chance to solidify itself, was robbed of its intellectual elite when on August 18, three days after the closure of the ghetto, 711 Jews fell victim to the "Intellectuals Action." The timing of the next step seems to have been more difficult to decide upon: on September 17, two days after the office of the Stadtkommissar had issued 5,000 work certificates ("Jordan-Scheine") to the Jewish Council, the Ältestenrat, all inhabitants of the so-called Small Ghetto were ordered to assemble, presumably for the purpose of undergoing a "selection"; shortly afterwards, however, the order was canceled. The Germans struck again on September 26, killing 1,608 Jews, among them 615 women and 581 children, at Fort IV. On October 4, together with the burning of the hospital for contagious diseases, the Small Ghetto was finally liquidated; 1,845 Jews, among them 818 children, were led away to Fort IX, where they were shot one day later. At the end of the month, the Germans targeted what they regarded as "useless eaters" in the "Great Action" of October 28–29, 1941, which reduced the ghetto population by nearly 9,200 persons, including more than 4,200 children, in mass shootings at Fort IX. Only about 17,000 people—the "work Jews" and their families—remained in the Kovno Ghetto.[21]

Hitler's decision late that fall to have Jews from the Reich deported to ghettos in the East—the start of transports that continued until late in the war—posed a special problem for local German officers. Lacking clear orders from Berlin (central headquarters appeared little concerned with what was to be done with these transports), German authorities in the Ostland had to make hasty decisions about the arrival of thousands of German Jews. In Riga and Minsk, deported Jews went into the ghettos after room had been made by killing local Jews. In Kovno, members of the Ältestenrat were informed by the Germans about new arrivals but awaited for them in vain; the deportees were sent straight to the mass graves of Fort IX without ever passing through the ghetto gate.

Even if the behavior of a German official or incoming news on the course of the war occasionally gave rise to hope, the members of Kovno's Ältestenrat were aware that the Germans saw the ghetto as a transit station established to exploit a limited number of Jews until the time of their ultimate annihilation. Although sometimes hidden behind the facades of ghetto life, the German threat was omnipresent. Its most obvious signs were economic exploitation by forced labor and the deliberate denial of basic needs—sufficient food, proper clothing, medical care, and a perspective of hope. For the time being, those deemed physically fit were allowed to stay together with their families as this, according to Jäger, promised to have a positive impact on their "joy in work" (Arbeitsfreudigkeit).[22]

In the absence of logic, nobody could anticipate the course of events. Indeed, no objective criteria existed to distinguish a "useful worker" from a "useless eater." Special certificates issued by the Germans, like the Jordan-Scheine, were of vital importance one day and, following a change of whim, altogether useless the next. Being called for a "special assignment" could mean moving into a privileged job or, as in the case of the "Intellectuals Action," out to the killing fields of Fort IX. The Germans made only one message certain: their orders were to be obeyed. The Germans had appointed the Jewish councils to implement these orders. The Ältestenrat in Kovno was flooded with regulations regarding all kinds of issues, from the trivial to the most crucial. By May 1942, the Kovno Ältestenrat had already received more than 2,500 orders, primarily from the offices of the Stadtkommissar and the local commander of the Security Police and the SD.[23] In the end, everyone, not just those persons the Germans deemed to be "superfluous"—the elderly, children, women (especially pregnant women), and hospital inmates—lived constantly on the verge of annihilation. A German order issued on July 24, 1942, made it perfectly clear that the ghetto was to have no future: "Pregnancies and births in the ghetto are prohibited; pregnancies have to be terminated; pregnant women will be shot."[24] For the German keepers of the ghetto, the mere acts of living and giving life represented noncompliance with their orders.

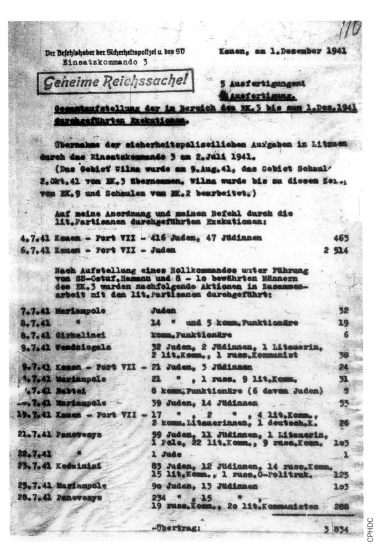

A page from the report compiled by SS-Colonel Karl Jäger in December 1941, listing dates, locations, and gender of persons killed during major "actions" in Kovno

Two Jewish ghetto policemen guard the abandoned belongings of deportees from the Kovno Ghetto to Estonian labor camps. October 1943

The Lithuanian case demonstrates that the dynamics of the process leading up to the "Final Solution" were, during and after the summer of 1941, generated to a large extent within the regional setting. Significantly, politicians and bureaucrats in Berlin never failed to take notice of events in Lohse's sphere of influence, even during a period of relative stabilization. (In Kovno the so-called quiet period lasted from after the "Great Action" [October 1941] to fall 1943.) They evaluated, with consistent interest, the execution statistics compiled by Stahlecker and Jäger. Lessons learned by the Germans in the East provided Berlin with clues for tackling even larger problems. At the Wannsee Conference of late January 1942, convened to coordinate the smooth, Europe-wide implementation of the "Final Solution," Heydrich noted that Estonia was the only area under German rule already "free of Jews." As far as ruthlessness, zeal, and determination were concerned, what Stahlecker's men had done in the Baltic States was clearly regarded as exemplary.

The liquidation of the ghettos in the *Ostland,* like preceding events, was a result of regional developments in conjunction with interference from Berlin. Over time it became obvious that German control in the occupied territory, and even in the ghettos, was anything but total. After mid-1942 the anti-Nazi partisan movement gained strength. In the remaining ghettos, clandestine groups were formed that looked for ways out of the impasse, either by organizing resistance cells or by preparing escape routes. Despite the great risks involved, Jews fled the ghetto and joined those already in hiding in the forests. Existing partisan groups did not always accept Jews as members, especially when there were a large number of women and children among them. As reflected in reports by Jäger's successor as commander of the Security Police and the SD in Lithuania, it remained a central task of the German Security Police and its accomplices to track down and kill Jews hiding in the forests. The Jews were perceived as the driving force behind the partisans—or, in Himmler's terminology, behind the "bandits."[25] If the struggle for survival in the ghettos had little to do with logic, their final destruction did: it was seen by the Germans as an integral element of anti-partisan warfare as well as of the aim to leave no trace of Jewish existence. This applied even retrogressively. From late 1942 on, as part of a coordinated effort to destroy the evidence of their crimes, the Germans started to dig up mass graves and to burn corpses all over Lithuania.

In June 1943 Himmler ordered "that all Jews still remaining in ghettos in the *Ostland* area be collected in concentration camps"; those "not required" were "to be evacuated to the East," i.e., killed.[26] Partly due to the civil administration's unwillingness to lose its most important source of income, implementation of the order was delayed beyond the August 1 deadline. On September 15, authority over "Jewish matters" in Kovno began to shift to the SS. Subsequently, the conditions of life for Jews deteriorated from bad to worse. The deportation of about 2,800 Kovno Jews to labor camps in Estonia and the killing, in late March 1944, of 1,300 persons during the so-called "Children's Action" foreboded the end.[27]

With Soviet troops approaching the city, the remaining Jews in the Baltic States were deported in early July 1944 to concentration camps in the Reich—men to Dachau, women to Stutthof. There and during the ensuing death marches, more were to die. Only a few evaded being deported and managed to survive the destruction of the former ghettos. Of the approximately 50,000 Jewish prisoners of the concentration camps in the *Reichskommissariat Ostland,* only 2,500 lived to see the end of the war. When the Red Army liberated Kovno on August 1, 1944, the Germans involved in "Jewish affairs" in the city had long gone, taking with them not only the spoils of their work, but also their knowledge of how they had implemented the "Final Solution" in Lithuania.

Jürgen Matthäus is a historian at the United States Holocaust Memorial Museum and author of numerous articles on German anti-Jewish policy and the Holocaust in eastern Europe.

Notes

1. See instructions by Reinhard Heydrich, Chief of the Reich Security Main Office, on policy and operations concerning the Jews in occupied Poland, September 21, 1939, reprinted in Yitzhak Arad, Yisrael Gutman, and Abraham Margaliot, eds., *Documents on the Holocaust: Selected Sources on the Destruction of the Jews of Germany and Austria, Poland, and the Soviet Union* (Jerusalem, 1981), 173–78.

2. See Raul Hilberg, "The Ghetto As a Form of Government," *Annals of the American Academy of Political and Social Science* 450 (July 1980): 98–112.

3. See Arad, Gutman, and Margaliot, *Documents on the Holocaust,* 185–87.

4. Report by Stahlecker on the activities of *Einsatzgruppe A* before October 15, 1941, Center for the Preservation of Historical-Documentary Collections (CPHDC, formerly *Osobyi arkhiv*), Moscow, *fond* 500, *opis* 4, file 93 (copy at U.S. Holocaust Memorial Museum Archives [USHMMA], RG 11.001M.01, *Reichssicherheitshauptamt* [RSHA]–SD, Berlin [*Osobyi fond* no. 500] [mss.], reel 14) (hereafter cited as Stahlecker report, October 15, 1941). Similar figures are given in Stahlecker's second report covering the period from October 16, 1941, to January 31, 1942: CPHDC, *fond* 500, *opis* 4, file 91 (copy at USHMMA, RG 11.001M.01, reel 14).

5. "Gesamtaufstellung der im Bereiche des EK 3 bis jetzt durchgeführten Exekutionen" [Complete list of executions carried out in the *Einsatzkommando 3* zone to the present], September 10, 1941, Central State Archive, Riga, *fond* 1026, *opis* 1, file 3, (copy at USHMMA, RG 18-002M, Selected records from the Latvian Central State Historical Archive–Riga, 1941–1945 [microform] mss., reel 16); "Gesamtaufstellung der im Bereich des EK 3 bis zum 1. Dezember 1941 durchgeführten Exekutionen" [Complete list of executions carried out in the *Einsatzkommando 3* zone up to 1 December 1941], December 1, 1941, CPHDC, *fond* 500, *opis* 1, file 25 (copy at USHMMA, RG 11.001M, Selected records from the "Osobyi" Archive [Moscow], reel 1); "Exekutionen bis zum 1. Februar 1942 durch das EK 3" [Executions up to 1 February 1942 by *Einsatzkommando 3*], February 9, 1942, CPHDC, *fond* 500, *opis* 1, file 25, fol. 128 (copy at USHMMA, RG 11.001M, reel 1); fragmentary report by *Einsatzkommando 3* on Jews in Lithuania, n.d. [February 1942], Central State Archive, Riga, *fond* 1026, *opis* 1, file 3 (copy at USHMMA, RG 18.002M, reel 16) (hereafter cited as *Einsatzkommando 3* report, February 1942).

6. *Stapostelle* Tilsit to RSHA IV, July 1, 1941, CPHDC, *fond* 500, *opis* 1, file 758, fols. 2–5 (copy at USHMMA, RG 11.001M.01, reel 10).

7. "Ereignismeldung UdSSR, Nr. 8" [Operational situational report USSR, no. 8], June 30, 1941, Nuremberg document NO-4543, in *The Einsatzgruppen Reports: Selections from the Dispatches of the Nazi Death Squads' Campaign Against the Jews in Occupied Territories of the Soviet Union July 1941–January 1943,* ed. Yitzhak Arad, Shmuel Karkowski, and Shmuel Spector (New York, 1989), 1; "Gesamtaufstellung," September 10, 1941.

8. Stahlecker report, October 15, 1941.

9. See Yitzhak Arad, *Ghetto in Flames: The Struggle and Destruction of the Jews in Vilna in the Holocaust* (New York, 1982), 37–38.

10. "Ereignismeldung UdSSR, Nr. 14," July 6, 1941, Nuremberg document NO-2944, in *Einsatzgruppen Reports,* ed. Arad, Karkowski, and Spector, 10–12.

11. "Gesamtaufstellung," December 1, 1941, fol. 116.

12. Ibid.; "Exekutionen," February 9, 1942; *Einsatzkommando 3* report, February 1942. In his first report, Stahlecker claimed that 71,105 Jews had been killed in Lithuania by October 15, 1941, some 3,800 of those during the pogroms.

13. For the events surrounding the ghettoization order, see "Ereignismeldung UdSSR, Nr. 19," July 11, 1941, Nuremberg document NO-2934, in *Einsatzgruppen Reports,* ed. Arad, Karkowski, and Spector, 16–19; Stahlecker report, October 15, 1941; Avraham Tory, *Surviving the Holocaust: The Kovno Ghetto Diary,* ed. Martin Gilbert (Cambridge, Mass., 1990), 9f.

14. Smaller ghettos had also been established in Swieciany and a number of other towns in Lithuania. Most of them had been liquidated by the end of 1941. See Dina Porat, "The Holocaust in Lithuania: Some Unique Aspects," in *The Final Solution: Origins and Implementation,* ed. David Cessarani (London, 1994), 159–74.

15. See Christian Streit, *Keine Kameraden: Die Wehrmacht und die sowjetischen Kriegsgefangenen, 1941–45* [No comrades: the German armed forces and the Soviet prisoners of war, 1941–45] (Stuttgart, 1978), 9–10.

16. Statement by Gustav Hörmann at Historical Commission Landsberg, September 2, 1946, Sammlung Versch. Heft 5, Zentrale Stelle der Landesjustizverwaltungen, Ludwigsburg.

17. "Die Zivilverwaltung in den besetzten Ostgebieten" [The civil administration in the the occupied eastern territories] (the so-called Brown folder), part I: Reichskommissariat Ostland, n.d. [summer 1941], Bundesarchiv Potsdam, R43II/685a, p. 35.

18. *Reichskommissar Ostland,* August 2, 1941, Central State Archive, Riga, *fond* 1026, *opis* 1, file 3, fol. 283ff. (copy at USHMMA, RG 18-002M, reel 16).

19. *Reichskommissar Ostland* to *Generalkommissare,* August 18, 1941, ibid., fol. 241–46; draft of letter by Stahlecker to Lohse, August 6, 1941, ibid., fol. 234–36, 296–98.

20. Stahlecker to *Einsatzkommandos,* August 29, 1941, ibid., fol. 303.

21. "Gesamtaufstellung," December 1, 1941, fol. 111–17. Numerical information in German contemporary documents often represents estimates or shows a tendency toward being inflated in order to impress superiors in Berlin. Here, for example, *Einsatzkommando 3* reports 711 intellectuals killed in the "Intellectuals Action"; sources from within the ghetto record 534 victims. Such discrepancies do not invalidate the usefulness of the German sources for the task of reconstructing the scope of mass murder.

22. *Einsatzkommando 3* report, February 1942, fol. 269.

23. See the compilation of German orders, Yad Vashem Archives, Jerusalem, file 048 B12/4.

24. Ibid. This order is paraphrased in Tory, *Surviving the Holocaust,* 114.

25. See Konrad Kwiet, "'Juden und Banditen': SS-Ereignismeldungen aus Litauen 1943/1944" ["Jews and bandits": SS operational situation reports from Lithuania, 1943–44] in *Jahrbuch für Antisemitismusforschung* [Yearbook for the study of antisemitism] 2 (1993): 405–20.

26. Order by Himmler, June 21, 1943, in Arad, Gutman, and Margaliot, *Documents on the Holocaust,* 456–57.

27. See Arad, *Ghetto in Flames,* 436–37.

Solon Beinfeld

View of old town Kovno photographed from the Aleksotas district across the Nemunas River

When Soviet forces entered Kovno on August 1, 1944, ending three years of German rule in the city, they found a scene of horror and desolation in the ruins of what had been the Kovno Ghetto. Not a structure remained standing; everywhere, in the streets and in depressions in the ground, there lay charred corpses. The bodies were those of Jews who had tried to evade the final deportation from the ghetto two weeks earlier, expecting that the Red Army would arrive in a few days. But the Germans, using fire and explosives, had destroyed the physical ghetto and nearly all of its last hidden inhabitants. In so doing, they put an end to the history of the distinguished Jewish community that had flourished for generations on this site.

In one sense, however, the Germans had miscalculated. For the Jews of the Kovno Ghetto had made sure, by every form of documentation, that their history and the memory of Jewish Kovno would not be lost. It is from this defiant record that we draw our narrative.

From the time Jews first settled in Kovno in the fifteenth century until well into the eighteenth century, efforts to create an organized Jewish community were repeatedly interrupted by expulsions. Nevertheless, Jewish life and religion settled across the Vilija (Neris) River in a district called Slobodka. After Lithuania became part of the

Russian Empire following the partitions of Poland in 1793 and 1795, residency restrictions imposed until 1861 made Slobodka virtually a Jewish ghetto.

Kovno's Jewish population began to grow rapidly in the last decades of the nineteenth century. By 1897 the Jews constituted 36 percent of the local population of some 70,000, more than Russians and Poles, and much more than Lithuanians who numbered just 6.8 percent of the total. During this period Kovno, which by then included Slobodka, emerged as a center of eastern European Jewish life. Its rabbi, Isaac Elhanan Spektor, was perhaps the greatest Jewish religious scholar of his day. The Slobodka yeshiva served as a center of the *Musar* movement, which emphasized ethics and individual morality in the study of Torah. Kovno was the home of the first modern Hebrew novelist, Abraham Mapu (1808–68) whose *Ahavat Tzion* (Love of Zion), an extremely popular biblical romance, inspired countless Jewish youth with enthusiasm for the ancient homeland.[1]

Despite its rising importance even before World War I, it was only in the interwar years 1919–39 that Kovno became the real center of Lithuanian Jewry and its traditions. This was the result of the bitterly disputed Vilna [Vilnius] question: Polish annexation of

A first-grade class of Jewish children wearing crowns marked with letters from the Hebrew alphabet

parts of Lithuania in 1920 not only cut off Vilna, the "Jerusalem of Lithuania," from its Lithuanian political and cultural hinterland, but the ensuing break in Polish-Lithuanian diplomatic relations separated Lithuanian Jewry from the much larger Jewish community of Poland. The near-total lack of contact between the two countries meant that the Jews of independent Lithuania were thrown back on their own resources. Kovno, the largest community, became their "capital," as it was of Lithuania as a whole.

The Jews of Kovno showed great resourcefulness during the chaotic years after World War I. Tens of thousands of Jews had been expelled from Kovno and adjacent provinces by the Russian authorities during the war—on the grounds that they were pro-German!— and many more had fled the war zone. With peace and repatriation, as one community activist later recalled, "a world of problems had to be solved. The wounds of the expulsion had to be healed somehow. [Aid] societies sprang up like mushrooms after rain," establishing, among other services, "medical facilities that could have been the health department of a large country."[2] One hopeful sign was that at the outset of this period, it appeared that Lithuania would set an example for the other new states of eastern Europe in its toleration and respect for its minority population. In the days of tsarist rule, the Lithuanians were reputed to have good relations with their Jewish neighbors, sharing with them a sense of oppression under Russian

rule. Lithuanian Jews were strong supporters of Lithuanian independence, and when it was achieved Lithuania went further than other states in the region in granting Jewish autonomy, as manifested by the establishment of a Ministry of Jewish Affairs and a Jewish National Council. Yiddish and Hebrew were recognized as the official languages of the Jewish community.

Branch office of the Jewish bank in prewar Kovno, with signs in both Yiddish and Lithuanian

But this era of good feelings did not last long. With the Vilna region incorporated into Poland in 1922, Lithuania became a relatively homogeneous society. There was no more need to present the country as heterogeneous. Jewish support, once crucial to the Lithuanian case for retaining Vilna, was now superfluous. By 1924, both the Ministry for Jewish Affairs and the Jewish National Council were abolished.[3] In 1926, the democratic government in the country was overthrown and replaced by the much more authoritarian and nationalistic regime of Antanas Smetona.

This new phase coincided with the rise of a Lithuanian urban middle class that saw the Jews as competitors. Its members supported the Smetona government's "quietly" antisemitic policy of ousting Jews from the economic positions they had held as artisans, merchants, and the like. To be sure, the Smetona regime did not tolerate overt acts of antisemitic violence, for fear of foreign reaction. But by the late 1920s, and especially during the 1930s with the rise of antisemitic influences from neighboring Germany, the Jewish situation in Lithuania had seriously deteriorated. Only the Jewish educational system remained autonomous, an important exception. Economically, the loss of opportunity and of access to higher education meant a Jewish youth without a future. Only emigration, despite restrictions in many countries (notably the United States), remained an option. Thousands left for South Africa, South America, and above all Palestine, to the extent that the British would allow it.

Despite the bleak outlook for Lithuanian Jewry in those years, the cultural vitality of Lithuania's Jews was not diminished. Though they numbered no more than about 160,000, what they lacked

Members of the popular Zionist youth group *Hapoel*, gathering for a rally. 1935

Boys at prayer at the Rabbi Spektor Children's House. 1927

in quantity they made up in quality. The historic traditions of the *Litvak* world were maintained, a culture that was both firmly rooted in religious Orthodoxy (Hasidism was largely absent) and open to modernizing tendencies. But this modernism was itself strongly Jewish—Zionist, Yiddishist, and so forth. No major European Jewish community seemed so immune to assimilation. Yiddish was the first language of virtually all Lithuanian Jews, and Hebrew was widely used. The Jewish educational network, in which the vast majority of the community's children were enrolled, encompassed numerous Hebrew-language Zionist schools, alongside more traditional religious schools (including world-famous yeshivas) and Yiddish-language schools run by leftist groups.[4]

In the center of this intense Jewish life stood Kovno, where despite the rapid growth of the Lithuanian population, Jews still made up nearly a third of the city's population. The community supported three Yiddish daily newspapers, numerous other periodicals, and both a Yiddish and a Hebrew theater. There were Jewish sport clubs, youth organizations, charities, and political and professional associations of every sort. The Kovno Central Jewish Cooperative Bank was at the heart of a network of Jewish People's Banks and cooperatives throughout Lithuania. A Polish Jewish visitor, seeing Kovno for the first time, was astounded at the ease and naturalness with which Kovno Jews lived their lives entirely within their own culture and language: young and old, doctors and lawyers, lovers and schoolchildren, all speaking Yiddish. "Walking the Kovno streets," he later wrote, "you had the impression . . . that it was a completely Jewish city. Perhaps it really was—in every respect—the most Jewish city in the world."[5]

The equilibrium of Jewish Kovno and Jewish Lithuania was abruptly shaken by the outbreak of World War II. The course of the war in this corner of eastern Europe was at first very different from events in neighboring lands. Lithuania remained neutral when Nazi Germany and later Soviet Russia attacked Poland, and when Great Britain and France declared war on Germany. Neutrality brought a measure of prosperity. More surprisingly, the Soviets, who had taken Vilna from the Poles in September 1939, unexpectedly turned it over to Lithuania the following month; the long-deferred Lithuanian dream of regaining their historical capital was realized. Nevertheless, this precarious position between Soviet and German expansion was deeply disturbing. For Jews especially, the new situation was fraught with danger. Millions of their Polish brethren had fallen into the hands of the Germans, who wasted no time in displaying an unprecedented brutality towards them. The situation in the Soviet-occupied areas of Poland appeared almost as dire, with arrests and purges of "enemies" of the new regime. The Lithuanian Jews, spared for the moment, had to assume a special role as the only "free" community in eastern Europe. The annexation of Vilna and its region had added some 100,000 Jews to the population, 75,000 of them in Vilna alone. In addition to the native Vilna Jews, this included a considerable refugee population of Polish Jews, fleeing both the Nazi and the Soviet zones, who needed assistance in the necessities of life and in obtaining papers to travel onward to other destinations. Among these refugees were leading personalities of Polish Jewry—rabbis, writers, scholars, party activists of every sort, and whole groups of Zionist youth who had been preparing for emigration to Palestine. Caring for this large population (they numbered some

Members of the Kovno literary community

YIVO

"Pogroms against Jews throughout Germany"—headline of the November 11, 1938, edition of
Folksblat, one of Kovno's Yiddish daily newspapers

14,000 to 15,000 people in 1940) was no easy matter. But once again Lithuanian Jews organized themselves for relief of the victims of war. One refugee recalls with what energy the "Jews of Kovno scrambled to assist the tens of thousands of refugees" and sent representatives of the major Jewish aid organizations to Vilna at the very moment the city came under Lithuanian rule in 1939.[6]

Against this background of desperate refugees from both Hitler and Stalin, unable to find a way out of eastern Europe, two foreign diplomats stationed in Kovno stand out as examples of humanity in a dark time. The Dutch consul, Jan Zwartendijk, was willing to stamp passports with the official-looking statement that no entry visas were necessary to travel to the Dutch overseas possessions of Curaçao and Surinam. On the basis of these "non-visas," the Japanese consul, Chiune Sugihara, issued over a thousand transit visas that enabled people to go to Japan and beyond via the Trans-Siberian Railway. Difficulties with the Soviets, whose influence in Lithuania was considerable, were smoothed over in part through the intervention of Dr. Elkhanan Elkes, a Kovno physician with many contacts in the diplomatic community.[7]

The increase in the Russian presence in Lithuania, both military and diplomatic, was in conformity with the secret amendment to the Molotov-Ribbentrop Pact, which in September 1939 had transferred Lithuania from the German to the Soviet "sphere of influence." It was also a prelude to the complete Soviet takeover of Lithuania (and the other Baltic States) that took place between June and August 1940, in several stages, beginning with the march of Soviet troops into Vilna, Kovno, and other Lithuanian towns on June 15, 1940. Two days later, a pro-Soviet government was installed and elections called for July 14. These rigged elections, in which virtually 100 percent of the electorate was reported to have voted for government candidates, produced a legislature that a week later unanimously proclaimed Lithuania a Soviet republic and demanded annexation to the USSR. This demand was "granted" by Moscow on August 6, 1940, completing the process of the destruction of

Lithuanian independence and the transformation of the country into an integral part of the Soviet Union.[8]

The brutal and cynical annexation of the country, accompanied by arrests, confiscations, and the disappearance of free institutions, was a tragedy for all elements of Lithuanian society. The Jewish population suffered no less than any other group. The elaborate structure of Jewish communal organizations was demolished virtually overnight, and Jewish property and economic activity were particularly severely affected by Soviet nationalization measures. Nevertheless, the Soviet takeover was viewed somewhat differently by Jews and non-Jews in Lithuania, and this difference was to have fateful consequences in the near future. For Jews, Soviet rule, however distasteful, was preferable to the only apparent alternative—Nazi rule. With the Soviets in control, the danger that tiny Lithuania would be taken over by neighboring Nazi Germany seemed to have been averted. This argument carried no weight with most Lithuanians, for whom the Soviet annexation was an affront to their national sentiment. Some extreme nationalists began to look to Germany as a potential liberator and easily fell in with the Nazi doctrine that Bolshevism was a "Jewish" ideology and that the Jews were responsible for the end of Lithuanian sovereignty.

To be sure, there were Jewish Communists, relatively few in number but highly visible, who genuinely and enthusiastically welcomed the new regime. They were far outweighed by those Jews who saw Soviet rule as a tragedy—Zionists and all lovers of Hebrew-language culture, Orthodox Jews, democratic socialists who understood all too well what perils they faced under Stalinism. But in general the Jewish population accepted a Soviet Lithuania as the lesser of two evils. Some Jews even benefited from conditions under the new regime to the extent that a kind of rough equality had been imposed on the population. Higher education was opened to Jewish youth for the first time on an equal basis, and Jewish talents were widely employed in government and party offices in positions that had never been open to Jews before. Jews in positions of power were a novelty in Lithuania; this, too, strengthened the misleading notion that the Jews were devoted to the Communist occupiers and the more fallacious idea that the Communist regime itself was essentially Jewish. Even quite moderate Lithuanians seemed incensed by what they considered Jewish "betrayal" of the country. Extremist nationalists, influenced by Nazi antisemitic propaganda, began to talk openly of a day of reckoning when German bullets would "liberate" Lithuania from the Jewish-Bolshevik yoke.[9] Lithuanian Jews sensed this mood, and even the most anti-Communist among them understood that their fate was bound up with the continuation of Soviet rule.[10]

For the moment, there were worries enough simply trying to survive under Communist rule. The Jewish middle class was hard hit by nationalization—over eighty percent of enterprises confiscated in Lithuania in fall 1940 belonged to Jews.[11] The Jewish press, political parties, schools, and other cultural institutions were all subjected to a process of rigid Sovietization. What emerged bore little resemblance to the vibrant and varied culture of the pre-Soviet period. Jewish religious practice, by definition, was made difficult. In secular affairs, by March 1941 only the Communist *Der Emes* (Truth) of Kovno remained of the Yiddish daily press. Jewish education—devoid of Jewish content—was permitted in Yiddish only; the "reactionary" Hebrew language was banned. In Kovno, where there had been six Jewish high schools before the occupation, there were now just two.[12] Theater enjoyed a relatively privileged position, but the Kovno Jewish Theater existed only from March to June 1941; it was closed by the authorities shortly before the German attack.[13]

Throughout the Soviet interlude, non-Communist Jewish political activists of every stripe, whether Zionist or socialist, whether natives or refugees, were subject to arrest, imprisonment, and deportation. In this respect the Jews, whom the Soviet regime "favored" in the eyes of Lithuanian antisemites, were treated in no way differently from the rest of the population. Among those arrested were Leib Garfunkel, future member of the Kovno Ghetto *Ältestenrat* and postwar historian of the ghetto; and Menachem Begin, the future prime minister of Israel, then a refugee from Poland. The culmination of the persecution came with the wholesale arrests and deportations to camps in the Soviet interior beginning at daybreak on June 14, 1941. These arrests, evidently intended to clear the western border areas of the Soviet Union, including Lithuania, of "unreliable" elements as the likelihood of a war with Nazi Germany became more apparent, created panic in all segments of society. As one young Kovno Jew later recalled, "It was a terrible day. Hundreds of friends of mine were among the deportees, since all of them were either Zionists or from well-to do families. Without wasting much time, our family went into hiding."[14] Whole families were taken away by the thousands, Jews and non-Jewish Lithuanians alike. The numbers deported from Lithuania totaled at least 30,000, perhaps fifteen percent of whom were Jews, a proportion much higher than that of Jews in the population as a whole. Included in the Jewish groups singled out for deportation on the orders of Soviet Lithuania's NKVD (People's Commissariat for Internal Affairs) were Zionists, Bundists (Jewish socialists), and Jewish war veterans, not to mention individuals with capitalist, Trotskyite, or various other suspect backgrounds.[15] Despite the large number

Candidates for the Zionist Socialist Party, headed by Leib Garfunkel, later the deputy chairman of the Kovno Ghetto *Ältestenrat*

of Jews among the victims, Lithuanian antisemites, encouraged by pro-Nazi émigrés in Berlin, spread the story that this was Jewish "revenge" against Lithuania. These allegations were apparently widely believed. Anti-Jewish sentiment grew day by day among the Lithuanian population, while the émigré members of the Lithuanian Activist Front in Berlin, sensing that the long-awaited hour was approaching, urged bloody vengeance against the Jews in the propaganda that they slipped across the border from Germany.

This was the psychological situation in the wake of the mass deportations, when barely a week later, on June 22, 1941, the German armies crossed the Soviet border, and German planes rained bombs from the cloudless summer sky. The Second World War, which had hitherto spared Lithuania from physical destruction, had arrived.

All sources that describe the opening hours and days of the invasion agree that panic spread quickly among the Jewish population as it became immediately evident that the Soviet army would make no effort to defend Kovno. All those with any connection to the collapsing Soviet regime, all those who had experienced Nazi rule in Poland before coming to Lithuania, knew that flight was their only salvation. They and thousands of other Jews clogged the roads and attempted to get on departing vehicles and the last trains leaving the city. But even those who were able to get as far as the pre-1940 Soviet border were in most cases turned back by the Russian military authorities—it was evidently feared there were spies among them. Those who then attempted to return to Kovno had to face the murderous situation that had developed in the countryside in the wake of the Soviet retreat. Jews were already being killed on the roads by Lithuanian "partisans" as a nationalist revolt, long planned in connection with the German invasion, spread across the land.[16] In Kovno itself—to which many Jews had fled from the small towns in the region, hoping to find safety in numbers—the situation was just as bad.

By June 23, the day after the German attack, the last Soviet forces had left the city, but the Germans had not yet arrived. In this temporary power vacuum, an "independent" Lithuania was proclaimed over Kovno radio. Pro-Nazi partisans patrolled the streets of the city, and the terrorization of the defenseless Jewish population began. Armed bands of young men roamed the streets, arresting Jews, breaking into Jewish homes, robbing, beating, humiliating, and taking people to unknown destinations. No help was forthcoming from friendly Lithuanians. As one survivor recalled after the war,

> And let it be stated at this point that, in these first fateful days for the Kovno Jews, when the above-mentioned atrocities were taking place in full view of the public, there was not to be heard—to the shame of the Lithuanian people!—one Lithuanian voice that dared to condemn the horrifying mass violence against the Jews on the part of the Lithuanian Hitlerites.[17]

This refrain was to be heard again, as the Jews viewed with astonishment the hostility, or at best the indifference, of their Lithuanian neighbors. Some Jews even looked forward to the arrival of the Germans, hoping that at least their presence would put an end to the lawlessness and violence. But when the Germans did arrive, on June 24, the violence only increased. In the district of Vilijampole,

known for centuries to Jews as Slobodka, a massive pogrom took place on the night of June 25–26, in which over eight hundred Jews were butchered in the most savage manner. On the next day, in a sadistic spectacle, dozens of Jews were beaten to death in two garages in the center of Kovno while jeering spectators looked on. Meanwhile, thousands of arrested Jews, men and women, were being held at Fort VII, one of the forts built in tsarist times and converted during the interwar period into prisons. The fate of those arrested was for a long time unknown. The women were eventually released, after being viciously abused; the men were shot.

For a time, in early July, the violence appeared to die down. But the Jewish population of Kovno still lived in fear. A survivor describes the emotional state in the brief pause:

> True, there were no more systematic raids on Jewish homes . . . but nevertheless for a Jew—especially a man—to appear on the streets was fraught with peril. Jews in those days were afraid not only of being arrested but of being rounded up for labor by the Germans or the Lithuanian partisans, since at work Jews were brutally beaten and harassed. Jews therefore sat trembling and grief-stricken in hiding and uneasily awaited further developments.[18]

These were not slow in coming.

On July 10, the Jews of Kovno learned of the establishment of a ghetto in Vilijampole-Slobodka, a poor area of mixed Jewish and Lithuanian population, with small wooden houses lacking adequate sanitary facilities, and in any case not nearly large enough to accommodate the whole Jewish population of Kovno. A Jewish Committee,

Elkhanan Elkes, chairman of the *Ältestenrat* in the Kovno Ghetto (*left*), with Moshe Berman, head of the new ghetto hospital

Kadish/BH

with prominent Jewish communal leaders among its members, was constituted to oversee the transfer to the ghetto, to be completed by August 15. The committee tried to persuade the municipal government and the Germans to abandon the Slobodka plan and place the ghetto instead within Kovno itself, where most Jews lived and where most Jewish communal institutions were located.[19] When this met with no response, the committee tried to influence the drawing of the boundaries of the ghetto in Slobodka, since the Lithuanian municipal authorities were constantly pushing for a reduction in its size. The result was a shrunken ghetto in two sections, a "Large Ghetto" and a "Small Ghetto," divided by Paneriu Street, over which a small bridge was eventually constructed.

The relatively long time granted to the Jews of Kovno to move into their ghetto (in nearby Vilna the Jews were given no more than half an hour), failed to provide for an orderly transfer. Instead there was a wild scramble for living space in the designated zone. Wealthy Jews attempted to "buy" desirable quarters from departing Lithuanians. Many poorer people were unable to find any room at all. But by the first week in August, the melancholy procession of carts and wagons carrying the possessions of Jewish households over the Vilija bridge to Slobodka had largely ended.

On August 15, 1941, the ghetto was closed as scheduled, encircling almost 30,000 inhabitants. It was, like all the Nazi imposed ghettos of eastern Europe, "closed" in the literal sense of the word. Unlike the medieval ghettos, the Jews not only had to reside in the reserved area but had to remain there on penalty of death unless, as laborers, they were escorted outside to places of work and back again. Within the ghetto, the Jewish Committee, whose original function had been to attempt some kind of rational planning for the transfer of the Jewish population from the city and to find housing for the thousands that besieged its office, now, by German order, had to transform itself into an *Ältestenrat* (Council of Elders) to run the internal affairs of the ghetto, and to choose a chairman. The Jewish leaders of Kovno met on August 4 and persuaded the extremely reluctant Elkhanan Elkes to accept the unenviable position of chairman. All other community leaders had refused the job; Elkes accepted it only after a moving appeal by Rabbi Yakov Shmukler.[20]

The Jews of Kovno had hoped that in the cramped and primitive Slobodka ghetto they would at least be left alone. Instead, a new series of calamities began. The "Intellectuals Action" of August 18 cost 534 lives—the first of a series of "actions," or anti-Jewish operations, that would punctuate the history of the Kovno Ghetto. A period of "confiscations" followed—wild house-to-house searches and robberies accompanied by violence and murder—until everything of value had been looted from the ghetto.

On September 15 SA-Captain Fritz Jordan, the "expert" on Jewish affairs for the German civil administration (*Stadtkommissariat*), brought to the ghetto 5,000 certificates (*Scheine*) to be distributed to skilled workers who could be employed at German and Lithuanian military and civilian enterprises. To the Jews in the ghetto, the significance of these *Jordan-Scheine* was not entirely clear, but it was understood that it would be desirable to have one. There was chaos at the *Ältestenrat* offices when the council, after some hesitation, decided it had no alternative but to distribute them. The certificates

indeed were honored during some of the ensuing "actions," justifying their popular name of "life certificates." In the brutal "action" against the Small Ghetto on October 4, during which the Small Ghetto was liquidated and the institutions located within it destroyed (the hospital for contagious diseases was set on fire and burned to the ground with its patients and staff locked inside), only the holders of *Jordan-Scheine* were spared. All others were taken to Fort IX and shot. Altogether the Small Ghetto lost about half its population, some 1,800 people.

The culmination of this series of "actions" came with the "Great Action" of October 28, 1941. The *Ältestenrat* was told on October 27 that all Jews were to assemble in Demokratu Square early the next morning, for what Master-Sergeant Helmut Rauca, the Gestapo officer in charge of Jewish affairs, assured the council was to be merely an administrative division of the population into heavy laborers and others. The *Ältestenrat* sensed that something more serious was afoot. Some members urged non-compliance. After a passionate debate, it was decided to seek the advice of Chief Rabbi Avraham Duber Kahana-Shapiro; after long deliberation, the rabbi ruled that the order should be posted. When the notices went up on October 27, there was a frantic rush to obtain, if not the precious *Jordan-Scheine,* then at least some labor document or even armband to show that one was a "useful" worker. But in the macabre mass "selection" that took place on the square that fateful day, little attention was paid to documents. With the exception of the *Ältestenrat*

Jewish merchants at the Kovno marketplace before the war

Jewish forced laborers smuggling food into the ghetto to supplement the starvation rations allocated by the German civil administration

and the Jewish Ghetto Police, all inhabitants had to pass before Rauca (and Jordan himself), who sent them to the right or to the left on the basis of their appearance or some other trivial criterion. Many bonafide laborers ended up on the right or "bad" side. By the end of the long day, some 9,200 people, about 30 percent of the ghetto population, had been taken from the right side of the square to the former Small Ghetto. In the morning they were marched off in a long procession to Fort IX, where their fate was execution by shooting, their bodies thrown into freshly dug pits.[21]

The "Great Action" left the ghetto stunned and despairing. There was not a family that had not lost members. Grief paralyzed the will to go on. Who could now believe that salvation lay in labor for the Germans? Rauca and Jordan tried reassurance: Jordan deposited a 10,000-Reichsmark check to the account of the *Ältestenrat*, to be distributed to the workers at the Aleksotas military airfield. And indeed life had to go on. As winter approached, problems of food and fuel became critical. The meager food rations (one-half of those given to Lithuanians) could not sustain life, even if every rotten vegetable and potato peel were somehow utilized. Only smuggling food into the ghetto through the heavily guarded gate could stave off starvation. Firewood was even harder to smuggle, and as the bitter cold of a northern winter set in, ghetto inhabitants were reduced to demolishing dwellings for fuel. A survivor recalls the frantic search for firewood:

> I decided that I'd rather be shot than freeze to death. . . . A couple of streets over, there was a block of houses with wooden fences between them. . . . It was so cold that I had difficulty breathing, but within half an hour I had removed about twenty planks and dragged them home.[22]

Despite all this, after the "Great Action" a certain period of stability and even of modest improvement in the lives of the inmates began to set in, though hunger, fatigue, and fear continued to stalk the ghetto as before. The period of stabilization, lasting roughly from fall 1941 to fall 1943, was never without its harassing measures. There were further reductions in the size of the ghetto and deportations for labor in Riga. Nevertheless, in comparison with earlier periods of mass killings, this relatively quiet period permitted a certain revival of social life, including political and cultural activity. In this "era," the surviving Jews of Kovno undertook to reconstitute themselves as a community under the most unfavorable conditions imaginable. They had long been familiar with organizing to meet needs in a crisis situation. This crisis surpassed in severity and duration all previous experiences. Nevertheless, the effort was made, and with a degree of success.

Central to this effort, and to the sheer survival of the Kovno Ghetto, were the major institutions of the *Ältestenrat*, which in effect was charged with running the affairs of a small city. This internal administration was obviously a necessity if the ghetto was not to perish of its own accord; nevertheless the ghetto inhabitants were very divided in their opinions of this "ruling body." Some inmates argued that the *Ältestenrat* was essential to provide direct contact with the Germans (bypassing the hostile Lithuanians) in order to moderate their policies, to arrange for the utilization of Jewish labor, and in general to represent the interests of the ghetto and to apportion the burdens of ghetto life as best as possible under the circumstances. Opponents of the *Ältestenrat* argued just as forcefully that it was in essence a tool of the Germans, and that in principle no such institution should have been created. Even in practice, the argument runs, the *Ältestenrat* was far from being an idealistic

In the old city of prewar Kovno, Jewish tradesmen and artisans pose for a photographer.

body; it served in the first instance the interests of its own members, who enjoyed various privileges and exemptions.

Criticism of the *Ältestenrat*, justified or no, did not extend to its chairman, Elkhanan Elkes. This dignified and serious man, whom even the Germans treated with a certain respect, was believed by the majority of the population to be doing all he could for the ghetto. In fact, however, Elkes had little to do with the day-to-day running of ghetto affairs. This he left to his subordinates. His task was to represent the ghetto to the outside world of hostile German and Lithuanian authorities, and this difficult assignment, by all accounts, he carried out well.[23]

The Jewish Ghetto Police was the most important of the *Ältestenrat*'s branches, and also the oldest. Preliminary discussions about the formation of a body to maintain order preceded even the establishment of the ghetto. It was clear from the start that some such force would be needed, and it was rumored that Jewish police were a feature of the ghettos in German-occupied Poland. But it had not been easy to recruit volunteers for so unprecedented an organization, one whose functions and relationship to the German authorities was unclear. A mobilization of army veterans, sportsmen, and other suitable young men had been necessary. An attempt was made to recruit people of all classes and shades of political opinion, and in the early days at least, there was a good deal of idealism and sense of responsibility to the welfare of the community as a whole among the members of the police.[24] Once the ghetto was closed, the police had to deal with immediate problems, in particular the catastrophic housing situation that was causing friction and even serious disturbances among the inmates. Food distribution had also to be overseen by the police, as did fulfillment of the labor service. It became necessary to reorganize the police on a more rational basis. A Central Administration was established to deal with general policy, with the instruction of recruits, and with running the ghetto jails located alongside local precinct offices for each area of the ghetto. The police were made responsible for dispensing justice in criminal cases and even in civil disputes among inmates. The police also had to carry out all sorts of duties required by the Germans, such as escorting labor brigades to and from work, conducting inspections at the ghetto gate, and even at times participating in "actions." It is hardly surprising that the police were unpopular in the ghetto. They did not always refrain from the use of violence in carrying out their orders. Their privileged position, protection from deportation, and the corruption of some policemen were understandably resented. One survivor recalls,

> We didn't want anything to do with members of the police. . . . To meet up with one of them could only mean trouble. We suffered from the blows and kicks of the police and being dragged out of our homes into one working brigade or another, not knowing if we would return. This is why we felt so bitter as we watched the Jewish police living well while we did the back-breaking labor. . . . We saw them working hand in hand with the Germans.[25]

The police were well aware of the attitude of the population, but insisted that without force it would be impossible to maintain order. Despite its unpopularity, the police force was obeyed. Its military qualities could be put to other uses as well. On one notable occasion, in November 1942, the police assembled to swear loyalty to the *Ältestenrat*—itself a significant gesture since in other ghettos the Jewish police often acted independently of "civilian" control and at times, as in Vilna, overthrew it. They marched and sang Jewish national songs from their days in Jewish schools and youth groups, while the audience, tears in its eyes, joined in. As the anonymous authors of the "History of the Vilijampole Jewish Ghetto Police" pointed out, the ceremony might look like "playing at soldiers" under ghetto conditions, but in reality it was intended as a "moment of national demonstration, solidarity, pride, and hope."[26]

The ghetto had from the start to deal with the insoluble problem that there was not enough living space in its territory. In the early period of resettlement from the city, *rezervatn* (communal dormitories) had to be created simply to give people a roof over their heads. Even the "actions" of fall 1941, which cost the ghetto one-third its inhabitants, did not "solve" the housing crisis because the area of the ghetto was constantly being reduced. After each reduction, the Housing Office had to find room for the expellees in the remaining ghetto space, and the transfers usually had to be carried out very quickly. The problem of unfairness in housing also proved impossible to solve. In addition to the usual small, primitive wooden houses in the ghetto area, into each of which several families were crowded, there were a few modern apartment blocks, built just before the war. These were quickly filled by wealthier inmates and *yales* (ghetto slang for big shots). This pattern prevailed to the end.

Food was a never-ending problem for the ghetto. The vegetable gardens along the Vilija River were the only internal source of food but not a very important one. All else had to come from outside. The only legal supply was in the form of allocations by the German civil administration. The ghetto's Food Supply Office was entrusted with the distribution of these official rations that amounted to only half the already restricted wartime ration generally available to Lithuanian civilians. No provision was made for fats except to airfield workers and some other heavy laborers, who received 20 grams (2/3 oz.) weekly as part of their supplementary ration. The meat was mainly horse meat. But even these paltry rations were never delivered in full; German bureaucrats routinely skimmed a percentage off the shipments for the ghetto and pocketed the difference. The Food Supply Office maintained a warehouse where the rations were kept and an additional potato depot when such were available. The occasional supplements of (mostly rotten) potatoes were a precious commodity, regardless of their state. Even the peels were used in the preparation of ingenious "recipes." But however ingenious its inmates, the ghetto would not have lasted long on these starvation rations, used mainly to prepare the ubiquitous *yushnik* (literally, "pig swill"), the thin stew that served as the ghetto staple. Only the large-scale smuggling of food from outside made survival possible.

Poverty was a fact of life in the ghetto, affecting virtually the entire population. But some inmates were much worse off than others, with literally nothing to their names. A Welfare Office was established in the wake of the "Great Action" of October 1941, when the Germans "graciously" granted the *Ältestenrat* the possessions of those victims who had left no close relatives behind. This made it possible, once the better items had been skimmed off as "gifts" to various Germans, to distribute clothing to the airfield workers and other needy individuals. Later it was possible to obtain a little food from the Food Supply Office for charitable distribution, as well as some of what had been confiscated from unlucky smugglers at the ghetto gate. Some of the workers in "good" labor brigades taxed themselves voluntarily for the Welfare Office. In summer 1942 a soup kitchen was established that provided free or subsidized lunches of the unappetizing *yushnik*; beneficiaries had to bring their own bread. The office was also able to provide the poor with a little firewood in winter. One principle was always kept in mind by the dispensers of charity: while applying for help was a familiar experience for those who had been poor before the war, for middle class inmates it was a new and humiliating circumstance. To them, assistance was given as discreetly and anonymously as possible.

The poverty, inadequate nutrition, and overcrowded living quarters of the ghetto population created a particularly difficult situation for

A forced labor brigade returns to the ghetto.

the ghetto's Health Office. The spread of diseases among the inmates carried the potential of providing the Germans with an easy excuse to liquidate the ghetto altogether. At the same time, the conditions of ghetto life made the prevention and treatment of disease a seemingly impossible task. In any case, the creation of a hospital was a vital necessity, and two separate facilities were set up. Both were in the territory of the Small Ghetto, and both were lost during its liquidation. The facility for contagious diseases was destroyed by arson, as has been mentioned. The facility for surgery and internal medicine had to be abandoned as well. After this atrocity, it was feared to establish a new hospital in the Large Ghetto, yet there was no alternative but to start over. The "new" ghetto hospital was furnished with whatever instruments the ghetto doctors had kept hidden during the robberies of August and September 1941. Since pregnancy was made a capital crime in 1942, there could be no official maternity ward; not surprisingly, there was also no department of infectious diseases. Some cases of such diseases, including the dreaded typhus, did indeed occur, but they were either treated at home or in the hospital under some other medical name. Astonishingly, there were no real epidemics in the Kovno Ghetto, thanks in large measure to the draconian enforcement of

hygiene by the Sanitation Service of the Ghetto Police. The Health Office maintained an x-ray cabinet, an outpatient clinic (including a dental office), a delousing station, a psychiatric ward, and medical substations in various ghetto institutions and places of work.

The ghetto had a Statistics Office, which kept track of all the demographic and other "changes" that occurred after an "action" or a reduction in the ghetto's boundaries. Marriages, real and fictitious, were common—it was not good to be alone in the ghetto. Much of this documentation has survived, a major source of our knowledge of ghetto life. The Kovno Ghetto even had an excellent graphics office, the Paint and Sign Workshop, that produced posters and signs for *Ältestenrat* offices and charts and graphs illustrating the activities of the ghetto administration, some of which survived the war. It also provided models for official forms (like labor cards) and, on at least one occasion, the models for toys that were produced in the ghetto for shipment to the children of the Third Reich.[27]

Education had always been one of the major concerns of Kovno Jewry, but before the stabilization of the ghetto few parents could think about the education of their children. An Education Office was established at the end of 1941, which undertook a registration of all children of school age. Not many, alas, had made it through the preceding "actions," and of these many had to stay home to take care of infants and keep house for their working parents. Nevertheless, education was made compulsory, at least in theory. Two schools were established with about two hundred students each, meeting in two shifts in their crowded premises. The educational background of the students was very uneven. A common curriculum was adopted, reflecting the strong Zionist influence on ghetto life, with Hebrew as the language of instruction. The schools, though cramped and spartan, provided almost the only moments of intellectual and spiritual diversion for the children of the ghetto. Their accomplishments were impressive under the circumstances, especially the holiday performances put on by the children for the benefit of the parents and other spectators.

In August 1942 the Germans authorities ordered the schools closed. This blow, though severe, did not quite mark the end of education in the ghetto. Illegal private education continued, and older children could be shifted to the Vocational School, which remained legal; its curriculum was expanded to include regular school subjects and Zionism. The Education Office was able, for a time, to run a ghetto library—until in February 1942 the "Book Action" resulted in the confiscation of all books in the ghetto, of whatever kind, in whatever language.

Varied and remarkable were the accomplishments of the Kovno Ghetto, but in the final analysis the basis for all its activities and all its hopes for survival was labor. From the very outset it had been made plain to the Jews that only their usefulness as a labor supply stood between them and the same fate that had befallen the rest of Lithuanian Jewry. The *Ältestenrat*, like many Jewish councils in eastern European ghettos, became a convert to the "rescue through labor" strategy early. It did everything in its power to mobilize the ghetto population as a labor force the Germans would consider essential for their war effort, thereby staving off destruction. Labor service was made obligatory for all males between the ages of 14

YIVO

Kovno kiosk plastered with posters in Lithuanian and Yiddish attest to the multiethnic, multilingual character of prewar Kovno. 1930s

Men gather outside the ghetto's *Ältestenrat* building for the latest pronouncements, work assignments, and news

and 60, and for females between the ages of 15 and 45 (later 55), with some exemptions for women with small children at home. This labor obligation could be fulfilled in several different ways, each viewed with different degrees of favor by the ghetto inhabitants.

The oldest, largest, and least desirable place of employment was the so-called Aerodrome, the military airfield in Aleksotas, about three miles from the ghetto to the south of Kovno. The airfield had been badly damaged by German bombs at the outset of the invasion of the Soviet Union, and the *Luftwaffe* needed to repair and expand it for its own use. In the first months of the ghetto, some 4,000 Jewish workers were employed there, under exceedingly difficult conditions. An exhausting march on foot from the ghetto was followed by a twelve-hour shift at heavy labor, both by day and by night. The work was heavy physical labor, made worse by the abusive overseers and by the fact that it had to be done in the open air, regardless of the weather or the season of the year. Worse still, since no civilians were present, there was no opportunity for bartering for food to smuggle into the ghetto. Naturally, no one wanted to work there. Though in theory all ghetto inhabitants had to put in at least some time at the detested Aerodrome, those with connections managed to get out of it. The *Aerodromshchiks* became a kind of ghetto proletariat. As a contemporary report put it, "There exists a sharp line of demarcation within the population of the ghetto: airfield workers and non-airfield workers, which coincides with the class distinctions in the population."[28]

Far more fortunate were the workers in the "city brigades," those employed by various German and Lithuanian military and civil enterprises in Kovno itself. As the war on the eastern front dragged on, and with many Lithuanians mobilized for labor in the Reich, a labor shortage developed that only Jewish labor could fill. Eventually some 150 such brigades came into existence, though the Aerodrome continued to be the largest single employer. At dawn each day, they

marched out to work through the ghetto gate, returning in the evening. In general, treatment was more humane in these brigades and the work less backbreaking. They had in addition the immense advantage of providing opportunities for obtaining food, which could usually be smuggled in through the ghetto gate, and any "surplus" could be sold at high prices. Membership in a "good" brigade was a coveted and jealously guarded prize in the ghetto labor economy.

Parallel to the expansion of the labor brigades was the growth of the "Large Workshops" located within the ghetto itself. They represented a kind of "joint venture" between the ghetto and the German civil administration in Kovno, with all the profits going to the latter. The German authorities provided the raw material, initially in the form of the valuables confiscated from the Jewish population of Kovno. The workshops were an ever-expanding enterprise, working by day and by night to carry out orders for clothing, baskets, brushes, carpentry, and the like. They provided work eventually for nearly 4,000 people and made use of the labor of those too old or too young or too ill to work in the city or at the airfield. In addition to producing goods for the Germans, one of their major "industries" was the sorting and repair of the clothing and valuables that had been taken from both the living and the dead among the Jews of Kovno. While the workshops could not be a source of food like the city brigades, they were free of German and Lithuanian overseers and involved no humiliating searches at the ghetto gate. As such they were also the preferred location for those inmates "wealthy" enough not to have to depend on smuggled food for their families.[29]

"It is hard to imagine more disturbing and inappropriate conditions for cultural activities than in the ghetto," wrote a survivor.[30] And yet, despite severe official restrictions, there occurred a partial renewal of the culture for which Jewish Kovno was renowned. Into this category fall the dramatic and choral performances at the Vocational School, the writings and lectures in literary and philosophical

A classroom for Jewish orphans maintained by the Jewish children's home in prewar Kovno

circles, and the religious study groups that carried on the traditions of the prewar yeshivas despite the ban on religious observance. The Ghetto Police played a unique role in the revival of culture through the Police Orchestra and the Police Culture House, where popular concerts were performed before large audiences. Perhaps most important of all was the concern for the history of the ghetto. Chaim Nachman Shapiro, the head of the Education Office, and Avraham Tory, the secretary of the *Ältestenrat*, amassed rich documentation for the use of future historians. Esther Lurie and other artists and the photographer George Kadish together produced a visual record unique in the history of the Holocaust. Slowly, the Kovno Ghetto was recovering its humanity and finding its own voice.

The period of stabilization lasted about 22 months. By early September 1943, there were signs of change. That month SS-Captain Wilhelm Goecke arrived in Kovno and visited the ghetto, hinting at an even more severe regime in the future than the SA-dominated German authorities the ghetto was accustomed to. In the course of the month, Goecke's presence became ever more pervasive. He began transferring workers from the city brigades to a small number of larger units. In early October came the horrifying news that the ghetto in nearby Vilna had been liquidated.[31] Kovno was to be spared that fate for the time being, but not much else. A new era of "actions" commenced in late October with massive deportations to Estonia, carried out with great brutality and costing the ghetto at least 2,700 people. Finally, on November 1, 1943, the Kovno Ghetto itself was officially transformed into a concentration camp, under the jurisdiction of the SS and of Captain Goecke. Between 7,000 and 8,000 Jews were now confined to a tiny area of the ghetto; the rest were quartered in camps at military installations around Kovno.

The destabilization of the ghetto in fall 1943 seemed to indicate that its days were numbered. Parents began to place their children outside the ghetto if they could, especially after the news reached Kovno in early November 1943 of an "action" against children and old people in Shavli [Šiauliai], the only other ghetto then remaining in Lithuania. Such "placement" was full of dangers and complications. At best, finding willing and reliable Christian families was difficult, even where money was available to compensate them. Delivering the children was itself very risky. If the money ran out, the child

might be returned to the ghetto, and there were cases of children who experienced this more than once. Language was often a problem, since many Jewish children were not fluent in Lithuanian. Despite all the difficulties and risks, however, dozens of families took this painful step, and hundreds of Jewish children were thus saved, showing that there was indeed another side to Jewish-Lithuanian relations.[32]

At the same time, many inmates turned to the creation of hiding places within the ghetto, known in Kovno as *malines*. These were typically bunkers, underground or concealed behind walls, where groups or individuals might hide during an "action." During the deportation to Estonian labor camps of October 1943, a number of persons with hiding places had saved themselves from deportation, and this "success story" inspired many to undertake the construction of *malines* of their own. These bunkers were often masterpieces of ingenuity, with entrances concealed behind wardrobes and false partitions, or under toilets and wells. They were provided with air, water, and food, and sometimes even had electricity. Some *malines* were "communal," involving all the inhabitants of a building; others were "ideological," for members of the same political movement. In the end, *malines* were unsuccessful as refuges. While they might with luck enable those within them to survive particular "actions," almost no *maline* survived the final liquidation of the ghetto.[33]

After the Germans closed all the ghetto schools in August 1942, education continued surreptitiously in underground schools and vocational training workshops.

The Jewish children's home in prewar Kovno

YIVO

To protect ghetto orphans, the *Ältestenrat* established a secret children's home on the grounds of the ghetto hospital.

Kadish/BH

During late 1943 and early 1944, the resistance movement in the Kovno Ghetto reached its high point. This movement had two wings, Zionist and pro-Soviet, which had merged by summer 1943 though their origins and orientations were very different. The Zionists were already experienced in underground activity, since they had been declared illegal by the Soviets in 1940. In November 1941, *Irgun Brit Tzion,* the "Organization of the Covenant of Zion," emerged, embracing most Zionist groups; its Hebrew language publication, *Nitzotz* (Spark), which had already existed clandestinely under the Soviets, began to appear. In April 1942, the Zionists created a broader umbrella organization, *Matzok* (from the initials for "Zionist Center, Vilijampole-Kovno" but also a word meaning "anguish"), whose membership included such ghetto notables as *Ältestenrat* Chairman Elkes and his deputy, Leib Garfunkel.

Around the same time as the formation of the Zionist underground, the pro-Soviet elements had begun to coalesce under the leadership of the writer Chaim Yelin into what became known as the Anti-Fascist Organization. If the Zionist groups drew their strength from the powerful tradition of Lithuanian Jewish Zionism, the leftist groups benefited from the fact that the Soviets were the Nazis' great enemy, whose victory alone could bring liberation. Soviet partisan activity behind the lines also promised a base for escape from the ghetto and the opportunity for participation in the armed struggle. Added to the differences between the Left and the Zionists were disagreements about whether armed resistance might not bring catastrophe for the ghetto. But young people, both Zionist and leftist, were impatient for armed struggle. The visit in July 1942 of the Polish emissary Irena Adamowicz, who brought word to the Kovno Ghetto of the existence of underground military preparations in the ghettos of Warsaw and Vilna, acted as a stimulus. In the course of 1943, following the German defeat at Stalingrad and the news of the doomed but heroic struggle in the Warsaw Ghetto uprising, excitement grew. In spring 1943, the liquidation of several small ghettos along the Lithuanian-Belorussian border brought to Kovno a small number of deportees bearing word of the existence of Soviet partisans in their region.

The Zionists and leftists fused into a single organization, the Jewish General Fighting Organization, in summer 1943. But there remained a kind of basic division of labor between them. The Zionists, who had the sympathy of the majority of the ghetto population, could be more effective inside the ghetto. The Left groups had better contacts with the pro-Soviet underground in Kovno itself and later with Soviet partisans in the forests. In September 1943, the Jewish paratrooper Gessia Glezer, a Soviet partisan, visited the Kovno Ghetto and held discussions with the leaders of the underground concerning the possibility of moving ghetto youth to partisan bases. The first such attempt, in October 1943, directed towards the Augustow [Augustavas] Forest south of Kovno, met with disaster. Only after contact was made with Soviet partisans in the Rudniki [Rudninkai] Forest much further south could a more or less regular movement of ghetto fighters begin.

The months between November 1943 and March 1944 were the high point of departures from the ghetto to the partisans. The saga of the Jewish partisans in the forests in and around Lithuania is a story in itself. From Kovno alone, hundreds of young people left, and all the resources of the *Ältestenrat* were put at their disposal. Money to buy arms, to provide transportation, and to bribe guards was raised in the ghetto, including by contributions from members of the "good" brigades. The ghetto police made every effort to assist in

A Kovno street peddler, 1920s

smuggling people and weapons in or out of the ghetto. The ghetto workshops produced German uniforms for purposes of disguise, plus warm clothing and the like for the use of departing fighters. Indeed, in this last phase the ghetto administration and The Organization came close to merging, with most leading members of the Ghetto Police serving in the underground, and simultaneously conducting a campaign within the ghetto against Jewish informers and criminal elements who might endanger the whole enterprise.[34]

The link between the ghetto police and the underground, of which the Germans inevitably got wind, proved to be the undoing of both and ushered in the last, terrible phase of the history of the Kovno Ghetto. On March 26, 1944, Goecke ordered the 130 members of the Ghetto Police to gather the next morning, allegedly to receive instructions regarding air raid procedures. The real purpose turned out to be the mass arrest of the Jewish police. After generally unsuccessful efforts to obtain, under torture, information regarding the activities of the underground, 36 of the policemen were executed at Fort IX. The same day, March 27, was simultaneously the first day of the nightmarish two-day "Children's Action," in which some 1,300 victims—children under the age of 12 as well as those over 55—were dragged from their homes and hiding places. In the aftermath of these two great tragedies, the last remnants of Kovno Ghetto "autonomy" were destroyed. The ghetto police were abolished and replaced by an *Ordnungsdienst* (Order Service) of dubious character. This frankly collaborationist body bore no resemblance to the ghetto police, which for all its unappealing side had nevertheless in general served the interests of the ghetto community.[35] The *Ältestenrat* was declared dissolved, with only Chairman Elkes remaining in "office" as *"Ober-Jude"* (Chief Jew).

The Kovno "camp" became a true concentration camp, with striped clothing for its inmates, collective responsibility (read: shooting) in cases of desertion, and other measures designed to make flight impossible. Under the circumstances, the activities of the underground were severely hampered. The arrest of its leader, Chaim Yelin, on April 6, 1944, and his subsequent murder made its efforts especially difficult.

The end came in midsummer 1944, just as Soviet armies were entering Lithuania. Concentration Camp Kauen was declared liquidated and its inmates evacuated over a six-day period, by train and by barge, from July 8 to July 13. With but a few exceptions, those who chose to try to wait it out concealed in *malines* perished. Goecke assured the deportees that families would be kept together in labor camps in Germany. Despite his promises, men and women (including the remaining children) were separated upon arrival at Stutthof, in Prussia. The men were taken on to satellite camps of Dachau in Bavaria. The long *via dolorosa* that these remnants of Kovno Jewry had to travel before a handful made it to the liberation of the concentration camps is a story in itself. So is their postwar interlude as displaced persons in Germany before they scattered by various routes, none of them easy, to new homes in Israel, America, and elsewhere. Few returned to Kovno; among those who had survived in the city against all the odds, few chose to remain. To be sure, a small community still exists in today's independent Lithuania. But it may be said that what really survived of Jewish Kovno and its ghetto is its

Kadish/BH

story, the story that the ghetto inmates wanted so badly to have told, and whose materials they have bequeathed us. In the words of Elkhanan Elkes, "Remember and never forget it all your days; and pass this memory as a sacred testament to future generations."[36]

Solon Beinfeld is author of numerous articles on the ghettos of Lithuania. He is Professor Emeritus of History at Washington University in St. Louis.

Notes

1. See Ezekiel I. Berlson, "Di yidishe kovne" [Jewish Kovno] in *Lite* [Lithuania], 2 vols. (New York, 1951; Tel Aviv, 1965), 1:1155–62.
2. Alte Arsh-Sudarsky, "Undzer kultur-gezelshaftlekhe tetikayt" [Our cultural and communal activity], in ibid., 2:463.
3. Ezra Mendelsohn, *The Jews of East Central Europe between the Wars* (Bloomington, Ind., 1983), 223.
4. Joseph Gar, *Umkum fun der yidisher kovne* [The destruction of Jewish Kovno] (Munich, 1948), 20.
5. Moyshe Mandelman, "In freyd un layd tsvishn litvishe yidn" [In joy and sorrow among Lithuanian Jews], in *Lite*, 1:1346–47.
6. Ibid., 1344–45; see also Joseph Gar, *Azoy iz es geshen in lite* [That is how it happened in Lithuania] (Tel Aviv, 1965), 50–52.
7. See in particular Zorach Warhaftig, "Curaçao and Japanese Visas," chap. 11 of *Refugee and Survivor Rescue Efforts during the Holocaust* (Jerusalem, 1988).
8. Dov Levin, *The Lesser of Two Evils: Eastern European Jewry under Soviet Rule, 1939–1941* (Philadelphia, 1995), 10–12.
8. Ibid., 36.
9. See the leaflet issued by the Lithuanian Activist Front, an exile group in Berlin, on March 19, 1941, reprinted in *Documents Accuse* (Vilnius, 1970), 123–24.
10. Leib Garfunkel, *Kovna ha-yehudit be-hurbanah* [The destruction of Kovno's Jewry] (Jerusalem, 1959), 25–26.
11. Levin, *Lesser of Two Evils*, 69.
12. Ibid., 96.
13. Ibid., 147.
14. William W. Mishell, *Kaddish for Kovno: Life and Death in a Lithuanian Ghetto* (Chicago, 1988), 9; see also Harry Gordon, *The Shadow of Death: The Holocaust in Lithuania* (Lexington, Ky., 1992), 20–21.
15. These orders are reproduced in Gar, *Azoy iz es geshen*, 143–46.
16. Garfunkel, *Kovna ha-yehudit be-hurbanah*, 29–30.
17. Gar, *Umkum fun der yidisher kovne*, 56.
18. Ibid., 45.
19. The memoranda are reproduced in Avraham Tory, *Surviving the Holocaust: The Kovno Ghetto Diary*, ed. Martin Gilbert (Cambridge, Mass., 1990), 14–17.
20. Ibid., 26-28; Garfunkel, *Kovna ha-yehudit be-hurbanah*, 47–48.
21. Tory, *Surviving the Holocaust*, 43–59.
22. Solly Ganor, *Light One Candle: A Survivor's Tale from Lithuania to Jerusalem* (New York, 1995), 194–95.
23. See the warm words of appreciation by Leib Garfunkel, Elkes's deputy and close collaborator, in *Kovna ha-yehudit be-hurbanah*, 245ff.
24. "History of the Vilijampole Jewish Ghetto Police," 1942–43, anonymous (in Yiddish), Archives of the YIVO Institute for Jewish Research, New York, Territorial Collection, Baltic: 3.0 Lita, 16–18.
25. Gordon, *Shadow of Death*, 74.
26. "History of the Vilijampole Jewish Ghetto Police," 249.
27. See Mishell, *Kaddish for Kovno*, 101ff. On the *Ältestenrat* and its institutions, the discussion here follows Joseph Gar, "Yidishe moysodes in kovner geto" [Jewish institutions in the Kovno Ghetto], *Umkum fun der yidisher kovne*, 277–394.
28. "The population and the labor force according to tables from the Statistics Office," May 31, 1942 (in Yiddish), Avraham and Pnina Tory, Israel.
29. On the Large Workshops, see Moshe Segalson, "Batei-ha-mlakhah ha-gdolim ba geto" [The large workshops in the ghetto] in *Yahadut Lita* [Lithuanian Jewry], 4 vols. (Tel Aviv, 1984), 4:110–12.
30. Samuel Greenhaus, "Dos kultur-lebn in kovner geto" [Cultural life in the Kovno Ghetto], in *Lite*, 1:1743.
31. Tory, *Surviving the Holocaust*, 481–84 (diary entry for September 28, 1943); 493–96 (October 9, 1943); and 500–501 (October 13, 1943).
32. Gar, *Umkum fun der yidisher kovne*, 170–74.
33. Ibid., 197–98.
34. On the Kovno Jewish resistance in general, see Dov Levin, *Fighting Back: Lithuanian Jewry's Armed Resistance to the Nazis, 1941–1945*, trans. Moshe Kohn and Diana Cohen (New York, 1985), 116–25.
35. Garfunkel, *Kovna ha-yehudit be-hurbanah*, 171–89.
36. Cited in Tory, *Surviving the Holocaust*, 506.

Part II
Inside the Kovno Ghetto

TRE VECKOR VID TYSKA FRONTER:

Judisk karavan.

Judarna i Kovno måste gå i körbanan. Observera Zionsstjärnan på bröstet! Därunder: den stora judeomflyttningen i staden är i full gång samt ett talande anslag: "Den som plundrar blir skjuten".

Wer plündert, wird erschossen!

ETT GHETTO SKAPAS.

Intryck från den stora judeomflyttningen i Kovno efter bolsjevikväldets fall och

These photos of Jews being forced to walk in the road, of Jews moving into the ghetto, and of a poster stating "Those who plunder will be shot" appeared in the Swedish newspaper *Aftonbladet* on August 14, 1941.

In cities throughout eastern Europe, the Germans cut Jews off from the general population and strictly confined them in areas known as ghettos. On July 10, 1941, Kovno's Jews who had survived the German invasion and Lithuanian pogroms were all ordered to relocate to the district of Vilijampole. Known to local Jews as Slobodka and to Jews worldwide for its once-influential academies of Jewish learning, Vilijampole was run-down and lacked running water. The order to relocate instituted the Kovno Ghetto. An outpouring of decrees thereafter deprived Jews of their mobility, property, and civil freedoms.

Some 25,000 Jews packed up whatever items they could take with them, moving both in fear of the powerful German forces and in hope of escaping the violent pro-German Lithuanian activists. Despite protests that Slobodka was too small, families were forced to double and triple up, crowding into living space that had previously accommodated just 12,000 people. Barbed wire defined the periphery, and armed guards patrolled the gates. Subsequent reductions in the physical size of the ghetto forced Jews to relocate again and again.

Hope that the ghetto would serve as a safe haven did not last long. The Germans began reducing the ghetto's total population of more than 29,000 through a series of mass murders. The first of these "actions," as the Germans deceptively called them, occurred on August 18, 1941, just three days after the Germans sealed the ghetto. Some 550 well-educated professionals, ordered by the Germans to report for work in the city's archives, were shot instead. In preparation for further "actions" to reduce the ghetto population to a core of laborers, on September 15 SA-Captain Fritz Jordan produced 5,000 work cards, known as *Jordan-Scheine* and widely but mistakenly regarded as lifesaving certificates, for the ghetto's Jewish leadership, the *Ältestenrat,* to distribute. About 1,000 Jews were rounded up on September 26 and shot in retaliation for an alleged shooting of a German police officer. On October 4, the Germans liquidated the Small Ghetto, an "action" that included sealing up and setting ablaze the hospital for contagious diseases, burning alive the patients and staff. Some 1,800 Jews lost their lives.

On October 27, the German authorities ordered the council to assemble all the Jews in Demokratu Square at 6:00 A.M. the next morning. Some wondered if the order was benign—an inventory, perhaps, in preparation for new work assignments. Others feared the worse. By the end of the day of October 28, some 9,200 Jews—about one-third of the ghetto's population and including more than 4,200 of its children— were separated from the rest. Still unsure of their fate, they were marched the next morning to Fort IX, a turn-of-the-century fortification on Kovno's outskirts. There, German troops and Lithuanian auxiliaries forced them to undress and lie in ditches dug by previous prisoners. The Jews were summarily shot at close range.

Fort IX remained an unrelenting threat, and occasional reality, for Kovno's Jews throughout the ghetto's three-year existence. Following the "Great Action" of October 28–29, it also became a killing site for train-loads of Jews from Germany, Austria, Czechoslovakia, and France. Tens of thousands of men, women, and children, mostly Jews, were murdered at Fort IX during the German occupation of Lithuania.

Ghetto Fighters' House, Israel

Theodor von Renteln *(center),* the German civil administrator for Lithuania, followed by his civilian First Lithuanian Adviser, Potros Kubilianis *(far right),* a pro-Nazi Lithuanian; undated

LCSA

"Order No. 15" from Kovno's Mayor Kazys Palčiauskas and Commandant Colonel Jurgis Bobelis that created the Kovno Ghetto, July 10, 1941

"Order No. 15" from Kovno's Lithuanian civil and military authorities, July 10, 1941

§1.

All persons of Jewish nationality who fled Kaunas do not have the right to return to Kaunas. Those who do return will be arrested.

Those who allow people of Jewish nationality returning to Kaunas to live in residences under their control will be punished. This rule applies to homeowners, managers of nationalized residences, and managers of other residences.

§2

All persons of Jewish nationality residing in the city of Kaunas are required to wear the following insignia on the left side of their chest starting on July 12 of this year [1941]: a yellow star of David 8 to 10 cm. in diameter. Persons of Jewish nationality are responsible to come up with the insignia themselves. There will be no exceptions based on sex or age.

Persons of Jewish nationality caught without the insignia will be arrested.

§3

Persons of Jewish nationality are allowed to walk on the streets or to appear in public from 6 A.M. to 8 P.M. At other hours, Jews caught in public places will be arrested.

§4

All persons of Jewish nationality residing within the city limits of Kaunas are required to move to Vilijampole, the suburb of Kaunas, between July and August 15 of this year. There will be no exceptions based on sex or age.

Families that are moving will be issued moving orders.

§5

To insure an orderly move, the staff of the housing administration office of Kaunas City will coordinate with representatives of the Jewish community to direct the implementation and sequence of the move. The implementation of the move will be supervised by officials of the Kaunas Military Headquarters and the Kaunas City Police. Those failing to move by the time required will be arrested.

§6

The move will be carried out at the expense of those being moved.

§7

Non-Jews living in Vilijampole have the right to move to other parts of Kaunas. The housing administrative office of Kaunas City will help them find apartments.

§8

Persons of Jewish nationality owning real estate in parts of Kaunas other than Vilijampole are required to liquidate that property, after first checking on the possibility of exchanging their property with Lithuanians in Vilijampole who plan to move out.

The Bureau of the Kaunas City Municipal government established for that purpose will coordinate the exchange and liquidation of real estate.

Persons of Jewish nationality who own firearms will turn them in immediately to the Military Headquarters at 34 Gedimino Street, and those owning radios will turn them in to the housing administration office at 9 Laisves Boulevard, third floor. Those who do not comply will be punished severely.

§9

Persons of Jewish extraction are not allowed to hire other nationalities.

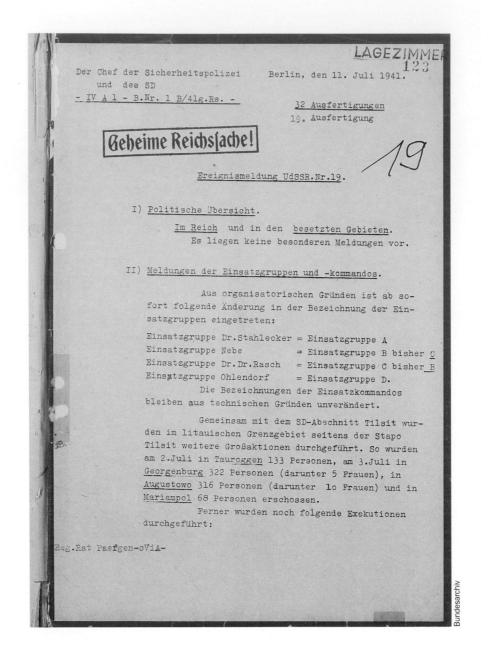

**First page of "Operation Situation Report USSR
No. 19" from the chief of the Security Police and
SD in Berlin that summarizes German activities
in the occupied Soviet Union as of July 11, 1941**

"Operation Situation Report USSR No. 19," July 11, 1941

In *Kovno* a total of 7,800 have now been killed—a portion through the pogrom, a portion shot
by Lithuanian commandos. All corpses have been disposed of. Continued mass shootings are no
longer possible. Instead I explained to a committee of Jews that up to now, we have not had a
reason to intervene in the internal conflicts between the Lithuanians and the Jews. The conditions
to undergo reorganization are:

Establish a Jewish ghetto. . . . The town *Vilijampole* has been designated to be the ghetto.

Į LAISVĘ

Nr. 30   Kaina 20 kap.

LEIDŽIA LIETUVIŲ AKTYVISTŲ FRONTAS

1941. VII. 28   Pirmadienis

Verordnung Nr. 1

1. Der jüdischen Bevölkerung wird das Betreten der Gehsteige untersagt. Die Juden haben den rechtsseitigen Rand der Fahrstrasse einzuhalten und hintereinander zu gehen.

2. Der jüdischen Bevölkerung wird der Aufenthalt auf Promenaden wegen und in allen öffentlichen Grünanlagen verboten. Desgleichen wird der jüdischen Bevölkerung die Benutzung der aufgestellten Ruhebänke untersagt.

3. Der jüdischen Bevölkerung wird die Benutzung aller öffentlichen Verkehrsmittel wie Autotaxen, Pferdedroschken und Autobusse, Personendampfer und ähnlicher Fahrzeuge untersagt. Die Eigentümer bezw. Halter aller öffentlichen Fahrzeuge sind verpflichtet, an sichtbarer Stelle der Fahrzeuge ein Plakat zu befestigen mit der Aufschrift: „Für Juden verboten".

4. Zuwiderhandelnde gegen diese Verordnung werden schärfstens bestraft.

5. Diese Verordnung tritt mit dem heutigen Tage in Kraft.

Kauen, den 28. Juli 1941.

Der Stadtkommissar
gez. CRAMER
SA—Oberführer

Privalomas nutarimas Nr. 1

1. Gyventojams žydams draudžiama naudotis šaligatviais. Žydai privalo eiti dešiniuoju kraštu važiuojamo kelio ir eiti vienas po kito.

2. Gyventojams žydams draudžiama naudotis visomis pasivaikščiojimo bei poilsio vietomis ir viešaisiais parkais bei skverais. Taip pat jiems draudžiama naudotis viešose vietose išstatytais suolais.

3. Gyventojams žydams draudžiama naudotis visomis viešosiomis susisiekimo priemonėmis, kaip auto taksi, vežikais, autobusais, garlaiviais ir pan. Visi viešojo naudojimo susisiekimo priemonių savininkai arba nuomotojai privalo nurodytų priemonių matomoje vietoje iškabinti skelbimą su užrašu: „Žydams draudžiama".

4. Nesilaikantieji šio nutarimo nuostatų bei jiems prieštaraujantieji bus griežtai baudžiami.

5. Šis nutarimas galioja nuo šios dienos.

Kaunas, 1941 m. liepos mėn. 28 d.

Miesto Komisaras
(pas.) CRAMER
S. A. Oberführer

LCSA

The Germans' "Order No. 1" restricting the Jews' activities in the city of Kovno, as published in the Lithuanian Activist Front newspaper *Į Laisve* [To freedom], July 28, 1941

"Order No. 1" from *Stadtkommissar* SA-Colonel Hans Cramer, July 28, 1941

1. The Jewish population is not allowed to walk on the sidewalk. Jews are to walk single file on the right side of the street.

2. The Jewish population is not allowed walk on the promenades and are not allowed in any public parks. Likewise, the Jewish population is not allowed to sit on public benches.

3. The Jewish population is not allowed to use any public transportation such as taxis, coaches, buses, boats, and similar vehicles of transportation. The proprietors and owners of all public vehicles of transportation must post a visible notice on the vehicle stating: "Jews Not Permitted."

4. Any violations of these orders will be severely punished.

5. These orders are to be enforced as of today.

"Public Announcement No. 2" from *Stadtkommissar* SA-Colonel Hans Cramer, July 31, 1941

The Jewish population, regardless of age and gender, is required to wear a yellow star of David 8–10 cm in diameter on the left chest as well as on the back.

Yellow star of David worn by ghetto prisoner

Meir Yelin USHMM, Gift of Dita Katz Zupowitz Sperling

Tory Collection

Carts loaded with the possessions of Kovno's Jews head toward the bridge to Slobodka while empty carts return to the city. July–August 1941

Diary of Elena Kutorgiene, August 1, 1941

In the morning I looked out the window and saw a long peasant wagon driving by. Amid the pathetic-looking tables, chairs, and mattresses that were piled up, I saw a Jewish doctor I know with his wife, who was hugging their two small children. Wagons carrying the Jews' household junk keep passing by all the time. The Lithuanian peasants and coachmen are charging the Jews exorbitant fees to transport their things. . . Along the street *in single file (!)—surely it had to be contrived!—*walk *Jews with yellow stars on their backs.*

Diary of Elena Kutorgiene, August 12, 1941

I was in the ghetto today. Barbed wire is strung along the streets on either side, almost up to the rooftops. In another place a wooden bridge has been built across a "Christian street" to keep the Jews who are crossing over from contaminating the Christian street. Pathetic, impoverished little houses. . . . Tormented faces. . . .Furniture and all kinds of household junk stand in vacant lots. Courtyards are filled with furniture that won't fit into the extremely cramped apartments. In a residential area *where about 5 thousand people used to live have been settled 25–30 thousand people*. I visited some doctors I know; two families are living in one little room nine meters square.

**Instructions from Kovno's Lithuanian authorities to implement their "Order No. 15,"
July 25, 1941**

§1

Jews moving to the assigned territory in Vilijampole are permitted to take along the items designated below:

1. Kitchen items.

All kitchen utensils, except for electric ones.

2. Dining room items.

One dining room table per family, one chair per person, two plates each, one cup or glass each plus a saucer, one fork, knife, and spoon each, and containers for condiments.

Note: Only inexpensive dishes should be taken.)

3. Bedroom items.

One bed for each person, with one set of bedding and three sets of sheets/pillowcases.

4. Clothes and footwear.

a) *For men* two suits, a summer and winter coat, two pairs of shoes, and four sets of underwear;

b) *For women* four dresses, a winter and summer coat, three pairs of shoes, four sets of underwear;

c) *For children* up to 14 years of age are allowed to take all their children's clothes and footwear; those over 14 years old will be allowed to take what adults are allowed to take.

Additionally, it is permitted to take along implements needed to work, with the exception of machinery that has been installed in a stationary way and other expensive apparatus (x-ray equipment, sterilization baths, and similar equipment).

§2

Items permitted in the first § must be taken during the period set aside for the family to move out.

Items not taken out during the time assigned for moving out, or items not designated in the first §, must be left in the apartments, which will be entered on the appropriate rosters by police officials. . . .

§4

The property left behind the Jews will be disposed of by the Mayor of Kaunas City, in coordination with the Police Chief of Kaunas City.

Ghetto writings of Chaim Yelin, 1941–42

Jews have fenced themselves in. Snatched from the streets, other dragged out of their houses, these Jews have, under the guard of bandits, built a fence around their "own land," their future living space. . . . They have planted beams of wood into the dried-out earth, stretched barbed wire, fenced around the designated streets with a high barbed-wire net. Between one parallel wire and the second must measure exactly twenty centimeters, and one meter between the vertical wires.

Kadish/BH

Kadish/BH

GEORGE KADISH

Photographing life in the Kovno Ghetto was an extremely risky venture. The Germans strictly prohibited it, and as with all defiant acts, they did not hesitate to murder offenders. George Kadish took every opportunity possible to document day-to-day life in the ghetto and, after his escape in 1944, the ghetto's final days. The results constitute one of the most significant photographic records of ghetto life during the Holocaust era.

George Kadish was born Zvi (Hirsh) Kadushin in Raseiniai, Lithuania, in 1910. After attending the local Hebrew school, he moved with his family to Kovno. At the Aleksotas University, located in one of Kovno's suburbs, he studied engineering in preparation for a teaching career and joined the rightist Zionist movement called *Betar*. In the years before the war, he taught mathematics, science, and electronics at a local Hebrew high school. His avocational interests, however, would have the most significant impact on his and others' lives. He started developing his interests in photography and began building his own cameras, including one designed for use on his trouser belt.

Acquiring and developing film secretly outside the ghetto were just as perilous as using hidden cameras inside. Kadish received orders to work as an engineer repairing x-ray machines for the German occupation forces in the city of Kovno. Once in the city, he discovered opportunities to barter for film and other necessary supplies. He developed his negatives at the German military hospital, using the same chemicals he used to develop x-ray film, and succeeded in smuggling them out in sets of crutches.

The subjects of Kadish's photographic portraits were varied, but he seemed especially interested in capturing the reality of the ghetto's daily life. In June 1941, witnessing the brutality of the initial pogroms, he photographed the Yiddish word *Nekoma* ("Revenge") found scrawled in blood on the door of a murdered Jew's apartment. Camera in hand, or whenever necessary, placed just so to record subjects through a buttonhole of his overcoat, he photographed Jews humiliated and tormented by Lithuanian and German guards in search for smuggled food, Jews dragging their belongings from one place to another on sleds or carts, Jews concentrated in forced work brigades, and so forth. Kadish also recorded the new regimen of regulated daily activities at the *Ältestenrat*'s food gardens and in schools, orphanages, and workshops. In addition to depicting the

George Kadish in Kovno after liberation

severe conditions of ghetto life, he had an insider's eye for portraiture, the desolation of deserted streets, and the intimacy of informal, improvised gatherings.

Among Kadish's last photographs from inside the ghetto are those recording the deportation of ghetto prisoners to work camps in Estonia. In July 1944, after escaping from the ghetto across the river, he photographed the ghetto's liquidation. Once the Germans fled, he returned to photograph the ghetto in ruins and the small groups who had survived the final days in hiding.

Kadish recognized early on the danger of losing his precious collection. He enlisted the assistance of Yehuda Zupowitz, a high-ranking officer in the ghetto's Jewish police, to help hide his negatives and prints. Zupowitz never revealed his knowledge of Kadish's work or the location of his collection, even during the "Police Action" of March 27, 1944, when Zupowitz was tortured and killed at the Fort IX prison. Kadish retrieved his collection of photographic negatives upon his return to the destroyed ghetto.

After Germany's surrender on May 8, 1945, Kadish left Lithuania with his extraordinary documentary trove for Germany. There, in the American Zone, he mounted exhibitions of his photographs for survivors residing in displaced persons camps. Since then, several museums, including New York's Jewish Museum, have formally exhibited his work.

The delivery of food to the ghetto

Jewish police at the gate

Kadish photographing through his buttonhole

On the streets of the ghetto

Laborers returning from work, photographed through Kadish's buttonhole

Jews awaiting housing assignments at the Housing Office

A labor brigade returning to the ghetto

Kadish/BH

This photograph of the Yiddish word *Nekoma,* "revenge," written in blood on the door of a murdered Jew in Slobodka, was among the first taken by George Kadish to document the Kovno Ghetto.

Over the sill of a window, George Kadish clandestinely photographed this gathering of a labor brigade.

Ghetto writings of Chaim Yelin, 1941–42

So this is the ghetto for Kovno's Jews—pious Slobodka with its yeshivas and study houses, with its scrupulously-observed sabbaths and holidays. Slobodka with its crooked, interconnected tangle of alleys. Old Slobodka—half-ruined cottages, hunch-backed little houses with roofs of moss-greened shingles, half-caved-in rafters, and walls split by the wind. . . . Jewish Slobodka with the spark of a small town, with its unique dialect; the poverty of Kovno, and also workers' families, revolutionary fighters. . .

Overlay map produced for the yearbook "Slobodka Ghetto 1942" showing the originally proposed boundaries

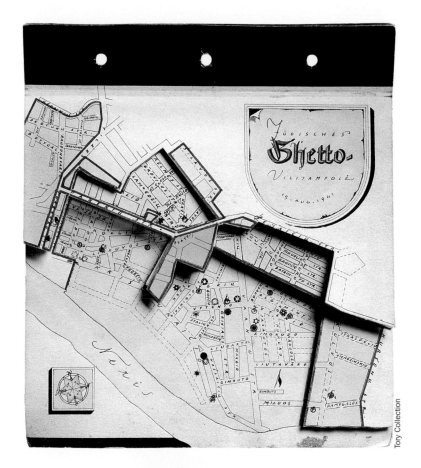

Tory Collection

Kadish/BH

On a ghetto street. The man on the right may be the writer Chaim Yelin, a leader of the Jewish resistance in the ghetto.

59

Tory Collection

Kadish/BH

Letter from the Jewish "Committee for the Transfer of Jews to Vilijampole" to the German authorities, July 10, 1941

Vilijampole is a small district in which up to now approximately 12,000 people have been living. . . . This district has no home for orphans or the aged, no hospitals, no plumbing, no sewage system, that is, no running water, and in no way provides the conditions for approximately 25,000 additional inhabitants. The concentration of so many people under such conditions would create a danger of sickness and an epidemic that could not be contained.

Jacob Lifschitz, *Mokklus Street,* **undated**
(pen and ink, 13¹/₄ x 9³/₄ in.)

Esther Lurie, *Ghetto Street Scene,* **1943**
(pen, ink, and watercolor, 8⁵/₈ x 7¹/₈ in.)

Ghetto writings of Chaim Yelin, 1941–42

New Slobodka—"Christian Slobodka," with its airy and sunny houses, with gardens and orchards and new apartment blocks, was originally supposed to be part of the ghetto. Someone, however, was not pleased with the Jews and soon cut out whole streets, took them out of the ghetto area, violently ripped them out and cut the ghetto into two parts. . . .

Now we encircle the Small Ghetto—a part of the left side of Paneriu Street, which extends its "how-do-you-do" to the Large Ghetto by way of a bridge. The bridge is six meters high, wooden, like an arch bent over the street. It leads upstairs, downstairs, connecting one part of Dvaro Street with the other, with Paneriu Street beneath, over which travel wagons and cars. Under the bridge Christian life goes on. Over the bridge walk the "criminals"—Jews.

The footbridge built to link the Large and Small Ghettos, fall 1941

Ghetto writings of Chaim Yelin, 1941–42

At 8:00 in the evening, people lock themselves in their houses. The scraping of doors and gates ceases. The children in the courtyard have been hushed. The streets are empty, vacated, although the day is not over. It will stretch on another couple of hours. Inside the houses it is hot and suffocating. In the houses by the fence they close the shutters early. A chain is run around them and is locked, or closed only with a lock. The doors are blocked with pegs. Through cracks in the wooden fences one looks at the barbed-wire fence.

Order from the Commander of the SD, October 27, 1941
All those living in the ghetto regardless of age or gender are ordered to leave their homes on October 28, 1941, and assemble at 6 A.M. on Demokratu Square. Those found in their homes will be immediately shot.

The *Ältestenrat* was to post in both German and Yiddish the announcement that the Jews of Kovno must assemble on Demokratu Square. This draft of the German text shows the council's struggle with wording the frightful order.

Meldung

Der Aeltestenrat wurde von den Machtorganen aufgefordert, der Ghettobevölkerung ~~mitzuteilen~~ folgenden Befehl der Machtorgane mitzuteilen:

Sämtliche Ghettoeinwohner, ohne irgendwelche Ausnahme, darunter auch Kinder und Kranke, sind verpflichtet, am Dienstag, den 28. Oktober 1941, nicht später als 6 Uhr früh, ihre Wohnungen zu verlassen und sich auf dem Platze, der sich zwischen den grossen Blocks und der Demokratu Strasse befindet, zu versammeln und sich laut Anordnung der Polizei ~~zu ordnen~~ aufzustellen.

Die Ghettoeinwohner müssen sich familienweise aufstellen, und zwar mit dem arbeitenden Familienhaupt an der Spitze.

Die Wohnungen, Schränke, Büfetts, Tische usw. dürfen nicht verschlossen werden.

Nach 6 Uhr morgens darf niemand in den Wohnungen bleiben. Diejenigen, die in ihren Wohnungen nach 6 Uhr früh angetroffen werden, werden auf der Stelle erschossen.

Vilijampolė, den 27. Oktober 1941.

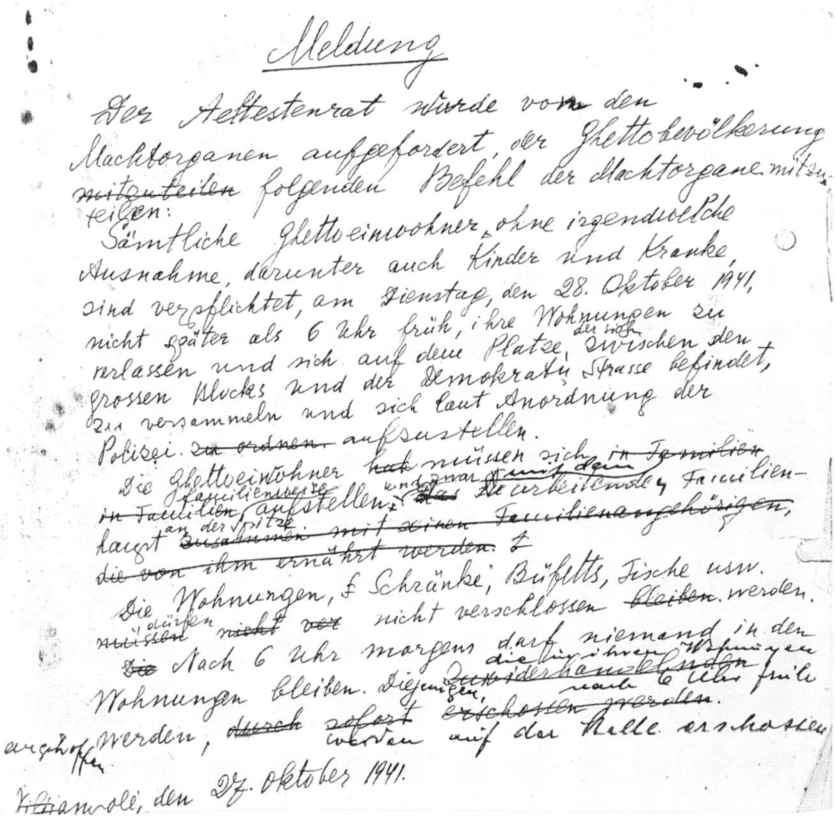

Yad Vashem

The final German wording of the *Ältestenrat*'s assembly announcement

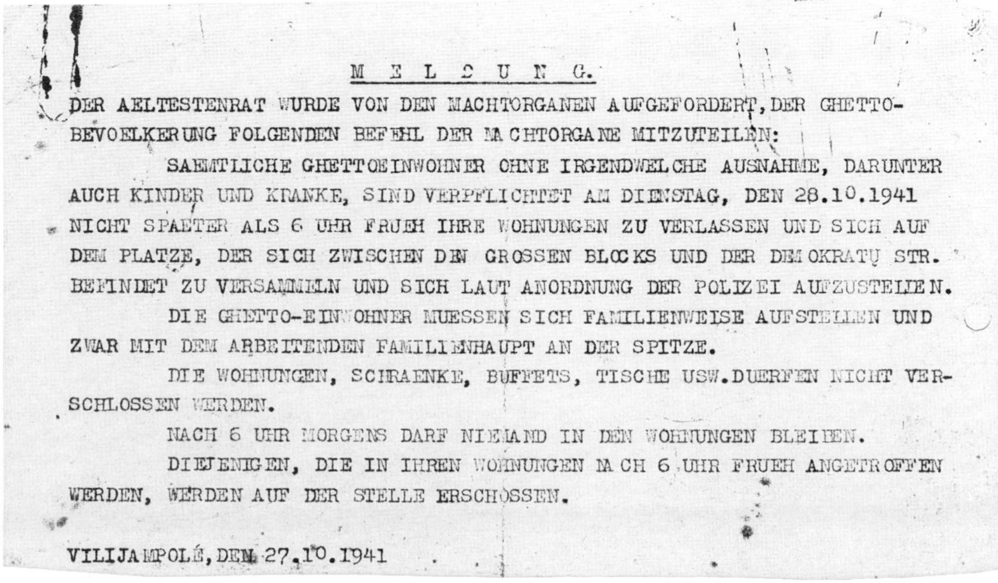

M E L D U N G.

DER AELTESTENRAT WURDE VON DEN MACHTORGANEN AUFGEFORDERT, DER GHETTO-BEVOELKERUNG FOLGENDEN BEFEHL DER MACHTORGANE MITZUTEILEN:

SAEMTLICHE GHETTOEINWOHNER OHNE IRGENDWELCHE AUSNAHME, DARUNTER AUCH KINDER UND KRANKE, SIND VERPFLICHTET AM DIENSTAG, DEN 28.10.1941 NICHT SPAETER ALS 6 UHR FRUEH IHRE WOHNUNGEN ZU VERLASSEN UND SICH AUF DEM PLATZE, DER SICH ZWISCHEN DEN GROSSEN BLOCKS UND DER DEMOKRATU STR. BEFINDET ZU VERSAMMELN UND SICH LAUT ANORDNUNG DER POLIZEI AUFZUSTELLEN.

DIE GHETTO-EINWOHNER MUESSEN SICH FAMILIENWEISE AUFSTELLEN UND ZWAR MIT DEM ARBEITENDEN FAMILIENHAUPT AN DER SPITZE.

DIE WOHNUNGEN, SCHRAENKE, BUFFETS, TISCHE USW. DUERFEN NICHT VERSCHLOSSEN WERDEN.

NACH 6 UHR MORGENS DARF NIEMAND IN DEN WOHNUNGEN BLEIBEN.

DIEJENIGEN, DIE IN IHREN WOHNUNGEN NACH 6 UHR FRUEH ANGETROFFEN WERDEN, WERDEN AUF DER STELLE ERSCHOSSEN.

VILIJAMPOLÉ, DEN 27.10.1941

Yad Vashem

Demokratu Square, Kovno Ghetto

Kadish/BH

Diary of Avraham Tory, October 28, 1941

Early on a dark autumn morning, the 30,000 Jews of the ghetto left their homes, abandoning their residences, their cupboards and dressers, their pantries and drawers; one was not permitted to lock anything. Outdoors, a wet, fine snow from a cloudy sky; a thin white layer covered the earth and the huge Demokratu Square toward which were streaming through the dark autumn morning men and women, young and old, people with children by the hand and in their arms, wrapped and bundled in cloths and rags; with tallow candles in their hands to light the way before them in the darkness. . . .

For the whole day they sorted the 30,000-head crowd on the square. To right and left, to right and left. It began to get dark; evening came, and the sorting had not come to an end. Rauca, the man from the Gestapo, stood in one place from which he separated to life and to death. In the fingers of his right hand was the fate of each individual on the square. If his finger pointed to the right—that fate was sealed; when he pointed left, then that meant life. When the finger would point left, the people went back undisturbed to the saved side. No one touched them anymore, not the Germans and not the partisans. But when the finger pointed to the right, the unfortunates were soon in a dilemma. Upon their heads and bodies was let loose a barrage of blows, with whips and daggers, with hard fists and iron-clad boots, with rifle butts and sticks. If one fell from the blows and lay where he fell, he was beaten so badly that he used his last strength to raise himself up; or two other unfortunates came to his side, took him under the arms, and dragged him along in the march from the square to the Small Ghetto. This meant—to death. Like a master of ceremonies at a parade, Rauca divided the people to the right and to the left very deftly and nimbly, sedately, with a smile on his face, refreshing himself from time to time with a sandwich wrapped in waxed paper. He shouldn't soil his fingers. . . . Every half-hour he demanded of his "people": "The count, the count, I must have the exact count.". . .

The day ended. No one remained on the huge square, but here and there were abandoned benches and chairs that older people had brought with them in the dark dawn and had sat on all day, until their row was called. Left orphaned on the square were cradles and little cots, from infants who had gone in the arms of their unfortunate parents to the right side—to death. Left lying on the ground, far to one side and in a far-flung corner, were several elderly or ill people for whom the day had been much too hard. The cold, the hunger, and especially the terror of waiting for the unknown had hastened their end. They had given up their souls and remained laying on the square. No one had to sort them; they had sorted themselves, no longer able, and perhaps no longer willing, to go through so much in the ghetto and particularly on this long gray day.

Two-thirds turned back towards home late at night (like Yom Kippur in a shtetl after the long fast, after crying and begging) exhausted, hungry, thirsty. Very many returned home broken, torn from their parents, a child, a wife, a brother, or a husband; almost everyone had lost someone to the accounting today. In every house someone was missed, as one misses one's own limb. Their own blood had run today, and they were left impoverished, orphaned, and alone. Each felt small and insecure. The corners of the empty house felt strange. One was afraid of the bed from which one had arisen at last dawn, with everyone together, father, brother, mother, child, who had not returned from the square. The homes of many had been looted by Lithuanian partisans and ordinary robbers. Robbed, the last bit of possessions taken away.

One-third went away from the square to the Small Ghetto, torn away, broken off, beaten black and blue. Most had not grasped what this signified. Others had hoped to begin something anew in the unknown situation. But what that something was, no one knew. Each hoped there would be something, some continuation; not to be cut off, broken off from their lives of before. In the Small Ghetto, there began a drama of tragedy and doubt. . . .

Esther Lurie, *Demokratu Square,* **undated**
(watercolor, pen, and ink, 6⁷/₈ x 8³/₄ in.)

Diary of Elena Kutorgiene, October 30, 1941

No one [in the Small Ghetto] suspected his fate. They thought they were being taken to other quarters (arguments even broke out on this account). They walked quietly, without resisting. At dawn a rumor began to spread that the prisoners of war being held at the Ninth Fort—the Fort of Death—were digging deep ditches. When the people started being taken there, they understood that this meant death. They began to cry and sob and scream . . . Those who tried to escape along the road were killed. Many of their bodies remained in the fields. The Germans took some of the people to the fort on trucks. There, they were forced to undress, and in groups of 300 they were pushed into the ditches that had been dug.

There they were killed—shot with automatic rifles and machine guns. Those who were doomed were kept naked in the cold for several hours. The children were thrown first into the ditches, often into water. Then the women were shot at the edge of the ditch, so that they would fall in. Then the men . . . Many were buried alive. All those who did the killing were drunk. An acquaintance told me today that all this was recounted to him by a German soldier who witnessed it. The soldier added that the day before he had written to his Catholic wife, saying: "Yesterday I became convinced that there is no God, because if He did exist, He would not allow what has taken place."

The next day the clothing of those who were murdered was brought out on trucks.

Diary of Avraham Tory, October 28, 1941

It was the first day after the downfall of the Kovno Jewish community, after the downfall of the Jewry of all Lithuania. On that day the concept of a Jewish settlement in Lithuania ceased to exist, a link was ripped out of the chain of Jewish history. After the "Great Action," the ghetto became melancholic; no one had any faith in the Gestapo's assurances that this was the last "action" and that there would be no more; that from now on everyone would remain alive, work, and exist. One only waited, like one who must go into the military: one does not want it, but it will come, it must come, it is unavoidable. From this very inevitability, people in the ghetto trembled. Ten thousand people were taken away in the "Great Action."

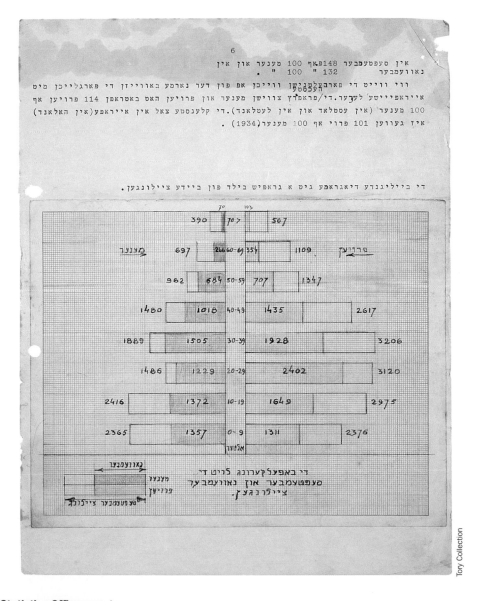

Tory Collection

This chart, from the ghetto's Statistics Office report "The September and November Census in 1941," reveals the population losses due mainly to the "Great Action" of October 28, 1941. The statistics are presented by age group *(center column)* and by gender, male *(left)* and female *(right)*.

Kadish/BH

Fort IX, August 1944

Diary of Elena Kutorgiene, December 4, 1941

Ten thousand foreign Jews have been brought here. I saw them walking with their suitcases. They were told they were being taken to work and ordered to bring their most valuable possessions with them. Then they were killed at the Ninth Fort. They say the young people among them, not suspecting anything, danced the night before. In the morning they were taken in groups of 50 to their death. Lithuania is now called the cemetery of Europe's Jews.

Deposition of Gestapo collaborator Ignas Velavicius-Vilius, December 20, 1945, and January 12, 1946

On December 11, 1941, at 5:00 A.M., I came . . . to Fort IX where 3,000 persons from Austria were already prepared to be shot. They were nearly all old women and children over the age of 2; the majority were disabled. . . . I ordered the prisoners to assemble in the courtyard in groups of 100 and undress to their underwear. In the freezing cold they were forced to run to the mass graves, where they climbed in, lay down, and were shot. In order to prevent the gunfire, the screaming, and the crying from being heard, truck engines ran continuously. In this treacherous way, the German guards and I led naked, freezing people—old people, women, and children—to their grave every 10–15 minutes, where they began to comprehend that they were about to be killed.

Personal papers of German Jews killed at Fort IX
in December 1941

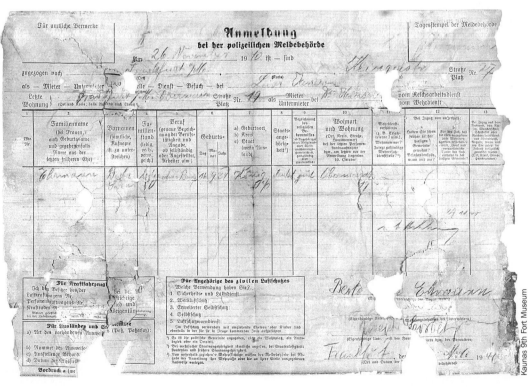

71

Luggage tags from the belongings of Jews
brought from Germany and Austria for execution
at Fort IX

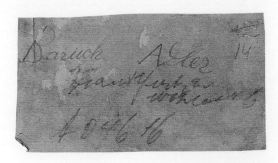

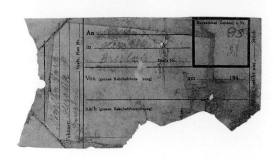

Erich Israel Sänger
geb. 27 Dezember 1922
Kennort. Ffm.
Kennummer A 7958

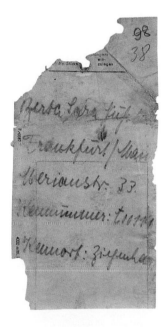

Samuel Weiss
III.
Sechsdrücker
3/2

15

Ständiger Wohnort

Straße
Platz Nr.

nach
(Bestimmungsbahnhof)

*) Angabe im deutschen Verkehr freigestellt,
im Auslandsverkehr stets notwendig

Name des Reisenden.

Ständiger Wohnort

Straße - Platz - Nr.

Von
Bahnhof
(Versand-
bahnhof)

am

nach
Bahnhof:
(Empfangs-
bahnhof)

Modantler
Heinrich Israel
Wien

A released prisoner's account of Fort IX, Diary of Avraham Tory, June 12, 1942

We were sitting in the afternoon. Suddenly a truck—women and men who had been here earlier for investigation—they did not have any things with them. No things. They knew that they had been brought here to be shot. The men: Zukhovitsh, Lipman, Zalmanovits, Lifshits, Zev, Loyfer, Berman; Mrs. Fridman and others. They all held up well. Berman cried. He had brought a prayer book with him. They spent the night. They stood in line for soup, took a little extra. The attitude of the guards toward them was as toward garbage.

List of Jews shot at Fort IX on June 3, 1942

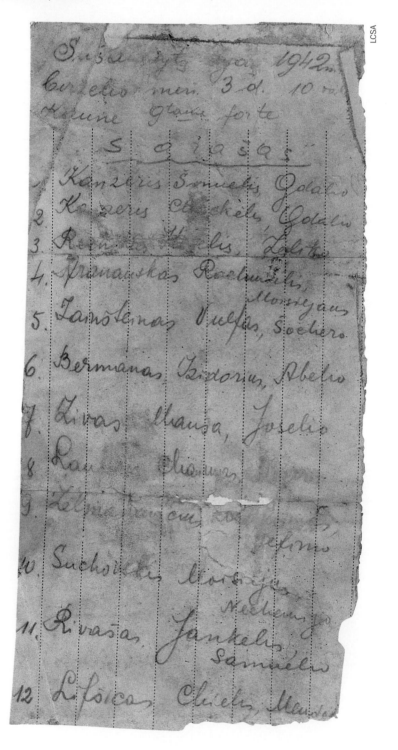

**Personal items of victims recovered during
excavation at Fort IX in 1962**

Diary of Tamara Lazerson, September 18, 1943

[My brother] Victor brought some bad news. It appears [our brother] RUDOLPH IS SHOT. Victor had met someone who had been with him in the Fort. No! I don't want it! I don't believe it. No! It can't be! The heart says no! My lips scream no! It takes only a few evil people. O God, how frightening it is. DEAR BROTHER, YOU ARE STILL ALIVE, I know. My heart is certain and it says NO! A silence, a terrifying silence. You walls, why are you so quiet? Shout, speak to me, calm my soul, just tell me one word, one precious word, "No!"

"Nightmares,"
by K. L. Yemo [Moshe Klein] *(excerpt)*

How can I fall asleep if execution
awaits me? How can I doze
in the lion's paw? Therefore I lie
with eyes open, conversing with my heart.

When will the hangman's hand smite me—
will it happen on a glorious night—
when the nightingale pours out its song
and herbs perfume the air?

On that luminous night we'll be led
to slaughter—sounds of weeping tearing
the heart; only the baby will be happy:
oh, we're going out for a stroll . . .

Or will it be a summer's end—air
overflowing with the land's blessings—
when the executioner decides
to do us in?

Or will it be on a dark autumn's night—
rain, cold as needle punctures
drizzling down our cheeks—
when we're all led to be butchered?

Or will it be in the midst of a grim
winter—the storm bursting into the house
making treasures of snow dance
and the cold freezing the spine.

*Klein, who wrote under the name K. L. Yemo,
was killed during the liquidation of the Kovno
Ghetto, July 1944*

The road to Fort IX

Following the "Great Action"—the summary murder in late October 1941 of nearly one-third of the ghetto's population—Kovno's grieving Jewish population slowly tried to put its life in order. It was to the *Ältestenrat,* the Jewish Council of Elders, that the ghetto's prisoners turned for a measure of relief from hunger and homelessness. The council's capacity to help, however, was severely limited. The *Ältestenrat* was, after all, an instrument of German coercion, used by the German authorities to communicate and enforce relentless directives. Some inmates criticized it as a privileged elite. Still, to the extent possible, the council attempted to ameliorate the dire conditions of daily survival.

The *Ältestenrat* supervised several offices for managing the ghetto's public order, allocating scarce resources, and controlling contagious disease. Except for offices responsible for schools and civil justice, which the Germans terminated in summer 1942, most council offices were active until the ghetto's conversion to a concentration camp in fall 1943. Even before the ghetto was sealed, the Germans ordered into existence a Jewish Ghetto Police. Like other offices, its role was profoundly ambiguous, acknowledged for its protection of order in the ghetto but also despised by many for enforcing onerous German directives, such as rounding up Jews for forced labor and for deportation.

For the German authorities, the ghetto's purpose was strictly utilitarian: to meet their constant demands for labor. The *Ältestenrat* therefore operated on two levels: to assure a steady labor supply for the German war effort and the region's economy as well as to provide relief from desperate physical and emotional want. The ghetto's Housing Office and Firefighters strove to keep the community adequately and safely housed, while the Health Office worked to protect it from typhus and other debilitating illnesses. Although only forty doctors worked in the open after the burning of the hospital for contagious diseases in early October 1941, medical officials enforced rigorous standards of cleanliness and sanitation; the police threw offenders in jail.

Exemplifying the council's hopeless predicament was its distribution of meager food and fuel rations. Food allocations amounted to just half the rations allowed to the Lithuanian population. Those who did not receive food at work could obtain coupons to the Welfare Office's soup kitchen. In addition, the council established community vegetable gardens.

The Germans targeted the ghetto's children from the start, killing more than 4,200 in the "Great Action," nearly half the victims. Too young to endure labor conditions, they existed precariously as expendable, "non-productive" prey. Still, in November 1941, the council set up schools despite the lack of teachers, books, and firewood, offering not only supervision but also a chance to train children in useful skills.

To meet incessant German labor demands in an orderly fashion, the *Ältestenrat* almost immediately established a Labor Office. As of December 1941, all Jews over the age of 16 had to work 12-hour days, most in regimented brigades outside ghetto boundaries. One-quarter of the ghetto—half of those able to work—labored under severe conditions at building and repairing the nearby Aleksotas military airfield, the most demanding of the corrosive toil that had come to characterize ghetto life.

Diary of Avraham Tory, June 5, 1943

The people come to the *Ältestenrat* seeking a chance to lighten their difficult lives—maybe to change from a hard workplace to a better one, to receive a furlough due to illness, to request a pair of wooden shoes, a pair of trousers to avoid going naked, an additional ration to supplement the watery *yushnik*, to request a chance for better housing, to moderate an order that the ghetto authorities had issued, and so on. They also come to the *Ältestenrat* to hear news, what the situation is. In this place the ghetto simmers.

Organizational chart of the *Ältestenrat,* from the yearbook "Slobodka Ghetto 1942." The items crossed out in red indicate departments that the Germans disbanded.

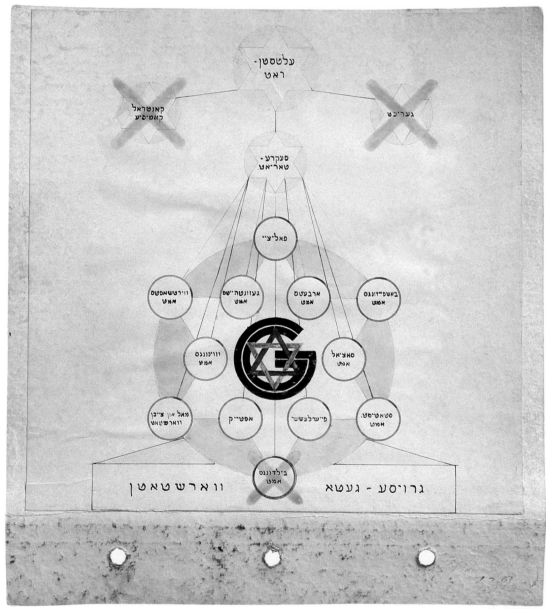

Members of the *Ältestenrat,* the ghetto's Jewish Council, 1943. *Left to right*: Avraham Tory, head of the Secretariat; Leib Garfunkel, deputy chairman; Dr. Elkhanan Elkes, chairman; Yakov Goldberg, head of the Labor Office; Zvi Levin, an adviser.

Tory Collection

Key to organizational chart of the *Ältestenrat*

Ältestenrat
(Jewish Council)

Control
Commission

Court

Secretariat

Police

Economic
Office

Health
Office

Labor
Office

Food
Supply
Office

Housing
Office

Welfare
Office

Paint and
Sign Work-
shop

Pharmacy

Firefighters

Statistics
Office

Education
Office

Large Ghetto Workshops

Armbands worn by officials of the Jewish ghetto community

Council of Elders of the Jewish Ghetto Community

Jewish Ghetto Police

Administrative Office of the Health Service

Ghetto Workshops

Jewish Ghetto Firefighters

"Slobodka Ghetto 1942" yearbook

An armband in the ghetto is not just a badge, a part of a uniform. In the days of "actions," people's lives were saved only thanks to their armbands. Thus, the ghetto residents stormed the *Ältestenrat* demanding armbands, and their value inflated. But in the "Great Action" of October 28, 1941, many ghetto residents died tragically in their armbands.

Esther Lurie, *The Jewish Council Building*, undated
(watercolor, pen, and ink, 7 x 8¹/₂ in.)

Lyrics from "Ghetto-Jew, Answer Me This," by Avrom Akselrod, 1942

Ghetto-Jew, ghetto-Jew, answer me this—
Who wants to play first fiddle here?
Who of the big shots wants to rule
Over us all just like a king?

(Chorus)
Tsimbale, tsimbale, play, ghetto Jew,
Play a song about ghetto big shots,
About "inspectors," about "chiefs"
Climbing so high in the ghetto ranks.

Which of the big shots can give you a card,
And maybe a pass to keep you alive,
And how many do you then have to pay,
In order to get in a decent brigade?

(Chorus)

How do the big shots eat their white pastries,
Cookies, warm bagels, rolls, and such,
Whiling their time at music and cards,
And "holidays" with actual tortes!

(Chorus)

Have the big shots worked at the airfield
With an ax, a crowbar, or spade?
Maybe our big shots would comprehend
Why we heap such curses on them.

(Chorus)

Who needs concerts amid such great sadness,
When hunger whines in every poor house.
Better to give the workers some soup,
And stop dancing at fancy-dress balls.

(Chorus)

Ghetto inhabitants gather outside the
Ältestenrat building to meet each other and
learn the latest news.

Insignia painted on leather and metal for
the *Ältestenrat*

ELKHANAN ELKES

Letter from Elkhanan Elkes to his children, October 19, 1943

I have stood at the head of the ghetto since the day of its founding. The community selected me and the authorities confirmed me as the head of the Council of Elders [Ältestenrat] along with my friend and colleague, the lawyer Leib Garfunkel. . . . We are steering our battered ship in the heart of the ocean while every day waves of persecutions and harsh decrees hasten to drown it. I've stood at my post with upright countenance, not pleading for mercy but demanding satisfaction, trusting in the honesty and justice of our claims.

Like other chairmen of ghetto Jewish councils in Nazi-occupied Europe, Elkhanan Elkes endeavored against impossible odds to navigate between coercive German orders and the Jewish community's interests. By most accounts, including those who otherwise disparaged the ghetto's Jewish leadership, he managed to gain the residents' respect and helped to preserve, at least during the period of relative calm (late 1941 to fall 1943), a significant measure of stability. In addition to fortifying residents' daily endurance, he encouraged writers, artists, and fellow council members to secretly document the severe tribulations of life in the Kovno Ghetto.

There is little in Elkes's background besides his intelligence and personal integrity to suggest that he would emerge as one of the exemplary Jewish figures in the Holocaust era. Before the war Elkes had achieved a reputation as a skilled physician in private practice and in service to the Bikur Holim Jewish hospital in the city of Kovno. Born in 1879 in Kalvarija, a small town in southern Lithuania (near the German border in what was then part of tsarist Russia) and educated in Kovno, Elkes received his medical degree in 1903 in neurology and several other specialties. After serving as a physician in the Russian army during World War I, he returned to Kovno and, in 1923, became head of the internal medicine department in Kovno's Jewish hospital. He also became the personal physician to Lithuania's prime minister, the German ambassador, and many others in the diplomatic community residing in Kovno, the capital of the newly independent Lithuanian Republic.

Members of the ghetto administration. Elkhanan Elkes, chairman of the *Ältestenrat,* is seated in the center.

Dr. Elkhanan Elkes *(front row, third from right)* among the staff of the Bikur Holim Jewish Hospital in Kovno, 1933

By the end of the 1930s, Elkes was widely known and admired among Kovno's Jews as a kind and good-humored doctor. But he was also a private man. Ideologically, Elkes was affiliated with the General Zionists, but he did not participate in organized political life.

The German invasion of Lithuania propelled Elkes to the forefront of political activity. The crucial moment came on August 4, 1941, when the Kovno Jewish community leaders urged Elkes to accept election as chairman of the German-mandated *Ältestenrat*. They felt that his personal character and contacts with Germans more than compensated for his age (he was 62), poor health, and political inexperience. Indeed, they considered his apolitical background an advantage. Elkes, protesting that he lacked administrative skill, reluctantly accepted this painful assignment.

Elkes utilized his facility with German authorities, and a certain respect he knew they had for him (they sometimes requested his medical service), to try to stave off assault. Due to an illness that kept him bed-ridden for most of 1942, he left running the ghetto's day-to-day administrative affairs in the hands of his deputy, Leib Garfunkel. Elkes acted chiefly as an intercessor for the ghetto with the German authorities, endeavoring to cancel or ameliorate their decrees. He took advantage

of the German-created ghetto workshops to provide work—a prerequisite for survival—for those residents who never would have endured the backbreaking rigor of forced labor. As recorded by the *Ältestenrat*'s secretary, Avraham Tory, Elkes struggled, in vain, to exert whatever pressure he felt he could by daring to remind the Germans that, after the war, they could be held accountable for their behavior. During the ghetto's final days, for example, as the Soviet Army approached Kovno, Elkes promised favorable postwar testimony in an effort to persuade SS-Captain Wilhelm Goecke, commandant of Concentration Camp Kauen (as the ghetto was recast) to spare the surviving Jews of Kovno.

For all his tenacity, Elkes ultimately had no choice but to preside over the ghetto's destruction. This

Imprint bearing Elkes's name taken from a stamp for official ghetto documents

became unmistakably clear early on, when in October 1941 he was given the order to assemble the entire ghetto population at Demokratu Square. After consulting with his *Ältestenrat* colleagues and with Chief Rabbi Avraham Duber Shapiro, Elkes decided that by obeying the order he might at least save part of the community. Even during the "Great Action" that ensued, he tried to win the release of 100 of the more than 9,000 victims selected for murder. For the effort, he was summarily beaten. Two years later, in his final letter to his children that recounts the ghetto's tragedies, he wrote: "Many shattered souls, widows and orphans, threadbare and hungry, are camping on our doorstep imploring us for help. My strength is ebbing. There is a desert inside me. My soul is scorched. I am naked and empty, and there are no words in my mouth."

All accounts of Elkes's life and leadership affirm his high moral standards and devotion to helping the Jewish community, however hopeless that task ultimately was. Under his leadership, the *Ältestenrat* maintained close relationships with the Jewish Ghetto Police, holding it to responsible behavior. He encouraged underground groups and, toward the end, helped make it possible for ghetto inmates to escape to the partisans in the forests.

In July 1944, Elkhanan Elkes was among the almost 2,100 men deported from Kovno via Stettin to the Dachau concentration camp, where he died on October 17, 1944. Even there, though very ill, he offered what medical assistance he could. Though his fall 1943 letter to his children and many of the records of his activities survive, his reputation as a deeply sympathetic and courageous figure is perhaps his most important legacy.

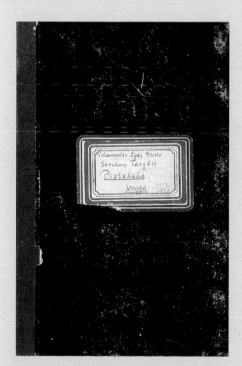 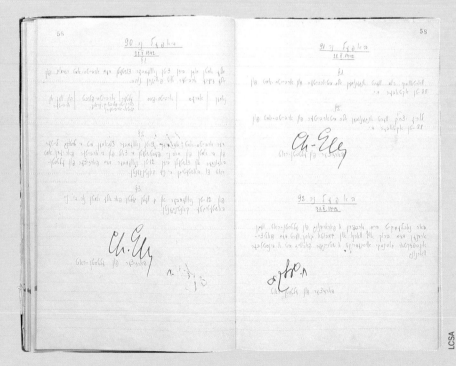

LCSA

"Proceedings Book" of the *Ältestenrat*. Here were recorded the decisions and orders of the council's meetings as issued over Elkes's signature.

"History of the Vilijampole Jewish Ghetto Police," 1942–43

It should be emphasized that in order to maintain more or less some kind of order and thereby head off our "dear" masters from having to come into the ghetto and make their order, which would involve casualties, we must have a strong hand; there must be an organization [a Jewish ghetto police] that keeps the population in line out of fear, for the good of all.

Members of Jewish Ghetto Police studying a map of the ghetto

Kadish/BH

Map of the ghetto as of October 1942 demarcating its three police precincts

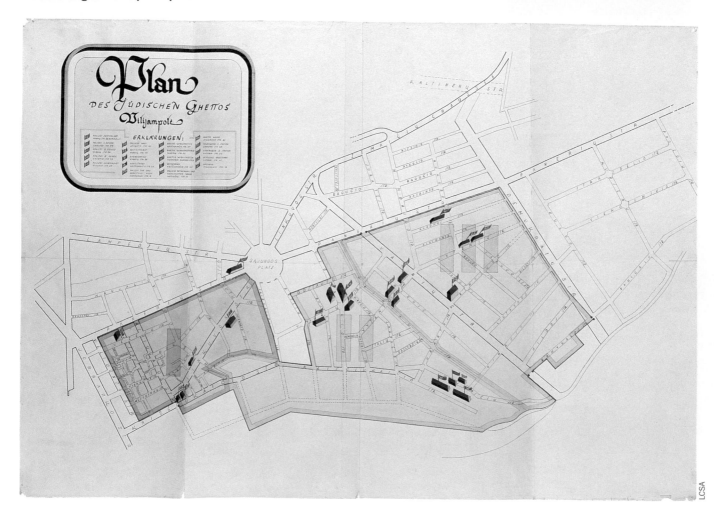

LCSA

Kadish/BH

Moshe Levin, chief of the Jewish Ghetto Police
(left), with two of his deputies, Yehuda Zupowitz
(center) and Tanchum Aronshtam *(right)*

LCSA

Police gather on main road

Kadish/BH

Policeman at the entrance of the ghetto
police criminal division offices. This office
was in charge of investigating crime in
the ghetto.

Recruitment poster for the Jewish Ghetto
Police. The poster specifically advertises for
former army veterans and asks potential
recruits to bring proof of military service.

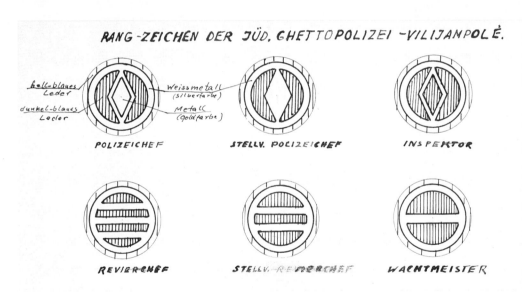

**Graphics Office designs for police
insignia**

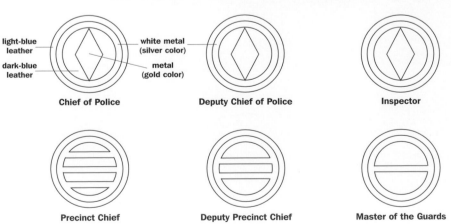

Rank Designation for the Jewish Ghetto Police—Vilijampole

light-blue
leather

white metal
(silver color)

dark-blue
leather

metal
(gold color)

Chief of Police

Deputy Chief of Police

Inspector

Precinct Chief

Deputy Precinct Chief

Master of the Guards

Police insignia designs recorded in the year-book "Slobodka Ghetto 1942"

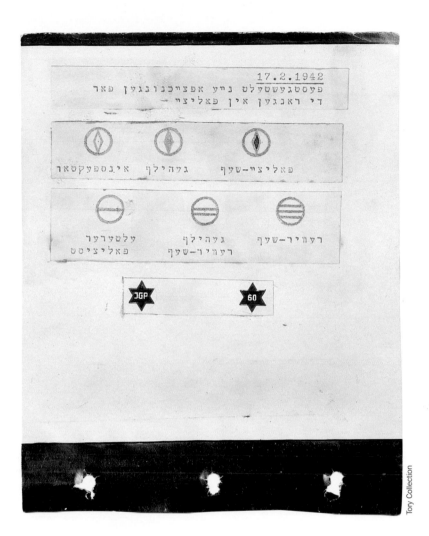

Samples of the police insignia made of leather and metal

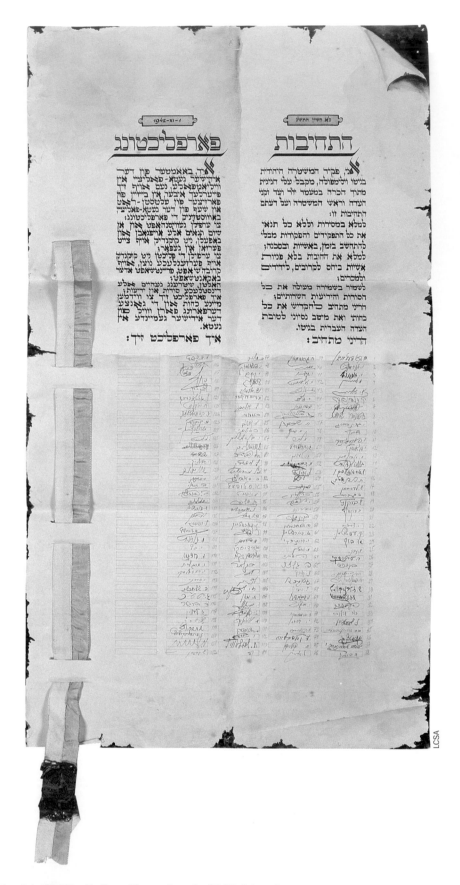

Oath of the Jewish Ghetto Police, November 1, 1942 *(above)*

I, a member of the Jewish Ghetto Police in Vilijampole, in the presence of the Chairman of the *Ältestenrat* and the Chief of Police, solemnly take upon myself this conscious oath: To conscientiously fulfill, without conditions, all assignments and orders, regardless of time, person, or danger; to fulfill this oath regardless of personal use, kinship, friendship, or acquaintanceship; to hold in strict confidence all secrets and information that I learn in this service. I pledge to dedicate my energies and all my efforts to the welfare of the Jewish community in the ghetto.

I pledge myself:

[signatures]

"The *Ältestenrat* and Its Offices," report, early 1942

The Ghetto Firefighters is made up of former Kovno and Slobodka Jewish volunteer firemen who were put into the ghetto in August and September 1941.

The main task of the firefighters is to protect the ghetto from destructive fires, and when fires should break out, to localize them. . . . The Ghetto Firefighters also has an array of other work. . . .

The firemen transported the wounded and sick to the ghetto hospital, which until October 4, 1941, was in the Small Ghetto. Today, due to the lack of transport, the sick are also carried to the hospital on stretchers by the firemen. . . .

They also built the fence along the new borders of the shrunken ghetto.

In pressing cases, for extra control and mobilization of workers, . . . the firemen also serve as police assistants.

During the big house-searches and confiscation "actions," the Jewish firefighters had an unusual task: searching for valuables in the wells where they were thrown by their owners, and taking the valuables to the assigned collection areas. This was to avert a catastrophe in the ghetto in cases where the valuables were already known to the authorities.

Firemen at work on the ghetto fence

Kadish/GK

"Slobodka Ghetto 1942" yearbook

The Firefighters are responsible for the barbed-wire fence around the entire ghetto. But approaching the ghetto fence can draw the death penalty. With their armbands, the Firefighters are recognizable, and the danger is lessened.

Armband illustrations from the yearbook "Slobodka Ghetto 1942" for the Jewish Ghetto Firefighters *(top)* and for the ghetto messengers *(center),* here described as 10- to 12-year-old boys who ran communications between the *Ältestenrat* and its offices

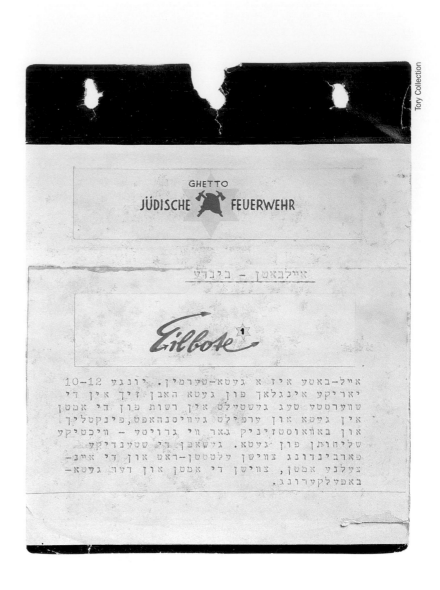

Members of the Jewish Ghetto Firefighters

"The *Ältestenrat* and Its Offices," report, early 1942

In the first days of July 1941, . . . the Jews in Kovno already felt very insecure and were in a hurry to get out of the city. Thousands of Jews besieged the Housing Office every day to arrange for a living space in Slobodka. A flight of elemental force began from the city. . . . Many Jews had to settle temporarily in study houses, synagogues, and other buildings that had been transformed into asylums. Thousands of Jews were simply left with their things in the courtyards, gardens, and fields.

Jews not already living in Vilijampole had to vacate their houses and move all their possessions to the ghetto.

Kadish/GK

Logo created by the Paint and Sign Workshop for the ghetto's Housing Office

USHMM

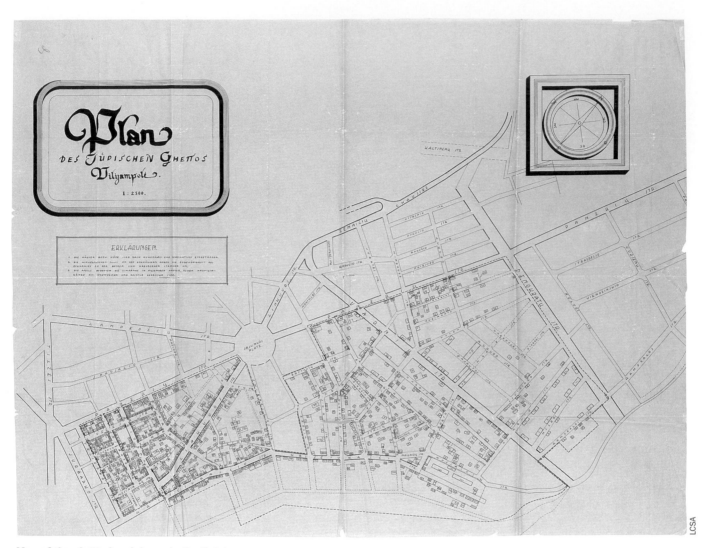

Map of the ghetto hand-drawn in the Paint
and Sign Workshop, with house numbers
written on each block

People wait outside Housing Office for
assistance

List compiled by the Housing Office for the year-book "Slobodka Ghetto 1942" showing street by street the number of dwellings, apartments, rooms, kitchens, square meters of space, population, and square meters per person. As of December 31, 1942, the 16,489 inhabitants of the ghetto averaged fewer than three square meters of living space each.

Wohnungsamt der jüdischen Ghetto-Gemeinde — Stand des Ghettos zum 31/XII 42

		Anzahl				Fläche in m²		Einwohnerzahl	Durchschnitts-fläche pro Person in m²
		Wohn-häuser	Wohn-ausgen	Zimmer	Küchen	Zimmer	Küchen		
1	Akmenes	1	3	3	3	41.4	20.60	22	1.88
2	Aldonos	11	22	49	20	464.1	158.85	160	2.92
3	Algimanto	4	6	10	5	126.-	35.30	41	3.57
4	Ariogalos	51	147	305	98	3539.95	605.45	1100	3.22
5	Auxuro	2	4	4	-	65.6	—	21	3.09
6	Bajoru	12	40	81	33	975.8	247.-	335	3.95
7	Broliu	4	13	18	10	198.75	61.40	77	3.24
8	Dailidziu	9	23	30	18	387.50	127.50	141	3.04
9	Demokratu	2	11	19	2	249.6	52.-	77	3.24
10	Dvaro	23	57	102	41	1157.09	255.65	377	3.07
11	Erzvilkos	5	9	16	5	176.45	23.80	64	2.76
12	Gimbuto	10	49	83	17	1068.-	217.50	343	3.11
13	Girucio	4	14	23	12	248.3	65.70	85	2.92
14	Gostauto	4	14	30	13	407.2	93.60	141	2.69
15	Griniaus	31	83	123	65	1413	542.60	533	2.65
16	Jaunucio	10	26	37	14	448.1	102.50	151	2.96
17	Jesiboto	28	68	153	49	1592.15	290.-	610	2.61
18	Joniskelio	2	3	5	3	49.-	13.60	20	2.45
19	Koxliu	22	57	116	40	1332.24	297.06	443	3.-
20	Krisciunaicio	102	232	568	256	6425.30	850.33	2238	2.87
21	Kriuxu	14	32	65	17	637.80	95.20	232	2.80
22	Linxmenu	9	22	41	11	432.80	82.40	152	2.84
23	Linxuvos	56	197	463	124	5889.27	799.65	1840	3.20
24	Liubarto	4	16	18	15	222.8	93.30	83	2.68
25	Liutovaro	9	23	29	11	350.8	79.30	139	2.51
26	Margio	18	56	81	36	987.-	194.50	322	3.06
27	Mesininku	15	37	86	22	979.85	123.-	320	3.06
28	Mildos	7	32	67	31	942.10	124.-	263	3.58
29	Mindaugo	6	18	34	15	408.85	102.-	127	3.22
30	Moxyxlos	18	35	85	20	846.70	126.40	298	2.84
31	Naslaiciu	7	17	25	14	313.10	80.40	110	2.84
32	Paneriu	38	120	241	98	2563.76	598.75	945	2.71
33	Puodziu	19	58	105	52	1200.78	884.12	378	3.17
34	Rabinu	10	22	45	20	452.30	130.40	169	2.70
35	Ramygalos	8	18	36	18	401.40	131.75	148	2.70
36	Sinagogos	2	7	17	6	162.25	36.90	46	3.52
37	Sintautu	2	2	6	2	54.90	17.40	20	2.74
38	Sxirgailos	4	17	24	13	352.20	93.-	122	2.88
39	Skirmanto	5	12	22	11	256.85	116.30	84	3.06
40	Staliu	11	27	35	17	406.50	136.20	156	3.60
41	Stulginskio	21	61	94	51	1073.20	291.30	381	2.82
42	Varguoles	1	1	1	1	12.-	6.-	3	4.-
43	Varniu	23	181	338	113	4673.65	904.05	1532	3.05
44	Voliuozos	7	12	33	11	335.30	62.-	109	3.26
45	Vezeju	28	78	167	66	1725.45	418.89	598	2.91
46	Viduriné	13	30	73	21	758.50	123.75	261	2.90
47	Vygriu	10	33	72	27	837.90	182.40	275	3.04
48	Vytenio	26	61	97	49	1057.70	355.60	397	2.64
		728	2106	4175	1565	48701.14	10464.60	16489	2.95

"Health Institutions in the Ghetto," report to the *Ältestenrat,* mid-1943

The region designated to be the ghetto was, from a hygienic point of view, the worst in the city.
. . . In the early days of the ghetto there were cases of typhoid fever, a few of diphtheria and
scarlet fever, and a lot of smallpox. It was urgently necessary that the sick be isolated, because
due to the extraordinary crowding the possibility of an epidemic was very great.

**In the ghetto hospital,
after 1941**

Kadish/GK

Tory Collection

**Armband illustrations and descriptions from
the yearbook "Slobodka Ghetto 1942" for the
Jewish Sanitation Service in the Ghetto** *(top)*
and the Ghetto Workshops *(center)*

"Slobodka Ghetto 1942" yearbook

The doctors and nurses of the Sanitation Service were often called on to attend to patients at night. To walk around in the ghetto after 10 P.M. is forbidden. With the armbands for the Sanitation Service, they can do their work even at night.

"Health Institutions in the Ghetto," report to the *Ältestenrat*, mid-1943

An important task of the Health Office was the Sanitation Service, thanks to which the ghetto was protected from epidemics and infectious diseases. The Sanitation Service stayed in constant contact with the Jewish Ghetto Police, fighting the untidiness of the residences and courtyards, establishing when and in what order to clean the courtyards, corridors, rooms, and streets, and how often to clean the toilets and septic pits.

Dr. Moses Brauns, head of the Sanitation Service, portrait by Josef Schlesinger, 1943
(pen and ink, 4³/8 x 3¹/2 in.)

Dr. Jacob Nochimowski, chief physician for the Labor Office, portrait by Josef Schlesinger, 1943
(pen and ink, 4 x 3³/8 in.)

Dr. Benjamin Zacharin, head of the Health Office, portrait by Josef Schlesinger, 1943
(pen and ink, 4¹/2 x 3¹/2 in.)

Tory Collection

Diagram indicating the illnesses that affected
women; from the report by Dr. Jacob Nochimowski
on labor and illness in the ghetto

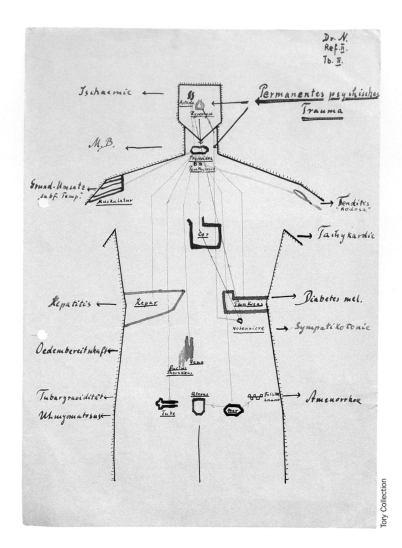

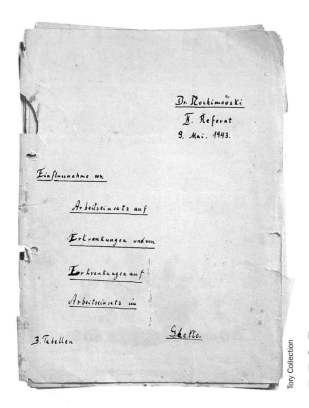

Report by Dr. Jacob Nochimowski, chief physician
of the Labor Office, on "The Effect of Work on
Illnesses and of Illnesses on Work in the Ghetto,"
May 9, 1943

Medical report by Dr. Jacob Nochimowski, May 9, 1943

During the course of the summer, when clogs were issued, injured feet, prevalent equally
among women and men, took on another form. I shall call this "foot erosion." The tough leather
attached to impractical wooden soles with no give and with their hard edges caused deep and
painful cuts after a few hours or one day of wear. These wounds took a considerable time to
heal. Only later in the fall, when the shape of the clogs was changed and protective cloths were
used, was it possible to wear these without causing damage. This foot erosion resulting from
poor footwear and poor stockings over long marches, noted particularly in the calcaneus [heel],
malleolus [ankle], and hallux [great toe] regions, became a very significant reason for sick leave.

Memorandum from *Reichskommissar* Hinrich Lohse, August 13, 1941

The ghettos are to be given only as much food as the rest of the population can do without, but no more than the bare minimum necessary for the ghetto inmates.

"Order No. 1" from SA-Colonel Hans Cramer, August 25, 1942

As of August 26, 1942 the following new regulations regarding Jewish rations will be enacted:

1.) Designated rations per person for the ghetto inhabitants will be allotted weekly to the *Ältestenrat* in the following amounts:

Bread	700 grams [1.5 lb.]
Meat	125 grams [4 oz.]
Flour	112.5 grams [4 oz.]
Grains	75 grams [3 oz.]
Salt	50 grams [2 oz.]

2.) The *Ältestenrat* has the responsibility for the free, fair, and orderly distribution of these amounts.

3.) When the weekly rations are received, the German administrator of the ghetto workshops is to be immediately informed for the purpose of inspecting the amount and quality of the food supply.

4.) In addition to the above noted ration, an additional ration will be given to the Jewish inhabitants who work.

5.) Until further notice, the additional ration per person per week consists of:

Bread	700 grams [1.5 lb.]
Meat	125 grams [4 oz.]
Lard	20 grams [2/3 oz.]

6.) The additional ration as a rule will be distributed at the workplace.

7.) In case of exceptions, the additional rations along with a list of names will be given to the *Ältestenrat* who are responsible for the immediate distribution to those listed.

8.) Any unauthorized procurement of food is not allowed.

9.) Any attempt in the future to bring food into the ghetto will be severely punished.

Ration coupons distributed from Food
Supply Office

Staatbrig. Zusatzration
Fleisch 0,125 Kg.

VISIERT
Arbeitseinsatzstelle

C. No. 3555

Rb. 30,- Dreissig.

JÜDISCHES GHETTO
ARBEITSAMT
VILIJAMPOLE

ESSENKARTE

FRONTBAULEITUNG 3/1

Sonnabend

Freitag

Donnerstag

Mittwoch

Dienstag

Montag

Sonntag

Staatbrig. Zusatzration
Kartoffel 2,4 kg.

VISIERT
Arbeitseinsatzstelle

73673

Rb. 5,- Fünf

FRAUEN

JÜDISCHES GHETTO
ARBEITSAMT
VILIJAMPOLE

2197

MÄNNER

JÜDISCHES GHETTO
ARBEITSAMT
VILIJAMPOLE

C. No. 6388

Rb. 30,- Dreissig.

JÜDISCHES GHETTO
ARBEITSAMT
VILIJAMPOLE

"LUISE-KOHLE"

Name

Vorn.

Adr.

Gültig bis

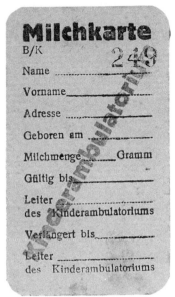

Milchkarte

B/K 249

Name ....

Vorname ....

Adresse ....

Geboren am ....

Milchmenge ....Gramm

Gültig bis ....

Leiter ....

des Kinderambulatoriums

Verlängert bis ....

Leiter ....

des Kinderambulatoriums

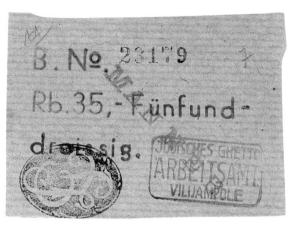

B. No. 23179

Rb. 35,- Fünfund-

dreissig.

JÜDISCHES GHETTO ARBEITSAMT VILIJAMPOLE

70911

Rb. 5,- Fünf

FRAUEN

ARBEITSAMT VILIJAMPOLE

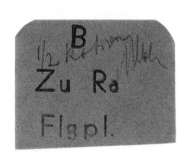

B

½

Zu Ra

Flgpl.

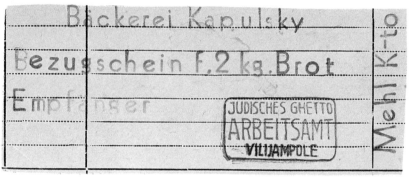

Bäckerei Kapulsky

Bezugschein f. 2 kg. Brot

Empfänger

JÜDISCHES GHETTO ARBEITSAMT VILIJAMPOLE

Mehl K-to

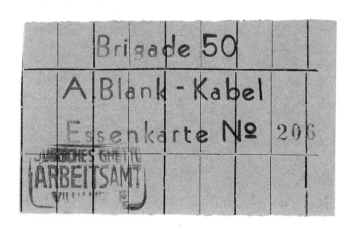

Brigade 50

A. Blank - Kabel

Essenkarte № 206

JÜDISCHES GHETTO ARBEITSAMT VILIJAMPOLE

26

Gut Noreikiskiai

JÜDISCHES GHETTO ARBEITSAMT VILIJAMPOLE

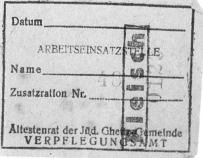

Datum ....

ARBEITSEINSATZSTELLE

Name ....

Zusatzration Nr. ....

Ältestenrat der Jüd. Ghetto-Gemeinde
VERPFLEGUNGSAMT

Datum ....

ARBEITSEINSATZSTELLE

Name ....

Zusatzration Nr. ....

Ältestenrat der Jüd. Ghetto-Gemeinde
VERPFLEGUNGSAMT

Fl. Küche 2

655 Mittag

JÜDISCHE ARBEI VILI

Imprint of a stamp for the Food
Supply Office

Ghetto residents wait in line for weekly rations
distributed through the council's Food Supply Office

Medical report by Dr. Jacob Nochimowski, May 9, 1943

With the establishment of bakeries, the lack of bread was overcome. The ghetto population,
starved for food, stilled their hunger solely with bread. Since the bakeries at the beginning baked
the bread thoroughly, eating bread did not lead to particular complications. . . . Soon, however,
the bakeries stopped baking bread thoroughly. As a result the bread was more difficult to digest,
was poorly absorbed.

Diary of Avraham Tory, March 30, 1943

In December of last year, after long months, the Germans consented for the first time to provide meat for the ghetto population: 3,054 kilograms—for the nearly 17 thousand souls. But
the meat was so bad that to touch it was disgusting, to say nothing of using it. We called in the
German manager of the workshops and ghetto commandant SA-Lieutenant Müller himself, that
they should see it and say themselves whether it could be eaten or not. They also agreed that it
was not edible. We questioned the German agents from the Maistas meat-packing company,
but each determined that the meat was fine, and that we must certainly eat it. That was written
in their records.

Bakers weigh flour in ghetto bakery.

Ghetto butchers at work. The Germans supplied
horse meat to feed the ghetto populace.

Digging potatoes

Raising tomatoes

Diary of Avraham Tory, May 4, 1943

Across the big field at Demokratu Square, a Jewish agriculturist drove two horses harnessed to a plow. Girls in green, red, blue, and multi-colored dresses in a neighboring field fashioned long, narrow beds, sowing seeds from paper bags in the freshly-turned earth. Some smoothed over the fertile black soil with their hands; others followed with a wooden rake, evening off the beds. A true, joyful spring scene, like we used to see during spring in a village outside the city, or even in a picture by a gifted painter. It is sunny, bright; it is spring here too, as it is all around. This peaceful pastoral scene has a barbed-wire fence around it—something not found in any landscape. No God-blessed artist has fantasized such a composition, a pastoral landscape with a barbed-wire fence.

"The Ältestenrat and Its Offices," report, early 1942

The soup kitchen, opened by the Welfare Office on April 8, 1942, gave out up to 800 warm meals a day, free, to poor workers and ghetto dwellers. The *yushnik*—as the ghetto dubbed the meager soup—from the Welfare Office was the only warm food of the day for the hungry poor and lonely people in the ghetto.

Waiting in line at the soup kitchen

Kadish/BH

Esther Lurie, *At the Communal Kitchen*, postwar, after 1942 original
(copperplate etching, 5¹⁄₄ x 4 in.)

Yad Vashem

Poster for the Welfare Office asking for donations
of used clothing for those in greater need

Logo of the Welfare Office

"The _Ältestenrat_ and Its Offices," report, early 1942

The Welfare Office gave out support in the form of money, . . . food supplies, fuel wood,
clothes, medicine, and so on, and also helped to arrange work positions for the needy, where
they could work by days.

Diary of Avraham Tory, July 17, 1943

We have no wood, not for the laundry, not for the bakery of the Welfare Office, not for the workers' soup, nor for the hospital or the bath and delousing institution. . . . Dr. Elkes reminded me
with that I must now begin negotiations with the German authorities about wood for the winter
for the entire ghetto population. . . . Wood in the ghetto is just as important, it is as much a
problem, as bread.

"The *Ältestenrat* and Its Offices," report, early 1942

A particular hindrance to learning in the early days was the hunger that dominated the ghetto and the lack of wood for heating the school. The students had to bring a piece of wood with them each day to heat the space. Still it was cold in the classes, and they had to sit wearing their coats; and it got so cold and there was no more wood, that the school had to be discontinued for the winter months.

Kadish/GK

The winter of 1941–42 was one of the coldest
on record in Kovno. The lack of firewood drove
the ghetto inmates to burn fences, furniture, and
virtually their homes in the effort to stay warm.

Residents distribute the ghetto's wood ration

Bringing home the family's wood ration

Diary of Tamara Lazerson, November 1, 1942

Time flies fast. Winter will begin this month, and that does not make us happy. We got some firewood today. It took a lot of work to haul it home. We plan to set up an iron stove, to consume less wood while producing more heat. But it will probably be difficult to stay supplied with wood. There is only enough until December. Hopefully the war will end after that.

Report of Dr. Chaim Nachman Shapiro, head of the Education Office, July 15, 1942

Whenever a few days passed without mishaps, the teachers would come immediately to the *Ältestenrat* to plead on behalf of the children's situation. They were growing up without Torah and without manners. Thus passed three months in the ghetto. Only after the "Great Action," when spirits had quieted somewhat, after repeated, soothing promises by the authorities, was an office for school affairs created on November 25.

Kadish/GK

USHMM

Logo of the Education Office

Studying in a ghetto school

**Yiddish and Hebrew mathematics textbooks
published in Kovno before the war**

GRAPHIC DESIGNER

PETER "FRITZ" GADIEL

During the early days of the ghetto, from August 15 to early October 1941, the *Ältestenrat*, saddled heavily with countless German regulations, gave its attention to informing inmates about the rigorous new order. Because the Germans prohibited radios and newspapers, the only alternative was posted announcements. For help in this critical undertaking, *Ältestenrat* Chairman Elkhanan Elkes turned to Peter ("Fritz") Gadiel to establish a graphics office, the Paint and Sign Workshop.

Gadiel, born in Germany in 1910, resided quite by accident in the city of Kovno when the Germans invaded Lithuania in June 1941. Married to Renée Silverman just two years earlier, he and his wife had settled in Kovno to join her relatives. By that time, Gadiel was well on his way to a promising career as a graphic artist. His training in his native Germany during the late 1920s and early 1930s had included study at the famed Bauhaus with Ludwig Mies van der Rohe. After Hitler's rise to power, however, Gadiel fled Germany. It was a journey by way of Holland and England that led him, in the end, into German hands and the Kovno Ghetto.

At first Elkes asked Gadiel to provide simple signs and posters, many communicating orders that meant life or death to ghetto residents. It was not long before Gadiel's Paint and Sign Workshop, employing cartographers, draftsmen, fine artists, and other graphic design-

Jewish Ghetto Police desk calendar, designed in Gadiel's graphics office

Lithuanian National Museum

ers, produced creative official ghetto insignia, armbands for the staffs of the *Ältestenrat* offices, the ghetto's currency, work passes, and many other requisite documents. The quality of the graphics presentation was striking: Gadiel experimented with different typefaces and design elements rooted in his Bauhaus training.

In due course, a number of other council offices came to rely on the talent in the graphics office. For the Jewish Ghetto Police, Gadiel's workshop produced recruitment posters, insignia of ranks, and the oath of

Tory Collection

Peter "Fritz" Gadiel *(center)*, in the ghetto gardens with Avraham Tory *(right)* and Rudolf Volsonok, head of the Residents Records Office created in 1942.

Paint and Sign Workshop's recruitment poster for the
Jewish Ghetto Police

Workshop-created posters on
display in the ghetto

Logo for the *Ältestenrat* of the Jewish Ghetto Community designed in Gadiel's workshop

renewed service commitment that all the ghetto police signed on November 1, 1942. The workshop also produced three of the most important official documentary artifacts that preserve the ghetto's history. Gadiel worked with the *Ältestenrat*'s secretary, Avraham Tory, to produce the visually arresting compilation of orders "And These Are the Laws—German Style" and the yearbook "Slobodka Ghetto 1942." Working with Rudolf Volsonok, the head of the Residents Records Office, Gadiel and his staff transformed written reports and statistical surveys into the memorial plaque "Numbers That Demand an Accounting!" that graphs the murder of Kovno's Jews from the start of the war to the end of December 1942.

Gadiel's department played a vital role in providing jobs for many who otherwise might well have been regarded by Germans as "useless" and fatally expendable. He assigned artists to projects requested by Germans stationed in Kovno, such as copying masterpieces of art for their private collections. Gadiel also directed a toy workshop, staffed by people including those either too old or too young for the labor brigades, that made wooden toys, dolls, and stuffed animals primarily for children in Germany.

For all its practical contributions, Gadiel's workshop on at least one occasion served as a cultural center when it presented an exhibition of ghetto art. Perhaps more importantly, however, the workshop also was a

records center. A sizable archive containing examples of nearly all of the ghetto's official drawings, certificates, forms, and stamp impressions was hidden there. This invaluable trove was retrieved by inmate Ephraim Gutman after the ghetto's liberation, who concealed it from the Soviets and conveyed it to Palestine.

Gadiel himself could not have saved his workshop's records. In July 1944, during the ghetto's liquidation, the Germans discovered him hiding with others in a bunker built within the workshop and deported him to Dachau. His wife, Renée, was deported to Stutthof. Though they both survived the German concentration camps, their three-year-old son, Raanan, who had been born in the ghetto, fell into German hands and, with other children, was taken to the ghetto's laundry, where they were killed.

Logo for the Ghetto Workshops

"History of the Vilijampole Jewish Ghetto Police," 1942–43

From the moment of the invasion of the German military and according to the general decrees, all Jews in all offices and enterprises were dismissed from positions they could no longer occupy. Jews were snatched from the streets and dragged from their houses . . . to clean toilets with their bare hands, to take off their shirts and wash the German tanks and trucks, to stand half-naked for hours in the frightful heat of the sun. . . . There were dozens and hundreds of cases of horrible sadism, cases which we do not even know about because many of the captured Jews never returned. As "wages" for their work, they were taken to the fort or to jail, from which they never returned. . . .

The Jewish Committee [for Transfer] intervened with the German authorities, that if workers were needed, the Jewish Committee would assemble the required number of people. After one such discussion, the Committee was promised that no more people would be snatched from the street, and that the Germans would come directly to the Jewish Committee.

Order from SA-Captain Fritz Jordan of the *Stadtkommissariat*, October 1, 1941

As from today, 1,000 men must be provided for work during the day, and 1,000 men for work at night, at the airfield.

Residents stand for roll call outside the council building.

LCSA

Labor brigade near the gate. The man in the long coat with the stick *(center)* is an official from the ghetto Labor Office.

Kadish/GK

LCSA

Jewish workers behind main gate waiting to be escorted to work

Diary of Avraham Tory, October 13, 1943

In the early-morning hours, the square by the ghetto gate is transformed into a slave market. Thousands of ghetto residents clamor noisily, pushing and shoving to get into the best brigades where it is easier to "make a package" or where the work is not so hard, and to avoid the brigades for the airfield, for the German construction company Grün and Bielfinger or for the *Waffen-SS*, where the work is hard and where one could receive a beating during work.

The Jewish Police and the officials of the Labor Office can hardly maintain order in such an uproar. The striving to get into a good brigade is stronger than all the efforts of the Jewish Police.

Jacob Lifschitz, *At a Table in the City Brigades Office,* 1941

(pen and ink, 9¹/2 x 13³/8 in.)

Two representatives of the Labor Office at the ghetto gate

"Proceedings Book" of the *Ältestenrat*, May 3, 1943

In order to insure that proper work requirements are followed and to increase the work force, the Labor Office supervisors were empowered to temporarily arrest all those individuals who were suspected of shirking their work responsibilities although they committed no crimes or violated specific laws.

Diary of Avraham Tory, June 5, 1943

Ghetto life is reflected mainly at the *Ältestenrat*, at the ghetto gate, and in the various work-brigades in the city and at the airfield. Not less than 60 percent of the people work every day in drudgery. . . . People are depressed, they collapse under the injurious yoke of the work, of trying to get through the gate. The constant fear about the coming day, the horror of extermination—all this drains everyone, sucks the last sap from each person's bones, dries up their minds, and erases any interest in life.

Labor Office logo

Aleksotas airfield work convoy schedule for women

Kadish/BH

Kadish/GK

Kadish/BH

שלום אברמוביץ – ולא יטבע זיר אני שעלטער 161

Kadish/GK

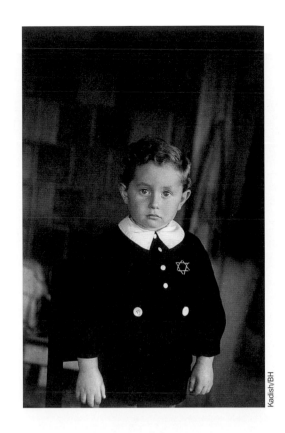

Kadish/BH

Kadish/BH

Kadish/GK

Kadish/BH

Kadish/BH

Kadish/BH

Kadish/BH

Amonth after the Fort IX massacre of Kovno's Jews in the "Great Action" (October 28–29, 1941), SS-Colonel Karl Jäger declared that those spared were needed for work. As a result, the ghetto's very existence came to depend on its utility to the Germans, giving rise to one of many paradoxes characterizing life in the Kovno Ghetto: forced labor, even as it impoverished the human will, was the key to the inmates' survival.

Day after relentless day, thousands of ghetto Jews assembled at the main gate for work assignments. Undernourished and all too often overexposed to the elements, they marched in brigades to various destinations in or near Kovno. At the Aleksotas military airfield, the largest and most detested work site, Jewish forced laborers endured an unusually severe routine of digging tunnels, hauling concrete, and loading and unloading aircraft.

Even though they acknowledged the necessity of dreadful work, the Jews did everything they could to keep from succumbing to considerable material deprivation. When possible, they engaged in smuggling, an activity that was officially punishable by death. Before leaving the ghetto, workers would conceal valuable household items—contraband for underground trade for food—to avoid detection at the main gate. Once in the city, they removed their Jewish stars and separated themselves from their brigades to mingle and trade more freely with the townspeople. The items they used for barter—anything from evening gowns to used wire—had survived the confiscations of some 75 percent of Jewish possessions during the ghetto's early days. A combination of luck, bribery, and the laxity of certain guards facilitated the flow of illegal goods to and from the ghetto for most of the ghetto's history.

A vital aspect of the ghetto's economy was the numerous workshops established by German authorities inside the ghetto at the *Ältestenrat*'s urging. Developed as small factories to make and repair products for the Germans and for the inmates, these workshops ultimately saved the lives of the "useless eaters": the infirm, the elderly, the underaged, most women at home with children, and anyone else deemed unsuitable for forced labor. Workshops made clothing and leather goods, even toys for children in Germany, but they also secretly channeled mess-kits, soap, and other items requisitioned by the German army to the ghetto population as well as to the ghetto's political underground.

A brigade of Jewish laborers returning from work

Order from the Labor Office, October 29, 1941 (the day after the "Great Action")
You are hereby notified that the work at the airfield will continue at the normal pace. All airfield workers must meet their columns and work their designated shifts punctually.

Report by SS-Colonel Karl Jäger, December 1, 1941
Today I can confirm that our objective, to solve the Jewish problem for Lithuania, has been achieved by *Einsatzkommando 3*. In Lithuania there are no more Jews, apart from Jewish workers and their families.

Diary of Avraham Tory, March 16, 1943
We often connect our fate to the huge demand for Jewish labor. . . . This is our trump card, this is our stronghold. When there was an impending "action," resettlement, or a regular reduction of the ghetto, right away the managers from all the work sites began to beg that the authorities should not take "their Jews" but leave them in peace; that they must leave the Jewish workers or there will be no production because they are useful. Many Jewish workers were saved in this way, though the "actions" were carried out anyway because such was the decree from Berlin, and the local authorities could not make any substantive changes. Instead of killing a Chaim, they killed a Baruch—but someone was killed. The interventions of the local employers were effective only to this extent.

Ghetto writings of Chaim Yelin, 1941–42

At every day's dawn, the broad neck of Meysim Street by the gate is filled with people. The arriving Jews tremble with the cold and the damp. They wait; the sorting should begin soon. . . .

The guards arrive to conduct the brigades into the city to their workplaces. There is tension at the gate. The Germans search for their "own" Jews. They want their regulars, especially the regular women. . . .

Sometimes a guard grabs up his gun, shoots into the air to frighten people, or sometimes fires into the crowd. You hear lamenting, shrieking. People begin to run. The Jewish police join the fray and command:

"In fours, in fours, arrange yourselves!". . .

The racket at the gate gradually quiets. The ghetto guards permit the Jews, arranged in fours, to go through the gate.

"Caps off!" scream the Jewish police.

All the Jews go through the gate with uncovered heads. The Germans are on the alert. If someone is late taking off his cap or puts it back on too soon, he gets a truncheon on his head, kicks to his behind. The ghetto guards drag him out of the line:

"What, you don't have time? What, you don't give a greeting, you dog you?!"

The Germans rest only when the "guilty" is bleeding from the teeth or his eyes are swollen or his head is split.

The Jews try to remove their caps at the required time.

Diary of Tamara Lazerson, January 23, 1944

Back to work again. The sentry, with his rifle, shepherds the women around like a herd of sheep everyday at the brigade. That is how the days, weeks, and months go by. It is always the same. Thus every day you go to the brigade, count the hours until noon, then lunch, a few more hours until five, then six, and finally the hour (God bless it!) when we go home. Then the road home. The spattering mud, wading through puddles, the cursing, and the groans of an exhausted existence. Finally, the gates. We are at the ghetto. We are finally home. You would think I would be happy about that, but no. Because tomorrow it will be the same all over again. The days run on, one into the other without change. It is the day of a manual laborer, a day of exhaustion.

During the period of relative calm, the number of brigades leaving the ghetto fluctuated with the German demand for labor, eventually forcing the *Ältestenrat* to recruit women, including mothers, and young teen-agers to fill the daily quotas.

Kadish/BH

Jacob Lifschitz, *The Downtrodden*, undated
(watercolor, 11³/₄ x 5⁷/₈ in.)

Labor brigades and their duties varied widely, from two women working as maids for the German military commandant to the thousands who toiled at the Aleksotas airfield. The larger brigades were divided into smaller columns for the march to and from their work sites.

Esther Lurie, *The Main Gate,* 1943

(pen and ink, 6⅞ x 8¾ in.)

Ghetto writings of Chaim Yelin, 1941–42

The hands of all those who dug the earth with spades were tied to their bellies with wire, leaving only their elbows free. On their backs was fashioned a hook, to which was connected a wire, like a rein. A German held each such wire, and pulled it to and fro. . . . The Jews had to dig in the earth like that all day. And when their spades were not full, because their hands were tied and because the Germans were constantly pulling at them from behind, to and fro, there was a hail of blows.

Diary of Avraham Tory, March 23, 1943

Jews going to work or returning from work must pass through the city, along certain streets and alleyways. Why must they run around in the city? The Germans cannot make peace with this. What are they, the lepers, doing mixing with the population? They were isolated—so they should disappear. Many wonder about this. By now there should not be any Jews. . . . The Führer himself has promised that the Jewish race will be exterminated—so why are they still coming here?

**Lyrics to "Jewish Brigades,"
by Avrom Akselrod, September 1941**

Bitter times have come upon us—
Times of hardship, and of pain,
Gone from us are sun and flowers,
Only labor cards remain.

(Chorus)
Jewish brigades
In patches we parade.
Our troubles we bear,
We never despair!

Inside the ghettos you confined us,
"Actions" take their grisly toll,
Turned us into slaves and robots
To destroy us is your goal.

(Chorus)

But we do not ask for pity,
Every promise is a lie.
At the Ninth Fort truth is shown us—
When you take us there to die.

(Chorus)

So we work for you and labor,
Blows and curses are our wage,
Guard dogs snarl at us and keep us—
Just like beasts inside a cage.

(Chorus)

Just because we do not whimper
When you beat us black and blue,
Do not think that broken bodies
Mean a broken spirit, too.

(Chorus)

Long enough you've robbed and stolen
Long enough our people killed—
Long enough the list of victims,
Too much blood has now been spilled.

(Chorus)

Brothers, we shall live to see it,
Our victory and spring,
Aching limbs will then be straightened
And a new song we will sing.

(Chorus)
Jewish brigades,
Boldly on parade,
Patches gone, and hand in hand,
March to our ancestral land.

Selected sites (■) of Jewish slave labor outside the ghetto

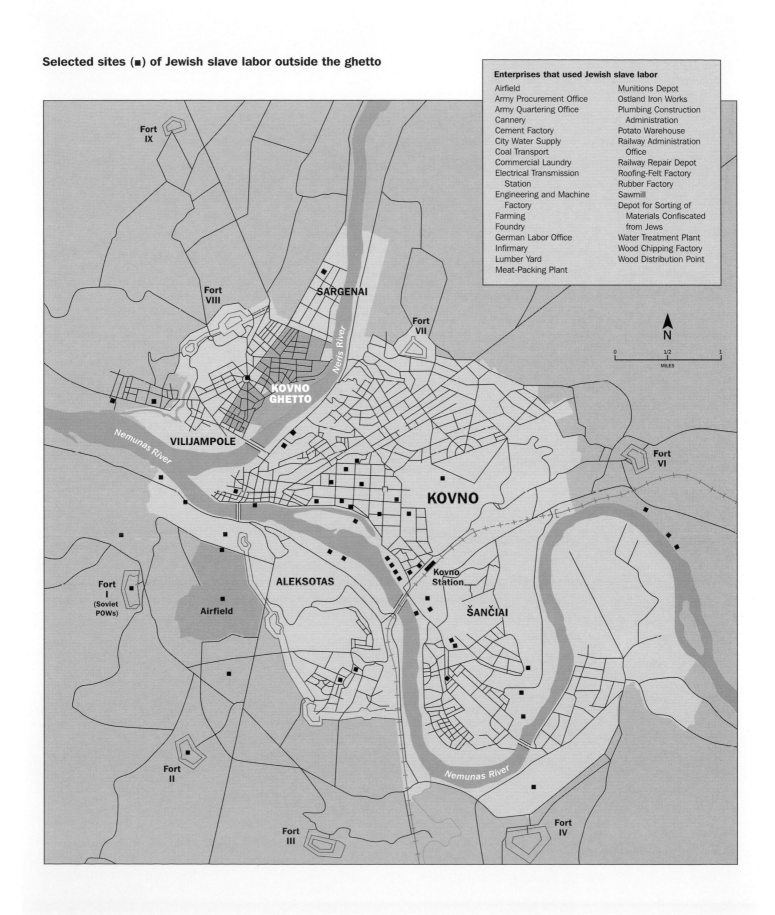

Enterprises that used Jewish slave labor

Airfield	Munitions Depot
Army Procurement Office	Ostland Iron Works
Army Quartering Office	Plumbing Construction
Cannery	Administration
Cement Factory	Potato Warehouse
City Water Supply	Railway Administration
Coal Transport	Office
Commercial Laundry	Railway Repair Depot
Electrical Transmission	Roofing-Felt Factory
Station	Rubber Factory
Engineering and Machine	Sawmill
Factory	Depot for Sorting of
Farming	Materials Confiscated
Foundry	from Jews
German Labor Office	Water Treatment Plant
Infirmary	Wood Chipping Factory
Lumber Yard	Wood Distribution Point
Meat-Packing Plant	

**Work assignment slips from the ghetto's
Labor Office**

LAMPEDŽIAI

A.K.№

Name

Vorn.

Adr.

Gültig bis

JÜDISCHES GHETTO
ARBEITSAMT
VILIJAMPOLE

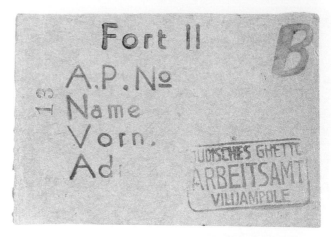

Fort II

A.P.№

Name

Vorn.

Adr

JÜDISCHES GHETTO
ARBEITSAMT
VILIJAMPOLE

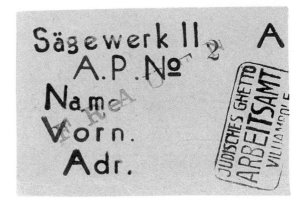

Sägewerk II

A.P.№

Name

Vorn.

Adr.

JÜDISCHES GHETTO
ARBEITSAMT
VILIJAMPOLE

60

Maistas

A.P.№

JÜDISCHES
ARBEITS

Kiek įmokėta	Išpild.	Atsakyta

45

„METALAS"

1,2 u.3 September

JÜDISCHES GHETTO
ARBEITSAMT
VILIJAMPOLE

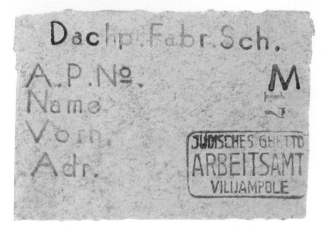

Dachp.Fabr.Sch.

A.P.№

Name

Vorn.

Adr.

JÜDISCHES GHETTO
ARBEITSAMT
VILIJAMPOLE

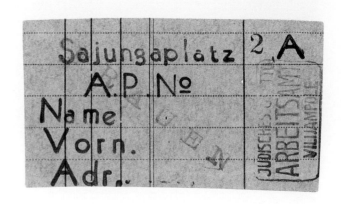

Sajungaplatz 2 A

A.P.№

Name

Vorn.

Adr.

JÜDISCHES
ARBEITSAMT
VILIJAMPOLE

5

Flack-Werkstätte

24, 25 u 26 August

JÜDISCHES GHETTO
ARBEITSAMT
VILIJAMPOLE

Munilager

A.P.No

JÜDISCHES G
ARBEITS
VILIJAMPOLE

37

Wasserstrassenbauverwaltung

25 u. 26 August

JÜDISCHES GHETTO
ARBEITSAMT
VILIJAMPOLE

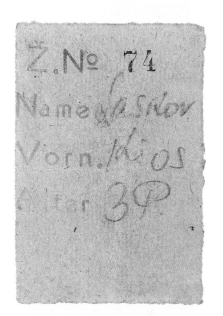

Z.No 74

Name Jashov

Vorn. Kios

Alter 39

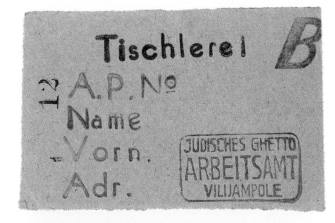

Tischlerei **B**

12

A.P.No

Name

Vorn.

Adr.

JÜDISCHES GHETTO
ARBEITSAMT
VILIJAMPOLE

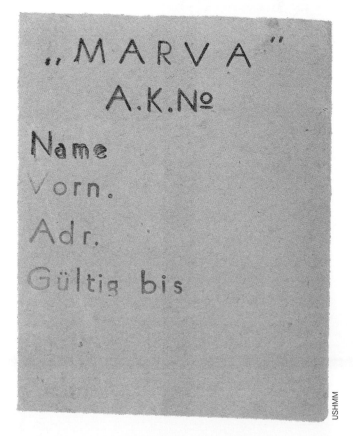

„MARVA"

A.K.No

Name

Vorn.

Adr.

Gültig bis

Kriegsschule Panem. **B**

16

A.P.No

Name

Vorn.

Adr.

JÜDISCHES GHETT
ARBEITSAMT
VILIJAMPOLE

Ghetto writings of Chaim Yelin, 1941–42

On the indicated day, at the appointed hour, men appear in the streets and alleys. All are going to the square beside the *Ältestenrat* building. They go grouped by skill, by streets, kinships, and friendships. Thus go doctors, nurses; there go tinsmiths, carpenters, painters, locksmiths, and various thrown-together and assembled groups—driven by a subconscious force. More than six thousand men gather at the square. It is clear that this has to do with work beyond the city brigades: these Jews will be employed at the airfield.

YIVO

Jews working at the military airfield in Aleksotas, the largest and most dreaded work site in support of the German war effort

Yad Vashem

Jacob Lifschitz, *Airfield Worker*, 1941
(pen and ink, 12^{1}/$_{2}$ x 9^{3}/$_{8}$ in.)

Lyrics to "Rise Up to the Airfield,"
by Shaul Shenker, September 1941

Seven days each week—no Sabbath day—
Heavy cares and labors on us weigh,
Near midnight to my home and bed I creep,
But soon I am wakened from my sleep:

"Rise up to the airfield!" cry police,
Knocking at my window without cease.
My head feels just as heavy as a stone,
I ache in every limb and every bone.
But like the ox that's driven to the field
I'm fearful of the lash and have to yield.

Blows and hunger—that describes my day.
Clothes all wet and muddy, shoes like clay,
Every night of endless sleep I dream,
But then I'm interrupted by the scream:
"Rise up to the airfield" . . .

I tremble from the cold, my feet are like lead,
As soon as I come home, I fall into bed.
Oh God! How good it feels in bed to lie!
At four o'clock comes morning and the cry:
"Rise up to the airfield" . . .

Report from the Statistics Office, May 31, 1942

There exists a sharp line of demarcation within the population of the ghetto: airfield workers and non-airfield workers, which coincides with the class distinctions in the population.

Graph from the yearbook "Slobodka Ghetto 1942" of the number of workers at the Aleksotas military airfield. The horizontal axis charts the months of the year, the vertical axis the number of workers per ten-day period. The green band denotes female workers, the blue band male workers, and the red band the composite of men and women together.

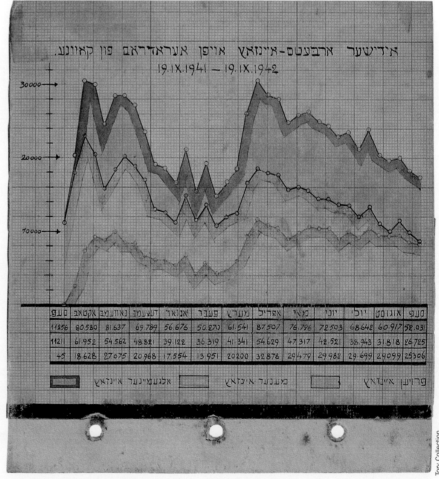

"Order No. 15" from Kovno's Lithuanian civil and military authorities, July 10, 1941

The Jews are forbidden from selling, using as collateral, or exchanging any real estate or other possessions. They are also forbidden from getting involved in any kind of trade.

Diary of Tamara Lazerson, September 14, 1942

I was accidentally drafted into the [labor] brigade. I was not far from the fish market. To my amazement, Jewish conversations and thoughts were solely about "packages." Although it is forbidden to bring anything into the ghetto or to buy anything, nevertheless our people take the risk to buy things. Later, hiding the food products in various places in their clothing, they sneak them in through the fence. Despite the controls, they bring through as much as five kilograms at a time, free and clear. Oh, what a nation! It will never die. Orders and injunctions cannot stop it. The Jewish nation will never carry them out. That is why it will always survive and will not surrender to annihilation.

"History of the Vilijampole Jewish Ghetto Police," 1942–43

So our singular life set in, the remarkable sources of livelihood—selling your clothes and eating them. We adapted to life . . . almost forgetting how things had once been different. We traded, bought, sold, negotiated, exchanged, made money off one another, got in each other's way, and lived.

Lithuanian guards conducting an inspection at the main gate while a Jewish policeman keeps order

Kadish/GK

Notice from SS-Colonel Karl Jäger to the *Ältestenrat,* March 11, 1942

On March 10, 1942, on my orders, 24 Jews were shot to death because, contrary to the regulations that were enacted for Jews, they engaged in extensive black marketeering with the Lithuanian population without their badges. This notice is to be announced to the Jews in a suitable way.

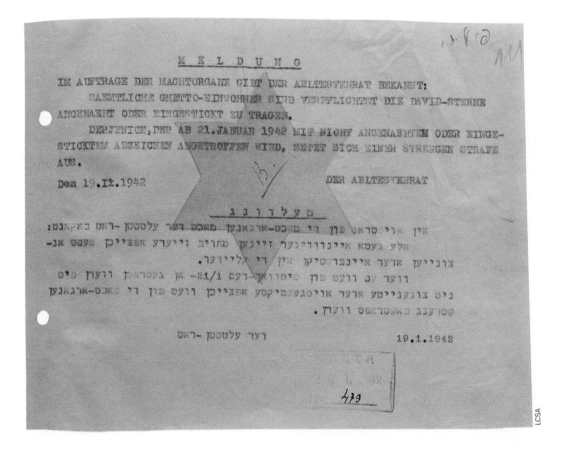

Announcement ordering Jews not to remove their yellow stars of David on penalty of "severe punishment." Workers often removed their loosely attached yellow badges, slipped away from their brigade, and conducted trade in the city.

The Jews of the Kovno Ghetto staved off starvation—a constant threat in other ghettos—primarily through smuggling by the city labor brigades.

For much of the ghetto's existence smuggling was carried out openly but illegally. Each act of smuggling defied the very real threats of discovery, arrest, and execution.

**Lyrics to "By the Ghetto Gate,"
by Avrom Akselrod, September 1941**

By the ghetto gate
burns a blazing fire
and searches go apace.
Jews are coming through
from their brigades,
and everyone's in a sweat.

(Chorus)
So should I go on?
Or should I stand still?
I don't know what to do.
The commandant
in the green coat
will take it all away.

A splinter of firewood,
cash to exchange,
he takes it on the fly.
Milk from a pan,
soup from a ladle,
you can kiss it good-bye!

(Chorus)

Friend with the stripe,
I have contraband,
help me out at the checkpoint.
For that I'll give you
all my booty today,
and then again tomorrow.

(Chorus)

Get ready to go,
stand right by me,
please don't creep ahead.
Go to the right guard:
Say "Everything's OK."
Here's your loaf of bread.

Diary of Avraham Tory, February 5, 1943

When the brigades went out today at dawn for their work in the city, the workers were strongly warned not to leave their work sites, not to buy newspapers, not to walk alone without a guard, not to buy and not to carry any "packages." Any divergence from this strong directive would involve the risk of the death penalty not only for oneself but also for the entire family. Everyone understood this very well; the ghetto paid too dearly yesterday—45 victims. A fresh common grave at Fort IX—of innocent little children, of pious and elderly people—was filled in yesterday. . . . No begging and no bidding, no explanation and no human appeal will help—the spectacle of authority must be played out so that no one can forget for even a minute that they are imprisoned, harnessed in a day-to-day yoke.

"By the Gate,"
author unknown, undated

By the gate at Ariagolas promenade,
a massive crowd is gathering.
Ghetto Jews assemble at dawn
to find a place in a labor brigade.

Women, men, in backpack and sack,
like horses in harness,
they hurry, push closer,
just to get through the gate.

A policeman, a Jew,
stands with the Germans,
protecting the peace—and
guarding that nary a "rabbit" steals through.

We have "rabbit"-catchers aplenty,
ordinary folk and great artists—
gate-watcher Aronshtam, "banana" in hand,
and, over all, the "chief" of Jewish labor.

He runs through the gate, he rechecks the
     cards;
he tells those to march, that one to wait.
He searches and screams—you could hear
     it in town.
A commotion, a racket—and it's only a show.

No crying helps, they don't have hearts,
no one goes without a pass.
The airfield is more important than all,
more important than bread or butter or *shmalts*.

If he catches a "rabbit" obligated to work
who isn't going to the airfield,
he's lost. He caught one, and
instead of the jail—his bones he easily broke.

So it is with "rabbits"—the men.
With women the chief is nicer:
A brigade leader's daughter wants to go to
     the city;
he slaps her face and sends her back home.

A "rabbit" was someone who tried to slip in or
out of a work brigade or someone who ran
away. A "banana" was a policeman's truncheon.

Report from the ghetto's Economic Office about the workshops, April 25, 1942. The report was forwarded to the *Ältestenrat* four days later.

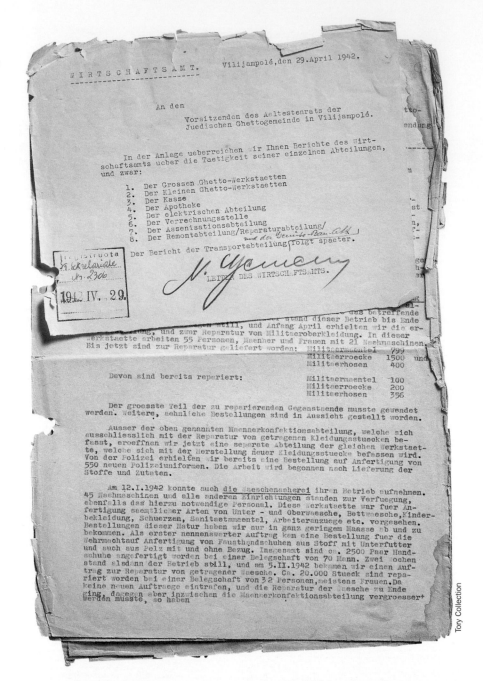

Report of the Economic Office, April 25, 1942

As of December 5, 1941, the Jewish Ghetto Community was ordered by the German district authorities for Kaunas to establish workshops for mass production as well as a laundry. . . . The ghetto workshops comprise 14 departments:

1. Men's garments, department for repairs
2. Men's garments, department for new clothes
3. Sewing workshop
4. Brush shop
5. Shoemaker shop
6. Laundry
7. Soap and candle shop
8. Wool-shearing shop
9. Sock-knitting shop
10. Children's toys workshop
11. Plumbing shop
12. Saddlery
13. Repair shop
14. Bandage shop

In the saddlery

ALI

The sewing workshop

Kadish/BH

Kadish/BH

At work in the plumbing shop

Diary of Avraham Tory, February 10, 1943

The large workshops are a political refuge, a bastion in the ghetto. Here 1,400 Jewish workers, master artisans, demonstrate their achievements and show that Jews are not only able to deceive, hoard, and be parasites—they can also operate and repair various machinery that cannot now be repaired in the city. The large workshops are an important accomplishment of the first order by the *Ältestenrat*, which, through their establishment, foresaw the great significance they would have when evil winds begin to blow, when the Germans begin to throw at us all the old sins, the old canards and litanies. . . . We hold on fast to the workshops . . . and to the work done there to show our accomplishments and to show that we contribute to the German *Wehrmacht* like no other such place.

A potter at work

Kadish/BH

Diary of Avraham Tory, March 28, 1943

In the ghetto itself there is now a pottery. *Stadtkommissar* Cramer is very taken with the pottery—they regularly show him their wares. He himself looks on with interest as Jews make from nothing—from mud or clay, with their own ten fingers, by the most primitive methods—all kinds of things: pots, jugs, pitchers, plates, and little pots, . . . even many kinds of playthings. A potter has been there since time immemorial. A family of Jewish potters lives there. It is their house. In this wooden house—on the same spot—their father, their grandfather, and great-grandfather lived and made pots, working for generations with that skill. Now, after all the "actions," only a few family members remain. . . . One brother renovated the place and reopened the pottery.

Kadish/BH

At work in the ghetto laundry

"Life," by K. Brenner, undated

Too dreadful, too hard
Is living like this.
Feeling you're sinking
Into the abyss.

A life of such sorrow
Has dulled my poor brain,
Seven months a laundress—
Have filled me with pain.

From morning till nighttime
I work at my task,
I stand at the washtub
And sadly I ask:
Where is the life that was joyous and glad?
Had I but known what a treasure I had!
Now is my life only evil and shame,
No longer human—"slave" is my name.
I dream of a place on a faraway shore
Where I can be sure that I'm human no more.
Here there are tyrants who murder and rage,
Who keep us confined in an barbed-wire cage.

They laughed as they robbed and they
    sneered as they killed,
While blood of our innocent brothers was
    spilled.
Life, where's your conscience, why cannot
    you hear
When blood of the innocent screams in your
    ear?

No more—I don't want it. I've had enough now.
I'd flee from this "life" if I only knew how.
Enough of the hunger, enough of the dread—
This is no life—I'm already dead.

Diary of Tamara Lazerson, February 26, 1944

Nothing special. I go to work, sleep, eat, and read a little. The same goes for yesterday, today, tomorrow, and the day after tomorrow. The same last week, the same next week.

In the ghetto gardens

The ghetto sawmill

Carrying supplies into the ghetto

Selling bread in the ghetto's "black market." This man was shot by the Germans a few days after this photo was taken.

Bringing in firewood

Jacob Lifschitz, ***The Little Market*, undated**
(pen and ink, 13½ x 9¾ in.)

Men sort potatoes harvested
from the ghetto gardens

Kadish/BH

Esther Lurie, *Children Carrying Branches*,
1956 after 1942 original
(pen and ink, 9³/4 x 14¹/4 in.)

Yad Vashem

Wood for heating and cooking was
second only to food as the most precious
commodity in the ghetto.

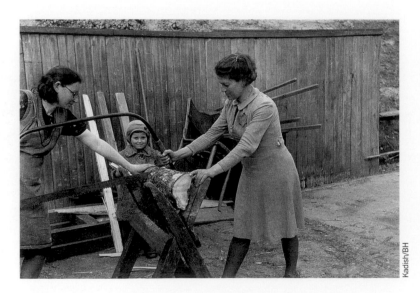

Kadish/BH

At the ghetto laundry

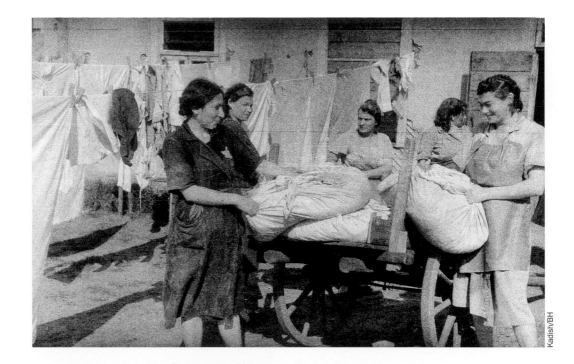

The Jewish police supervise and register the bread ration.

Repairing clothes

Diary of Avraham Tory, June 5, 1943

But little by little the mood changed. The people got accustomed to the gate, to the work, and to the injustice, and they gradually tried to lay aside the dangers of the time and, as possible, to forget themselves, not to think about the yoke. Some began to host dinners, drink liquor or wine, or get involved in community activities; still others found relief in poetry or got lost in study, etc. And so life gradually became a little more varied, took on different hues. The people became more invigorated, their approach became lighter, more routine. Except all this in general is forbidden by the authorities. It is forbidden to study, it is forbidden to hold gatherings or lectures, it is even forbidden to pray, and it is in truth forbidden to lift a glass or to eat a good meal. These are forbidden first of all because we are perceived to be slaves, and we are supposed to think that, too. Slaves do not need any of these things. . . .

But forbidden fruit is sweet. As strict as the authorities are, as draconian as their measures are, the desire for knowledge, for life, for spiritual nourishment is greater.

Throughout the years of the ghetto's existence, Kovno's Jews developed a culture to express, in Avraham Tory's words, "the desire for knowledge, for life, and for spiritual nourishment." This desire, drawing strength from their traditions and prewar accomplishments, made it possible for inmates to endure and even defy German-imposed restrictions and privations.

From its earliest days, the *Ältestenrat* kept the ghetto's history in secret archives of documents and artifacts that included a compilation of decrees "And These Are the Laws—German Style," the yearbook "Slobodka Ghetto 1942," and the statistical graphs presented as a memorial plaque "Numbers That Demand an Accounting!" In addition to preserving these elaborate works, Avraham Tory, the head of the *Ältestenrat*'s Secretariat, collected formal office reports and records.

Many inmate artists, either commissioned by the *Ältestenrat* for its archives or on their own, sought to render buildings, street scenes, portraits, and key events. One event, the public hanging of a smuggler who shot at a German guard, appears in a number of paintings, diary entries, reports, and photographs, vividly reflecting the shared experience of all those recording the ghetto's story.

Music, too, offered an important means of expression in the ghetto. Several inmates wrote new lyrics to well-known melodies. Some thirty musicians formed an orchestra and performed in concerts. To make these concerts possible, the Jewish Ghetto Police employed the musicians in their ranks and sponsored their performances. Not a few inmates, however, felt these concerts crossed the line as inappropriate to the ghetto's circumstances.

Following the burning of the hospital for contagious diseases in October 1941, which killed patients and medical staff alike, ghetto inmates feared that the German authorities would respond to other outbreaks of contagious disease by killing the infected. To avoid this pretext for wholesale murder, doctors struggled to control a disease's virulence with whatever equipment and supplies they had illegally hidden or could smuggle. An occasional outbreak—a crisis for the entire community—made it necessary for doctors to conceal infected inmates. Doctors also sought to protect orphans, who were particularly vulnerable to German assault, in secret hospital wards. In the wake of the September 1942 German decree that pregnancy was punishable by death, doctors performed abortions to save women's lives.

The German and Lithuanian murder of rabbis and desecration of synagogues early in the war shattered the community. After all, Slobodka, the site of the ghetto, had been a world-renowned center of Jewish study and piety. Against this background, and the edict in February 1942 to confiscate all religious and secular books, Kovno's Jews sought ways to preserve their religious lives. They prayed in makeshift gathering places, studied in clandestine classes, and concealed ceremonial objects and sacred texts and scrolls. Forced by circumstances into behavior that undermined dietary and other rabbinic laws, Jews looked to the ghetto's rabbis for new sanctions. The rabbis' conclusions *(responsa)*, often recorded on scraps of paper torn from concrete sacks, together constituted codes of permissible religious observance under conditions of extraordinary adversity.

After the closing of schools in August 1942, children and adolescents went "underground" to continue their education. Although teen-agers were actively involved in the ghetto community—guarding the community's vegetable gardens, serving as messengers for the *Ältestenrat,* passing as eligible brigade workers—some studied Jewish and Zionist subjects without books in vocational schools and youth movements.

As conditions became more desperate in 1943–44, the Jews combined forces to organize an underground united front dedicated to the goal of destroying the Germans. Active resistance and dreams of armed revenge were, in fact, features of ghetto existence from the start. Jews had carried out acts of industrial sabotage at work sites and devised schemes to demolish the German guardhouse in the event of an uprising. Underground activists also participated in socialist cells, the Communist Anti-Fascist Organization, and Zionist youth movements devoted to promoting a Jewish national culture. Converging in the summer of 1943 to form the Jewish General Fighting Organization, men and women, many armed with illegal weapons snatched on the black market or from German supply depots, planned their hopeful escape from the ghetto. More than three hundred people succeeded in reaching the partisan units in surrounding forests.

The political underground did not operate alone. The *Ältestenrat* supplied it with money and protection; members of the Jewish Ghetto Police offered weapons training, and workshops outfitted fighters with clothing and mess kits. In the face of their forced compliance with German demands, many in the ghetto population were determined, no matter the cost, to keep themselves and their defiant spirits alive.

"Last Testament" of Avraham Tory, December 1942

In order to provide a notion of the ghetto, I have also gathered documents, placards, statutes, warnings, announcements, and decrees from the German authorities' domain and—separated by a thousand separations—announcements from the *Ältestenrat* in the ghetto and its departments, and resolutions of the Jewish Ghetto Court, which created precedents under exceptional conditions whose equivalent does not exist in any of the books of law and judgment in the world.

I have collected signs, symbols, works of graphic arts, song lyrics, and macabre jokes, which reflect as in a crooked mirror the life of the individual and the life of the community in the ghetto.

I have trifled with the fear of death that is directly tied to the very writing of each page and leaf of my diary, with the very collecting of the documentary material, hiding them and burying them.

The yearbook "Slobodka Ghetto 1942" preserves an almost daily record of that year's events in the ghetto, as well as folk songs, poetry, illustrations of ghetto insignia and armbands, and a sequence of overlay maps that record the ghetto's changing boundaries.

Yearbook map showing the streets of
Vilijampole to be included within the confines
of the Jewish ghetto

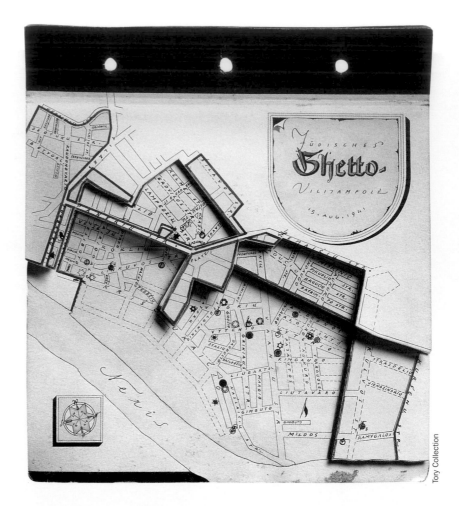

The ghetto in August 1941 at the time of its
closure. Several streets designated for the Jews
were excluded from the ghetto even before
any of Kovno's Jews moved in. The Large Ghetto
along the Neris River was connected to the
Small Ghetto *(upper left)* by a single footbridge.

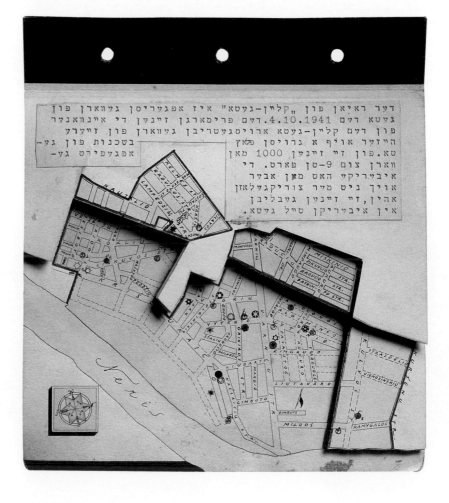

On October 4, 1941, the Small Ghetto was eliminated when the Germans murdered the district's Jewish population and burned the hospital for contagious diseases.

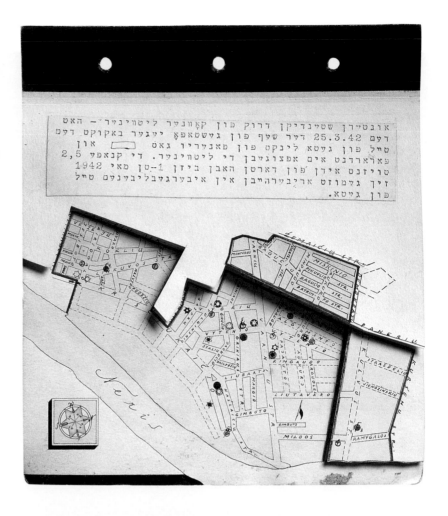

The third reduction, May 1, 1942

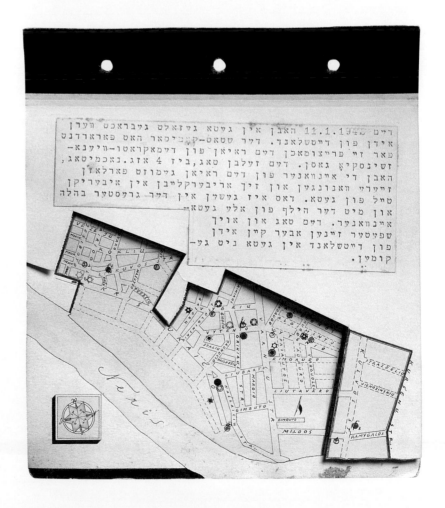

The Kovno Ghetto after the fourth reduction of October 5, 1942. There were no further reductions until after the SS took control of the ghetto in September 1943.

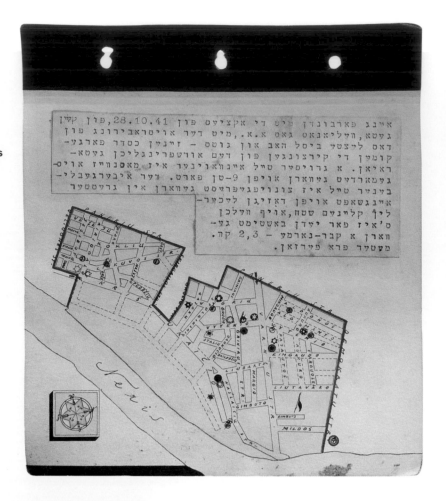

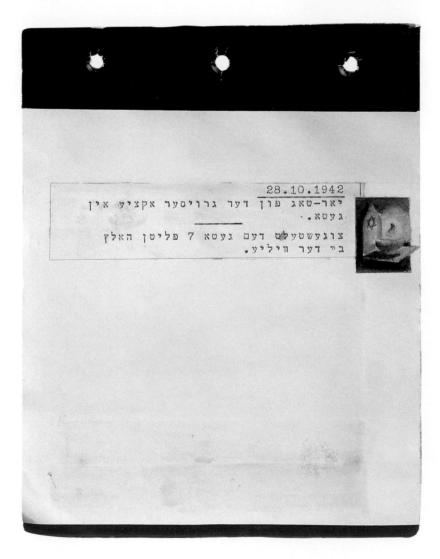

Yearbook entry illustrated with a memorial candle for October 28, 1942, marking the first anniversary of the "Great Action"

This folio contains the compilation of German orders to the *Ältestenrat* from July 1941 to May 1943, most of which were delivered orally. Making a play on words from the Book of Exodus 21:1, the Hebrew title on this front cover reads "And These Are the Laws—German Style, 1941–1943."

The back cover of the compilation, illustrated with
the symbol for a paragraph of law and the German
word *"Juden"* (Jews), represents the *Ältestenrat*'s
transmittal of German orders to the ghetto, here
termed "Disorder and Decrees, July 1941–May 1943."

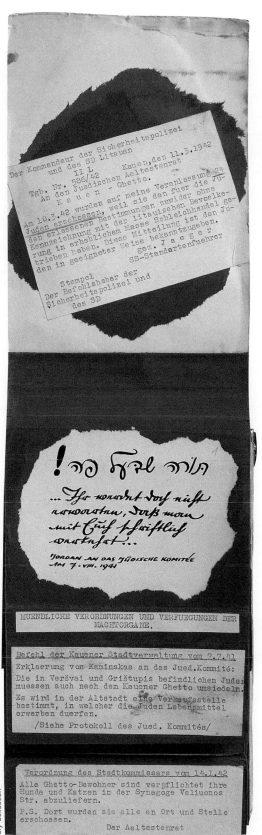

The inside of the front cover *(top)* is the announcement of the execution of 24 Jews on March 10, 1942. Beneath the Hebrew phrase *"Torah She-Be'al Peh,"* the common name for Jewish "oral law," is SA-Captain Fritz Jordan's comment of August 7, 1941: "You will not expect that one communicates with you in writing." The German typescript that follows begins: "Oral decrees and orders from the powers in authority."

Orders framed in black in the compilation indicate those that led to the death of Jews from the ghetto. Shown here are the October 3, 1941, order to burn the hospital for infectious diseases and destroy the Small Ghetto, and the October 27, 1941, order to assemble on Demokratu Square for the "Great Action."

wie Hafer, Heu, Stroh usw. muessen abgeliefert werden.

Der Aeltestenrat

Befehl des Hauptsturmf.Jordan vom 1.10.1941

Ab heute sind 1000 Maenner bei Tag und 1000 Maenner bei Nacht zur Arbeit auf dem Flugplatz zu stellen.

Der Aeltestenrat

Befehl des Kommandeurs des SD vom 3.10.41

Das Infektionskrankenhaus im Ghettos ist nebst Einrichtung, Kranken und Med.Personal in Brand zu setzen. Die Saeuglinge sind zum IX.Fort abzufuehren.

P.S. Am 4.10.41 ist der Befehl vollstreckt worden. Die Bewohner des Kleinen Ghetto sind zum Teil zum IX.Fort gebracht und zum Teil im uebriggebliebenen Ghettoteil untergebracht worden.

Der Aeltestenrat

Befehl des Kommandeurs des SD vom 27.10.41

Alle Ghetto-Bewohner ohne Unterschied des Alters und Geschlechts muessen am 28.10.41 ihre Haeuser verlassen und sich um 6 Uhr morgens auf dem Demokratu Platz befinden. Diejenigen, welche in den Haeusern vorgefunden werden, werden auf der Stelle erschossen.

Der Aeltestenrat

Verordnung des Stadtkommissars vom 8.11.41 durch Kaminskas

Saemtliche Ghetto-Einwohner sind verpflichtet Wagen, Droschken und Schlitten abzuliefern.

Der Aeltestenrat

Befehl des Kommandeurs des SD vom 27.12.41

Die Juden muessen ihre Pelze und Pelzwaren

This document entitled "Numbers That Demand an Accounting!" is a *trompe l'oeil* in the shape of a memorial plaque found in synagogues to mark the anniversaries of the deaths of loved ones. It unfolds to reveal graphics about the numbers of Kovno Jews murdered between June 22, 1941, and December 31, 1942.

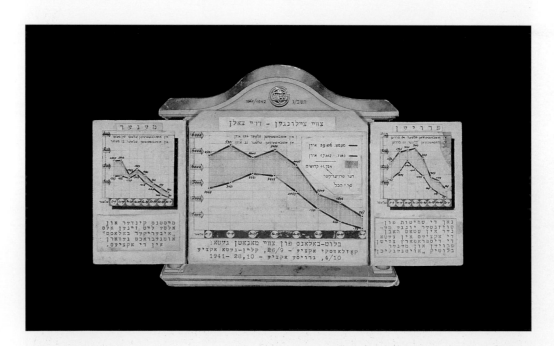

These graphs compare by age group the ghetto censuses of September 1941 *(in red)* and November 1941 *(in blue)* to show the losses from "actions" to the ghetto as a whole *(center)*, and to the population of men *(left)* and women *(right)*.

Under the heading that names the four biblical forms of capital punishment (death by stone, fire, sword, and strangulation) are enumerated the deaths by the ghetto's equivalents: 240 by natural causes, 646 by deportations, 336 by "accidental" shootings, and 12,199 by "actions."

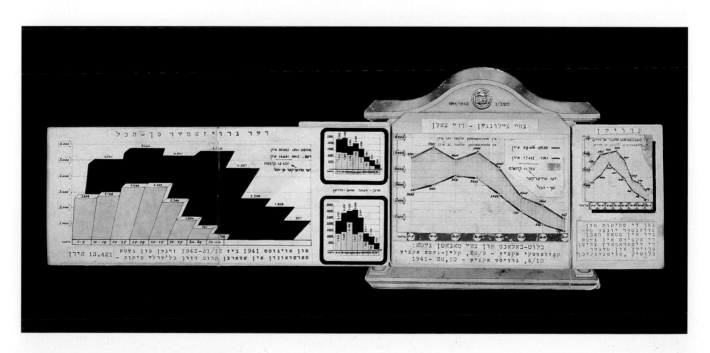

The three black-and-gray graphs compare the census of September 1941 with the population as of December 31, 1942, by age group, for the ghetto as a whole (left), for men (top), and for women (bottom).

This bar chart analyzes by age group and
gender the victims of the October 28, 1941,
"Great Action."

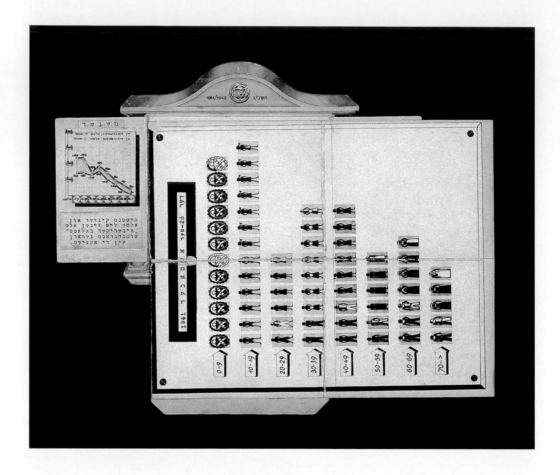

AVRAHAM TORY

"Last Testament" of Avraham Tory, December 1942

Driven by an inner force and by fear that there might be no remnant of the Kovno Jewish community who would be able to relate the shuddering of its death agony in the days of Nazi rule, I have pursued the writing of my diary in the ghetto, which I began on the first day of the outbreak of the war. . . .

With awe and reverence, I am hiding in this box what I have written, noted, and collected with fervor and dread. . . .

Next to the leadership of the *Ältestenrat*'s chairman, Elkhanan Elkes, and vice-chairman, Leib Garfunkel, Avraham Tory's role as an administrator and record-keeper was central to the ghetto's life and history. Tory was born Avraham Golub in 1909 in Lazdijai, Lithuania, then part of the tsarist Russia. (He replaced his Russian surname with a Hebrew one—both meaning "dove"—in 1950.) After attending a Hebrew high school in Marijampole, Lithuania, and participating in the General Zionist youth movement, he attended law school in Kovno and in the United States. Completing his law degree in Kovno, he worked in the 1930s at the University of Lithuania as an assistant for an authority on civil law, one of the

few professors at the time who was Jewish.

When the Soviets annexed Lithuania in 1940, Tory was working for the Soviet construction administration that was building military bases in Lithuania. The era's volatile politics, however, twice caused Tory to flee Kovno. The first time he went into hiding in Vilna [Vilnius] to escape the Soviet threat of arrest and deportation to Siberia for his Zionist "counter-revolutionary" sympathies. After the Soviets retreated in June 1941, permitting Tory to return, the dangers posed by the occupying German regime forced him to flee again. Prevented from crossing the Lithuanian-Russian border, he returned to Kovno and found himself with the rest of Kovno's Jews caught in ghetto captivity.

Like others, Tory began keeping a diary, writing entries at night (with the help of an assistant, Pnina Sheinzon) based on notes he took during the day. As a member of the administrative Secretariat for the newly formed *Ältestenrat,* his vantage point was unique. He became head of that office in May 1942 after his two predecessors were successively seized by German authorities (one perished in the "Great Action," the other

Avraham Tory with his assistant (and future wife), Pnina Sheinzon, in the ghetto, 1943

The diary of Avraham Tory

was imprisoned on charges of maintaining postal contact with the Vilna Ghetto). In this capacity Tory was able to report conversations between Elkes and Gestapo authorities. He provided the text that, in the hands of the graphic designers of the Paint and Sign Workshop, became two of the central documentary records of the ghetto, the compilation "And These Are the Laws—German Style" and the yearbook "Slobodka Ghetto 1942."

As head of the Secretariat, Tory was deeply involved in administering the day-to-day affairs of the ghetto and managing its secret archives. It is evidence of Tory's high regard for documenting the ghetto experience that he used his position to commission artists and requisition images—including 150 photographs—for the

archive. He also collected documents or their carbon copies from various *Ältestenrat* offices.

When the ghetto became a concentration camp in September 1943, reducing the council's influence with the Germans, Tory searched for any possible means of escape. Because of his ties to groups outside the ghetto, he managed to spirit Pnina and her daughter, Shulamit, to safety. He also made preparations to secure the five small wooden crates containing his own diary, the compilation of orders, the 1942 yearbook, the *Ältestenrat* office reports, art, and photographs in a bunker beneath Block C, the unfinished Soviet-built apartment house that had been used for a number of open and clandestine ghetto activities. He himself then escaped on

March 23, 1944, spending the final months of the war in hiding on a farm outside Kovno.

Immediately after Lithuania's and Kovno's liberation in August 1944, Tory returned to the ghetto in search of Block C, now reduced to rubble. He was able to retrieve only three of the crates he had hidden and took their contents to Poland. There, he turned over his diary and other documents to a member of *Brichah*, the organization helping Jews reach Palestine, who promised its safe passage to Bucharest. Seeking passage to Palestine, Tory traveled through Czechoslovakia, Hungary, Romania, Austria, and Italy, where he remained for two years. In October 1947, he arrived for good in Tel Aviv. With the help of the Israeli ambassador to Romania, Tory regained his diary and most of the cache of documents from the Kovno Ghetto.

Over the years, Tory has served Israel's legal profession with distinction, achieving recognition in 1969 when he took on responsibilities as secretary general of the International Association of Jewish Lawyers. Clearly, however, it was the publication of his diary and the preservation of other secret archive documents that have made the most durable impact. Consulted by investigators as evidence against Lithuanian and German perpetrators since the 1960s, the diary, published in Hebrew in 1983 and in English five years later as *Surviving the Holocaust: The Kovno Ghetto Diary*, serves as an extraordinary eyewitness account. It and the other documents Tory saved have substantially helped in rescuing from oblivion a significant part of the history of the Kovno Ghetto.

The "Last Testament" of Avraham Tory, December 1942. At the top of each crate he buried, Tory placed a copy of this statement in which he outlined the intention of his documentation and his hope that these documents might serve as evidence to bring the murderers of Kovno's Jews to justice.

Diary of Avraham Tory, July 25, 1943

We are obligated first of all to remember, remember and note events, people, and forms, images and moments, in words and in writing, in clay and in painting, in every place and in every manner that one can.

Esther Lurie responded to that call. She does it faithfully and completely.

Esther Lurie, *Ghetto Buildings,* **undated**
(watercolor, pen, and ink, 7 x 8¹/₂ in.)

Esther Lurie, *Man in the Ghetto*, 1943
(pen and ink, 6⁷/₈ x 4³/₈ in.)

Esther Lurie, *Deportation at the Main Gate*, 1943
(pen and ink, 11 x 14 in.)

"Dying Confession" of Jacob Lifschitz, July 5–6, 1944
The knife of the beast lies at our throat already. . . . Do not leave behind the few drawings of mine that you will find here.

Jacob Lifschitz, *The Ghetto,* undated
(watercolor, 12¹/₂ x 9¹/₂ in.)

Jacob Lifschitz, untitled, undated
(pen and ink, 13¹/₂ x 9³/₄ in.)

Jacob Lifschitz, untitled, undated
(pen and ink, 12¹/₂ x 9³/₄ in.)

Jacob Lifschitz, *Doorkeeper of the Labor Office*, undated
(pen and ink, 13¹/₄ x 9³/₈ in.)

Josef Schlesinger, unidentified portrait of an *Ältestenrat* messenger, 1943
(pen and ink, 6⁷/8 x 4³/8 in.)

Josef Schlesinger, untitled, 1943
(pen and ink, 7 x 8³/4 in.)

Nolik Schmidt, *Expulsion of the Inhabitants from Demokratu Square,* 1942
(watercolor, pen, and ink, 3⁹/16 x 5¹/2 in.)

"Slobodka Ghetto 1942" yearbook, January 11, 1942

At 12 o'clock noon, the chairman of the *Ältestenrat* . . . was given an order to vacate Demokratu Square by 4 o'clock P.M. for German Jews who were to arrive. . . . We waited all day, but they never came. The day was -30 degrees [C; -22°F].

ESTHER LURIE, JACOB LIFSCHITZ, JOSEF SCHLESINGER, AND BEN ZION "NOLIK" SCHMIDT

Within the confinement of the Kovno Ghetto, several artists drew and painted portraits and landscapes and even created copies of art masterpieces for the German overseers and others stationed in Kovno. Often they worked clandestinely to capture scenes of aggression and deportations.

Esther Lurie, self-portrait, undated
(pen and ink, 4¹/₁₆ x 3³/₁₆ in.)

Four artists left significant portraits of Kovno Jewry in captivity. Esther Lurie was perhaps the most influential. Drawing the attention early on of *Ältestenrat* Chairman Elkhanan Elkes, she eventually received a temporary work release from the council to allow her to document on commission the ghetto's existence for its "secret archives." By fall 1942 she was working regularly in collaboration with fellow artists, including several from the Paint and Sign Workshop. Lurie's stature as a leading artist in the ghetto is not surprising in light of her considerable previous formal training and accomplishment. Already as a young student in Riga—the capital of Latvia not far from the village of Liepaja where, in 1913, she was born—she showed promise and interest in drawing and design. Upon graduation from the Hebrew gymnasium, she joined her brother in Brussels, enrolling in a practical arts school to study theater design. Preferring more formal training, she moved on to the Academie Royale des Beaux Arts, the fine arts academy in Antwerp.

In 1934 Lurie joined part of her family in Tel Aviv, where they had settled a few years earlier. There she became a set designer for emerging theatrical companies. By 1938 she had exhibited her paintings in Jerusalem and Haifa and won the city of Tel Aviv's coveted Dizengoff Prize. Toward the end of 1938, Lurie returned to Antwerp for additional training, but as war threatened Western Europe, Lurie went east the following fall to join her sister in Kovno. There, she was caught in the expanding net of German terror and was forced into the ghetto.

The very act of drawing was Lurie's first sustained response to the confusion that occurred in the ghetto's early days. She first depicted displaced families trying desperately to set up living quarters in a former school of handicrafts among heavy machinery and industrial equipment. Other renderings during this period, including one of a girl and another of a group of individuals—each wearing the yellow star—capture disconsolate moods. It was her portrait of inmates frantically raiding the potato field that aroused the *Ältestenrat*'s interest in her work.

Lurie often conveyed crisis within ordinary, even quiet settings, as in her illustration of Demokratu Square *(p. 68)*, the scene of a massive, murderous "selection," rendered in empty stillness, or in a series of two water-

Jacob Lifschitz, self-portrait, 1943
(watercolor, 13⁵/₈ x 10¹/₈ in.)

Josef Schlesinger, self-portrait, 1943
(pen and ink, 4¹/₄ x 3¹/₈ in.)

Nolik Schmidt, his class picture at Kovno's
Shwabes Gymnasium before the war

colors and two pen-and-ink drawings showing sketchy figures on their way past peaceful suburban houses toward Kovno's Fort IX killing site.

Jacob Lifschitz, born in 1903, lived in Lithuania throughout his entire professional career. He studied at Kovno's Art Institute and, after joining its faculty, continued to teach engraving and print-making until his ghetto confinement. Well regarded for his technical skills, he illustrated books and teaching manuals and was active as an exhibiting artist. Lurie took note of his first and only solo exhibition (1940) in a laudatory review published in a local Yiddish newspaper.

Lifschitz did not seek a position supported by the ghetto's administration. Instead he resigned himself to assignments in labor brigades and in workshops devoted to producing nonmilitary goods. At the end of the day he retired to the attic of his house, where he lived with his wife and daughter, to paint with watercolors supplied by Lurie. His distorted use of perspective seems perfectly suited to depicting the ghetto as an uneasy world.

Lifschitz occasionally emerged from his private world to collaborate with Lurie for the secret archiving project. He eventually became Lurie's greatest collaborator. Both drew street scenes and inhabitants, often focusing on the same subject matter. However Lifschitz, cleaving to his own rules of perspective and his preference for distorted planes, seemed interested in capturing the pervading atmosphere—confusion in the city brigades office (p. 116), the starkness embracing a ghetto school, or bewilderment in the faces of children and ghetto officials.

A third artist active in the ghetto and also closely associated with Lurie was Josef Schlesinger. From the ghetto's first days he sought out the Paint and Sign Workshop, where he designed projects and most likely took part in the several clandestine art exhibitions held there. Born in Brno, Czechoslovakia, in 1919, Schlesinger began his training at the Prague Academy of Fine Arts

in 1938. Within the year he and his mother left German-occupied Czechoslovakia for Kovno, where his father managed a textile factory. There he continued his studies at the Arts Institute until his ghetto imprisonment.

Schlesinger, as evidenced by his surviving work, appears to have been assigned by the *Ältestenrat* to concentrate on producing portraits of ghetto administrators and police, as well as professionals among the inmates—doctors, lawyers, economists, agronomists, and so forth. He also produced sketches of at least two critical events. One portrayed the hanging of Nahum Meck in mid-November 1942 (p. 178). The other shows a huddled family set against a background of a deportation, probably to Estonia in 1943 (p. 167). Both were deposited in the council's secret archives.

Very little is known about the artist Ben Zion (Nolik) Schmidt. Though still a student at Kovno's Shwabes Hebrew School when he was forced into the ghetto, Schmidt was considered a promising member of the intimate circle of artists who worked in the ghetto's graphics shop. His 1942 depiction of the expulsion of Jews from Demokratu Square (p. 167), a German-enforced initiative intended to make room for the anticipated arrival of Jews from Germany, is the only surviving drawing he produced.

Indeed, most of the artists' work has been lost. The bulk of Lurie's 200-plus watercolors and sketches has

This photograph by Avraham Tory is of one of Esther Lurie's now-lost watercolors.
After the war, Lurie drew the grid on the photo in order to reproduce this work.

Esther Lurie, *The Wooden Bridge*, 1957 after 1941 original
(copperplate etching, $10^5/8$ x $14^1/2$ in.)

Jacob Lifschitz, untitled view of the Kovno Ghetto from the artist's attic room, undated
(watercolor, 7⁵/₈ x 12¹/₈ in.)

never been found and was probably destroyed, even though she took pains to bury it in ceramic jars for safe-keeping during the October 1943 deportation to Estonian labor camps. The small portion that did survive comprises several sketches and portraits that Tory buried in his secret crates. Eight watercolors and additional portrait sketches were found hidden with the Paint and Sign Workshop's archive. In the 1970s, five pen-and-ink drawings, scenes of deportation, were discovered by a Lithuanian family and returned to the artist. Lurie herself was deported in July 1944 to the concentration camp at Stutthof, Germany, and endured several labor camps until her liberation in January 1945. After a brief stay in Italy, where she exhibited her labor camp drawings, she returned to Israel. She has devoted much of her time since the war to reconstructing her ghetto art work on the basis of photographs Tory had taken of her pictures during one of the clandestine exhibitions.

At Lurie's urging Lifschitz buried his more than 75 watercolors and drawings, together with a few photographs, in ceramic pots she provided him just days before the ghetto's liquidation. Lifschitz did not survive his final internment, perishing in 1945 from starvation at the Dachau concentration camp. His wife escaped from the ghetto and, at war's end, recovered her husband's work from its burial place in the ghetto's cemetery as instructed in his will. She donated all but three watercolors to Yad Vashem, Israel's Holocaust memorial and museum, after she and her daughter emigrated to Israel in 1957.

Among Schlesinger's work only his illustrations of the Meck hanging and a scene from the Estonian deportation, plus composite portraits of youth and a policeman, a self-portrait, and a few formal portraits have survived. Deported to concentration camps in Germany during the ghetto's liquidation, he returned upon liberation to Prague to resume his studies and painting. From 1975 to 1988 he directed the Central Bohemian Galleries. Themes of war's upheaval and horror have appeared in his postwar art. Deep shadows, dark backgrounds, and oversized facial features characterizing his postwar portraits also emerge from his ghetto experiences.

Schmidt's surviving sketch of the Jews expelled from Demokratu Square is a beneficiary of Tory's hidden archive. The artist was not as fortunate. Trying to evade forced deportation during the ghetto's final days, Schmidt hid in the Paint and Sign Workshop bunker, where he perished in the ghetto's summary burning.

Diary of Tamara Lazerson, December 11, 1942

As a diversion, concerts are being held in the ghetto. Tomorrow, a dinner is being held for the doctors. There will be some sandwiches, a glass of tea, and a program made up of cultural works created in the ghetto. There are some excellent singers and poets. And that is how people forget where they are for one night, transporting themselves to an entirely different world. Although some people angrily object to what we are doing, they are wrong. A lot of people are composing something in the ghetto. My father wrote quite a few epigrams about our life. Victor wrote some prose, "One Day in the Ghetto."

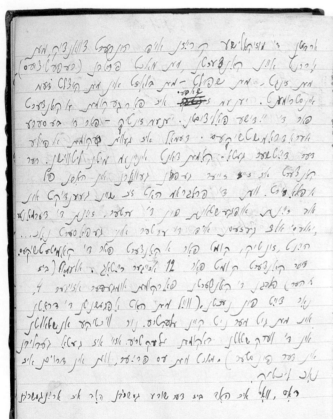

Diary of Ilya Gerber, December 28, 1942 *(above)*

Musical circles are working at 120%, concerts are organized, there are rehearsals, people sing, they play, they blow, and they tickle their instruments. . . .

Lyrics to "Lullaby,"
by K. L. Yemo [Moshe Klein], undated

Not by song will I put you to sleep,
my beloved, my tender one,
in my mouth there's no song, only
lamentations buried there by a God of wrath.

You came into the world when evil
has erased all lines of demarcation:
human blood—sewage water,
human life—not worth a garlic clove.

My son, when you came into the world
you were met by men of blood:
a yellow beast with his accomplice,
a drunken brute, the seed of Ham.

A human beast craves your blood,
my blameless, pure innocent—
What are prophets? What are saviors?
If that's how the world is.

A one-month-old is surrounded
by ruthless hunters—
They tear babies like you apart
as wolves rend lambs.

Your innocent eyes, your sweet babbling
seem to claim a debt from me:
"Look how soft and frail I am,
please protect me."

But how ashamed I am, my son,
gazing into your eyes—
not only can I not protect you—
I cannot protect myself.

To save my son's life by sacrificing my one—
do I lack courage?
If only I had a sword, a lance—
but I don't.

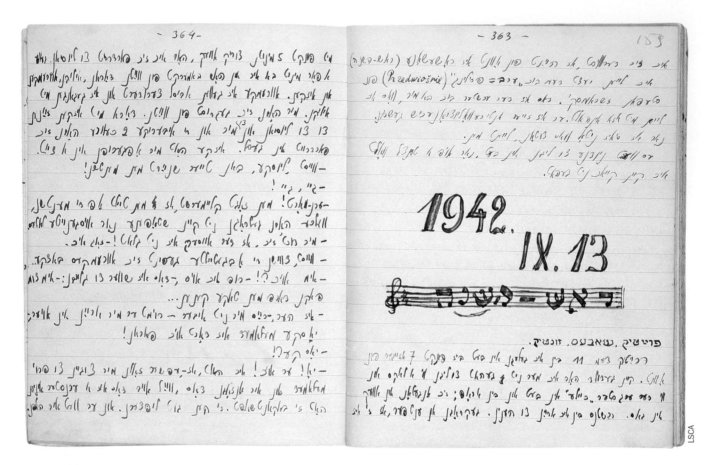

From the diary of Ilya Gerber, September 13, 1942.
The music staff of "notes" form Hebrew letters
spelling "Rosh Hashanah," the Jewish New Year.

As part of her ghetto record, Tamara Lazerson
wrote the Yiddish lyrics of ghetto songs in the Latin
alphabet of her native Lithuanian language. This is
her transcription of "By the Ghetto Gate" *(see p. 138*
for translation).

"Slobodka Ghetto 1942" yearbook, January 3, 1942

The *Ältestenrat* has given instructions for the activities of the Police House. The police will be organized by sections: for its own organization, and for artists. The institution of the Police House was necessary to legalize the orchestra.

Boris Stupel, a famous German Jewish violinist who had fled to Kovno after Hitler's rise to power, carries his violin in the ghetto.

Michael Hofmekler conducts a concert by the police orchestra.

Ticket for a concert at the Jewish Ghetto Police House

"History of the Vilijampole Jewish Ghetto Police," 1942–43

The matter of creating a concert hall in the ghetto brought about many commentaries and criticisms.

Some said that the ghetto is not the place for making concerts, that this is not the place for musical presentations and celebrations. We do not have the right, and we must not forget what we have gone through.

But on the other hand, it was later evident that the concerts carried a positive character in the sense that it is important that one in the ghetto have a few hours a week in which it is possible to forget a little, to rest a little from the daily nightmare, and to rise a little above the unremitting grayness into a finer world, which could fill one with hope and provide encouragement.

"In the Yeshiva,"
by Moshe Diskant, late 1942

In the yeshiva where the fear of G-d is great,
Where yeshiva students have spent their whole lives—
of this yeshiva they have made a concert-hall!

How can you forget that in the days of pogroms and slaughter,
when dogs of murderers had us in their power and grip.
when Jewish blood poured out like water—
where then could the pale yeshiva boy hide?

In the yeshiva, there was the house of refuge—
and that very building they have transformed into shame and mockery,
dressed the windows in green paper,
though it is difficult to cover over the blood spilled there.

The ghetto elite are invited into the decorated salon
and with them they bring the men who ordered—
our murder, degradation, and slaughter!
They enjoy intensifying the scene
with blue and white flags,
to hear the music, the pleasant tenor!

Only they don't know what they step upon,
on whose blood that was extinguished
without a why, without an indictment!

Don't you see that from the ornamented walls
martyred hands reach out,
and dance out with wild screaming,
"Get out of G-ds's house,
of the holy yeshiva,
where we have given up our lives with heart and love!
The music is not for us,
we cannot hear it,
we ask you not to disturb our holy rest!"

"Slobodka Ghetto 1942" yearbook, November 15, 1942

At 5 o'clock P.M., Commander Fleischmann of the Germans' Ghetto Guard detained a young Jewish man—Meck—crawling through the fence. Meck fired a gun three or four times into the air. Meck was immediately arrested and put into the Ghetto Guard's house. As compensation, the Security Service (SD) promptly arrested *Ältestenrat* members [Deputy Chairman Leib] Garfunkel, [Labor Office head Yakov] Goldberg, and [Secretary Avraham] Golub [Tory], and threatened to do away with them. That same evening, they were taken, with Meck, to SD headquarters.

Order from the Commander of the SD, November 17, 1942

Meck is to be publicly hanged in the ghetto on November 18. The gallows is to be built in the ghetto, and the execution is to be carried out by the Jewish Ghetto Police.

Order from the Commander of the SD, November 18, 1942

Meck should remain hanging on the gallows for 24 hours. All ghetto inhabitants are required to turn in all firearms.

Order from the Commander of the SD, November 19, 1942

The mother and sister of the hanged Meck are to be taken to Fort IX for execution.

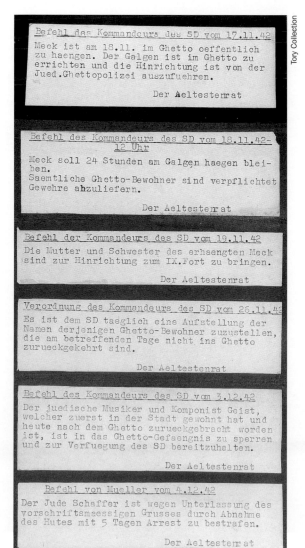

Tory Collection

The German-ordered fate of Nahum Meck, as recorded in the compilation "And These Are the Laws—German Style"

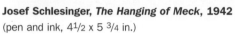

Josef Schlesinger, *The Hanging of Meck*, 1942
(pen and ink, 4^1/$_2$ x 5 ^{3}/$_4$ in.)

The Jewish Ghetto Police hang Nahum Meck
while German troops supervise and keep order.
The ghetto population is forced to witness.

"Slobodka Ghetto 1942" yearbook, November 18, 1942

At 12 noon today, the hanging of Meck was carried out publicly in the ghetto, opposite the *Ältestenrat* building and in sight of the SD, German and Lithuanian police, the Ghetto Guard, the *Stadtkommissariat*, and the Jewish Ghetto Police. The ghetto populace had to assemble at the site of the execution. The dead body must hang from the gallows for 24 hours.

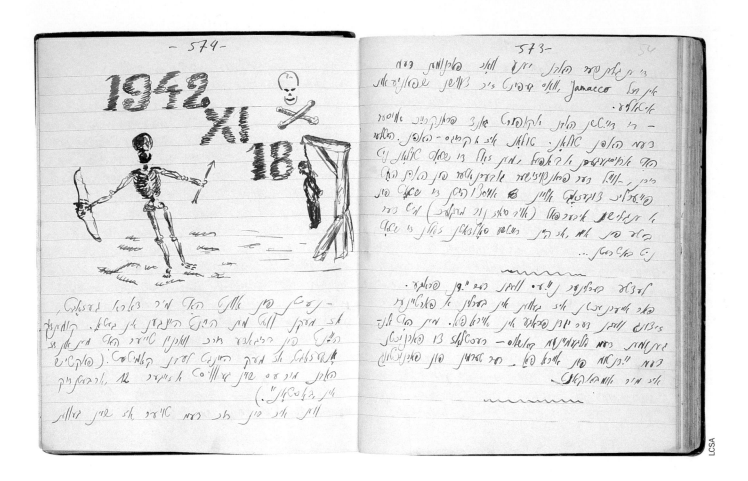

Diary of Ilya Gerber, November 18, 1942 *(above)*

Last night Dora told me that Meck will be hanged in the ghetto. Today, coming back with the brigade through Varniu Street, we were told that Meck is hanging near the *Ältestenrat*.

Diary of Tamara Lazerson, November 18, 1942

The poor wrongdoer, after horrible tortures, was publicly hanged next to the *Ältestenrat* building today. The Commandant personally drove people out of their houses to observe the chilling spectacle. I, being the mischievous girl that I am, was overcome by curiosity and also went down to watch the hanging. The spectacle was not so chilling after all. But I did feel sorry for the person who had visibly suffered so much. But others have said that we should not feel sorry for him, because with his idiotic act he could have gotten the whole ghetto wiped out.

Diary of Tamara Lazerson, November 19, 1942

Against my will, the sight of the hanging keeps coming back to me. What does all of one's life mean in front of death? Why live, why suffer, why struggle—death awaits in the end. We will disappear from the world without a trace.

Diary of Avraham Tory, February 25, 1943

We are not allowed to be sick. We must be healthy. . . . We must hide ourselves, bury our pain, bite our lips, and not let on to the world that it hurts us.

We need medical treatment like all the people of the world. No, for us it is dangerous. Dangerous not only for those who are actually sick—it is dangerous for all. If one is sick with typhoid or typhus, the Germans would use it to justify wiping out an entire district or maybe even the whole ghetto—a very good opportunity for them to get rid of it. We know that we must avoid this. We suffer and we keep silent.

Patients recuperating in the ghetto hospital

Kadish/GK

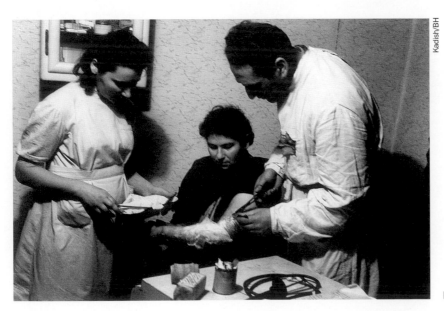

Kadish/BH

Dr. David Arolianski treats a patient in the clinic.

Even newborns wore the Jewish star.

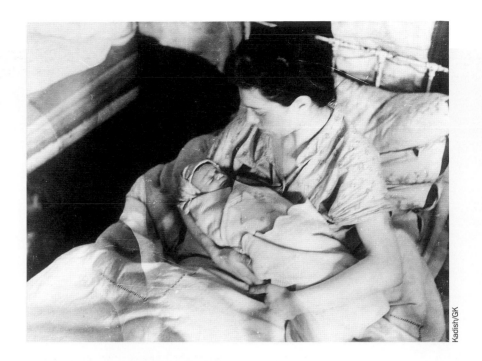

Kadish/GK

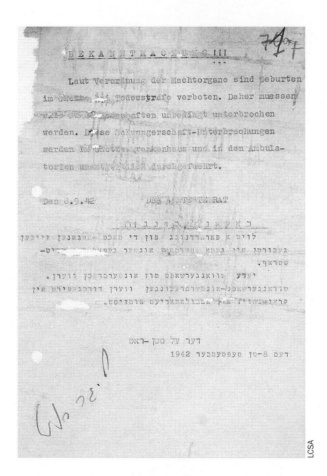

LCSA

Announcement from the *Ältestenrat*, September 8, 1942 *(above)*

According to an order from the organs of authority, giving birth in the ghetto is forbidden under punishment of death. Every pregnancy must be terminated. Termination of pregnancies will be carried out in the hospital and in the clinics free of charge.

"Health Institutions in the Ghetto," report to the *Ältestenrat*, mid-1943

There was a case when Rauca of the Gestapo chanced to see the wife of a policeman who was 8 months pregnant. He warned her that she would be shot if the baby was not killed.

Diary of Avraham Tory, February 18, 1943

Who should sponsor the 15 or 16 solitary, abandoned children—the sole survivors of the hospital children's ward that was completely destroyed by fire in the Small Ghetto? . . . These same children now are in the ghetto hospital and formally are said to be in its children's ward. . . . The fiction, the jest of the ghetto hospital has become an absolute necessity after the Germans, before God and witnesses, set fire to the contagious diseases hospital in the former Small Ghetto and destroyed the almost 180 children and suckling infants who were there. It was through a miracle that 8 to 10 children were saved, and we can no longer leave them without a children's home or orphanage, just as we can no longer go without a formal old-age home. But upon the creation of such institutions, the Germans would surely not hesitate to transport every last soul away from them to Fort IX. . . .

In light of these circumstances, we decided—without any trouble and there should be no questions—that children not placed with private families should be formally admitted to the hospital children's ward. In case this is scrutinized, we will have the pretext that these are sick children, and that they are here only temporarily.

Orphans hidden in a ghetto hospital ward

Kadish/BH

Diary of Avraham Tory, June 5, 1943

Slobodka for generations has been a center of Talmud and Torah study, of yeshivas and Jewish religious culture. I have more than once wanted to know how it appears now, in the time of the ghetto. Where are they, the former yeshiva-people, the diligent students and the rabbis? For the most part they, just like thousands of others, were taken as martyrs for the sanctification of God's name. Only a small handful remain. They come together over a page after work at Tiferes Bachurim, among the *Musarniks,* and in other tiny, secret synagogues, to study and to pray. They continue, protecting the flame so that it will not be overwhelmed.

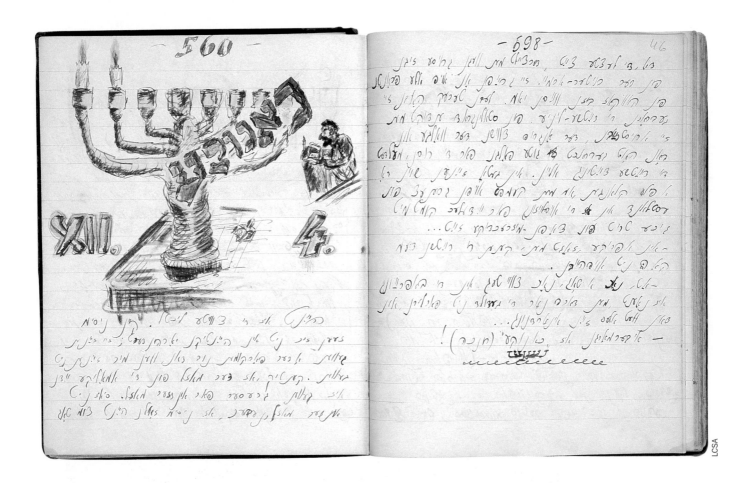

Diary of Ilya Gerber, December 4, 1942 *(above)*

Today is the second candle [of Hannukah]. There are no miracles to be seen in this century; they happened or took place only when we were not around. Apparently the luck of Jews of former times was better than our luck.

Order from *Einsatzstab Rosenberg* (German civilian units that plundered art) via the *Stadtkommissar,* February 27, 1942

All ghetto inhabitants are required to turn in all of their books, regardless of content or language.

Title pages from religious books hidden from the 1942 confiscations

This "Scroll of Esther," which recounts the unsuccessful plot to kill the Jews of ancient Persia and is read on the holiday of Purim, was hidden in the ghetto from the confiscations.

"History of the Vilijampole Jewish Ghetto Police," 1942–43

On the 26th of February it was announced that all ghetto residents were obliged to hand over all books in their possession. Collection points for the books were given, and as usual, the announcement in the name of the authorities made clear that, after the deadline for handing in books, house searches would be conducted by the Germans, and that if books were found, punishment would be severe. . . .

From out of the Jewish houses was carried the best that we possess, the greatest intellectual treasures, pearls of secular and Jewish literature; holy books fondled with great love and devotion by fathers and grandfathers; books that we had sometimes saved up for, in order to acquire this or that work; pages that can tell about the quiet groans of fathers and grandfathers as they sat bent over them and gleaned their vital strength, their spiritual food and force for a lean gray day; books that tell the suffering and joy of whole families, of whole eras and their various wanderings and forms; all this we had to collect for the Germans who want to finally take from us the last weapon we have: the book.

Carting away books during the confiscation

EPHRAIM OSHRY

Diary of Avraham Tory, June 5, 1943

Oshry teaches boys every day and, for older people, a page of Talmud. He holds "evenings" with the remaining rabbis, he consults with the Tiferes Bachurim school, and does no few other things, too, that, if the authorities knew, he would have met a violent death.

The Germans not only segregated Kovno's Jews from the outside world by forcing them into a ghetto; they also sought to cut them off from their traditions by forbidding many of their religious observances. Even under these hostile circumstances, Rabbi Ephraim Oshry exemplified the extraordinary determination to affirm the community's Jewish traditions. The role he played as a religious authority was partly due to chance: he was one of the few ghetto rabbis to survive to the end of the war (and beyond). At the time he and other Jews were ghettoized in 1941, Oshry already possessed considerable religious knowledge and training based on his deep immersion, before the war, in Kovno's vigorous Jewish academic life. In adapting religious practices to adverse and intractable ghetto conditions, Oshry showed remarkable resilience.

Oshry was born in 1914 in the small northeastern Lithuanian town called Kupishok. He studied Torah at the famous yeshiva of Ponevezh [Panevezys], a town close by, before moving on at age 17 to Kovno's Slobodka Yeshiva, a center of Jewish learning renowned throughout the Jewish world. Oshry excelled throughout the 1930s, studying in an advanced program devoted to training leaders for educational and religious institutions. He eventually served as an assistant to Kovno's chief rabbi, Avraham Duber Shapiro.

As a resident of Slobodka, Oshry witnessed the bloody massacre of Jews carried out by pro-Nazi Lithuanian nationalists after the Germans took control of Kovno in June 1941. Densely populated by pious Jews, Slobodka was the first place Lithuanian nationalists targeted for anti-Jewish assault. It became the site of the Kovno Ghetto two months later.

Oshry's dedication to his religion and to religious instruction and leadership in the ghetto appeared unshaken. The rabbi taught clandestine classes in Talmud to youths as well as to adults. When the Germans turned the synagogue he and his followers had used into a prison after the "Great Action" at the end of October, they moved to new quarters. He asked the

Ältestenrat to exempt youths from working on the Sabbath so that they could observe the Jewish day of rest whenever possible. He was the custodian of Kovno's religious library until the Germans' book confiscation in February 1942; in response to that order, Oshry and others did what they could to save as many of the treasured books in hiding places throughout the ghetto. Oshry frequently consulted these texts, including works from the valuable library of the Kovno's nineteenth-century chief rabbi, Yitzhak Elhanan Spektor, to help interpret Jewish law in light of hostile ghetto circumstances. Oshry took on other duties, such as heading the delousing baths for the Health Office's Sanitation Service, in order to remain employed and "useful" to the Germans.

Oshry worked alongside senior rabbis, including Rabbi Shapiro until his death in February 1943, in offering learned answers to a wide range of painful questions

Rabbi Ephraim Oshry shortly after the liberation of Kovno, wearing his Sanitation Service armband

Shofar, a ram's horn, used in the ghetto to call Jews together for Rosh Hashanah, the Jewish New Year

posed by pious, traditional Jews who could not observe the Sabbath, dietary laws, or other sacred ritual obligations. The practice of soliciting rabbinical advice *(responsa)* is itself traditional and an important aspect of Judaism. Oshry painstakingly searched the historic religious texts in his efforts to help others follow Jewish law under catastrophic conditions: How would Jews observe Passover without available ritual foods? Could Jews wear the clothes belonging to someone who had perished? Could Jews use stolen wool or torn fragments of a prayer shawl to fashion a sacred garment *(tzitzis)* in fulfillment of a biblical commandment?

Oshry's *responsa* constitute a precious spiritual and legal record that still spurs discussion today. The notes he kept on scraps of paper, which survived in buried cans, became the basis of a significant five-volume work he wrote in Hebrew after the war called *Questions and Responses from Out of the Depths.* He outlived

the ghetto's liquidation and arson by hiding with about 20 others for nearly a month in a bunker beneath the fires that raged through the Block C apartment building that had housed the delousing facility he supervised. After Kovno's liberation, he served Kovno's remnant Jewish community as its rabbi, burying the bodies of as many victims as he could. In addition to writing, Oshry dedicated himself to finding and caring for Holocaust-era orphaned children throughout Europe. His personal mission led to the founding in Rome of a yeshiva for this nearly-lost generation. After relocating to America, he wrote an account in Yiddish of the Holocaust years, translated and published in English in 1995 as *The Annihilation of Lithuanian Jewry.* He founded a yeshiva in the Bronx, New York City, and for many years served as the head of Beth HaMedrash HaGadol in New York City.

Questions of Jewish practices for Rabbi Oshry's *responsa*

May one use a slightly cracked *shofar* to announce Rosh Hashanah?

Might a Jew eat nonkosher food to prevent malnutrition?

Should critically ill patients fast on the holy day of Yom Kippur?

Must a Jew risk his life in order to pray every day and study Torah?

Responsa from the Holocaust of Rabbi Ephraim Oshry

Question: On 4 Elul 5701—August 27, 1941—the Germans captured stray dogs and cats and brought them into the Neier Kloiz, a house of study in Slobodka . . . where they shot them to death. . . . They proceeded to force a number of Jews to rip apart a Torah scroll with their own hands and to use the sheets of parchment to cover the carcasses of the shot animals. Other Jews were compelled to watch the Torah scroll being shredded and the Word of G-d defiled with the blood of these carcasses. . . .

The ghetto dwellers who heard the report of this horrifying insult to the Torah saw it as a sign that the fury of the Germans was being unleashed upon the entire community. It therefore seemed appropriate that all of us accept upon ourselves some form of penance and implore G–d to have mercy on His people and to tell Satan, "Enough!" Because the rabbi of Kovno [Avraham Duber Shapiro] was very ill then, he asked me to study the subject and to determine precisely what the people ought to do.

Response: Those who saw the scroll being torn were obligated to rend their garments. . . . Those who were forced to rend the Torah scroll with their own hands were obligated to fast, even though they had been forced to act at gun point. All those who witnessed this vile act also had to fast. But if they could not fast because of physical weakness due to the hunger and the other sufferings they bore daily in the ghetto, one could not obligate them to fast.

Torah scroll desecrated during the Slobodka pogroms, June 1941

Responsa from the Holocaust of Rabbi Ephraim Oshry

Question: Among the boys in the Tiferes Bachurim was an extraordinary boy from Kovno named Shereshevsky who dedicated himself totally to the study of Torah. Even though he was not yet bar-mitzvah, he was as precise as an adult in his fulfillment of *mitzvos* [the commandments]. This extraordinary boy asked me if he might be permitted to don *tefillin*, despite the fact that his bar-mitzvah was three months away.

New edicts by the German taskmasters were issued against us every day; especially upon Jewish children. Who could assure this boy that he would ever reach the age of 13 to fulfill the mitzvah? This was why he could not wait to don *tefillin*. . . .

Response: I ruled that the precious child who had such a great desire to merit the privilege of fulfilling this mitzvah because he feared he might not live to fulfill it if he waited to reach 13, certainly had authorization for donning.

Oshry Collection

Rabbi Oshry's *tefillin* (phylacteries) from the ghetto, each containing inscriptions from Torah and worn, one on the forehead and one on the left arm, during morning prayer.

Questions of life and death for Rabbi Oshry's *responsa*

Can a Jew endanger his own life in order to save fellow Jews?

May a person save himself by causing the death of a fellow Jew?

Is one permitted to commit suicide?

Can you take the property of murdered Jews who have no surviving heirs?

May a Jew cook on the Sabbath if he was working in the ghetto soup kitchen?

May a woman who has become pregnant have an abortion?

Can one eat in the presence of a corpse?

Can a Jew risk his life to join the partisans?

Can a Jew entrust his Jewish children to non-Jews?

The Jewish Police collecting bundles of clothing and other abandoned household items outside the *Ältestenrat* building after the deportation of more than 2,700 Kovno Jews to Estonian labor camps, October 26, 1943. The Welfare Office distributed these items to needy Jews in the ghetto.

Responsa from the Holocaust of Rabbi Ephraim Oshry

Question: In the Ninth Fort there was a storeroom of garments from Jews the Germans had murdered, and the pockets of those garments still contained personal letters, photographs, and other miscellaneous items which identified the garments as belonging to the murdered victims. . . . The clothes had no bloodstains, proof that the murderers had stripped their victims before killing them. [I was] asked whether those garments might be used again, since garments in which people were killed are forbidden to be worn.

Response: Since those garments had been removed before the victims were killed, they might be worn not only by the victims' heirs, but also by any other survivors as well. The martyred souls would unquestionably derive spiritual satisfaction in the world of the souls from the fact that their suffering captive brethren were garbed in warm garments that had once belonged to them.

Order from *Stadtkommissar* SA-Colonel Hans Cramer, August 25, 1942

Existing schools are to be closed immediately; the staff employed in the schools is to be directly integrated into the labor brigades. Any form of instruction as well as conducting religious exercises is immediately prohibited.

Diary of Avraham Tory, March 28, 1943

It is often truly heartbreaking to look at the young people. These 16- and 17-year-old boys and girls—just children and just developing themselves—their place is on a school bench. The ghetto is not the appropriate atmosphere for their development—no schools, no youth societies. . . . The unnerving changes of these times have left a recognizable mark—underfed, washed-out, their normal development disrupted, the normal foundations for their physical growth disrupted.

**"Ghetto Child,"
author unknown, ca. 1942**

Wretched body, skinny
Weak, shrunken;
Sunken chest
Downcast eyes.

Without fathers,
A miserable orphan
His meager body
Wrapped in rags.

Barefoot, naked,
Always hungry—
All day long here
Circling around.

Without freedom or laughter
And without springtime—
From an age, far from
Beauty or splendor.

A little Jew
And suffering so—
Satan has already
Tormented him.

Kadish/BH

"Slobodka Ghetto 1942" yearbook, September 13, 1942

Meeting of the *Ältestenrat;* the issue—schools. We should found a vocational training school with a broadened program of general studies.

Diary of Avraham Tory, April 26, 1943

Therefore we take great interest in knowing exactly what is going on in the vocational school, what they learn and how they learn. Under our auspices, the school accomplishes much more than the official "production" of artisans for the work force. That, too, but not only that. Under our auspices, beneath the cloak of the vocational education courses that they call official, our children receive a national-Jewish education in the spirit of our tradition and national aspirations.

Diary of Tamara Lazerson, April 4, 1943

I have not written for almost a month. I am now working at the vocational school. I am quite satisfied. The lectures are quite interesting. We take notes and study them. You wouldn't recognize me now, because I am studying and working for the cause of my fatherland: The Land of Israel! Today, I submitted one of my larger compositions for the wall newspaper. I concluded the article with the motto, "Forward to work, The Land of Israel awaits us." Generally, things are upbeat.

A vocational school. Training in sewing and other practical skills was supplemented with academic topics, Zionist education, and lectures to school the ghetto children despite the prohibitions by the German authorities.

Kadish/BH

Members of the ghetto's Zionist underground youth movement, *Irgun Brit Tzion,* the Organization of the Covenant of Zion, which pursued Hebrew cultural activities, published its own underground newspaper, and engaged in armed resistance activities

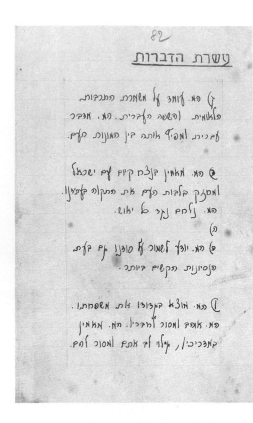
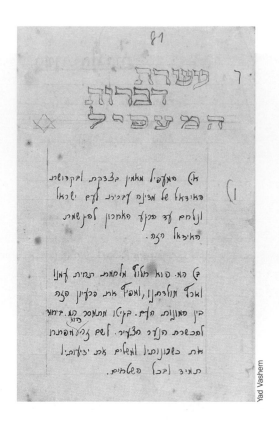

"Ten Commandments" of *Irgun Brit Tzion* unit "The Defiant Ones" [*HaMapilim*] *(above)*

The Defiant One—

1) believes in righteousness and the holiness of the ideal of a Hebrew state for the people of Israel, and will fight until the last moment to achieve this ideal.

2) is a pioneer in the war for the rebirth of our people and our homeland, and spreads this idea among the masses of the nation. In the ghetto, he devotes himself in particular to prepare the young people. To this end, he will use all his talents and always supplement his knowledge in all areas.

3) will stand for the preservation of the national culture and the Hebrew language. He speaks Hebrew and spreads it among the masses of the nation.

4) believes in the eternity of the Jewish people's existence and will strengthen the hope in our future in the hearts of the people. He fights all despair.

5) knows how to keep its secrets even during the time of our most difficult trials.

6) finds his family in the group. He loves and cares for his comrades and believes his leaders, is candid with them and devoted to them.

7) will always obey orders from his leaders and commanders without any hesitations.

8) is a man of order; he loves work. He possesses national pride and preserves this pride in a time of need.

9) is a man of truth, is cordial and good to all men. He is pure in his thoughts, words, and deeds.

10) remembers and always will remember the spilled blood of his brothers, and he will revenge this blood. He remembers and will remember the curse of the Hebrew people settled in Europe and will awaken the people to end the European exile. He mourns the nation's martyrs and will not go to any places of enjoyment in the ghetto.

TAMARA LAZERSON AND
ILYA GERBER

Two diary notebooks from the ghetto years, one written by a teen-age girl and one by a young man, reveal two very different personalities wrestling variously with daily torment. Tamara Lazerson started her ghetto diary in September 1941, when she was just 12 years old, and kept writing until (and after) her ghetto escape in April 1944. Only the second of her two notebooks, beginning in September 1942, survives. Ilya Gerber was 20 years old when he began his third notebook (the first two, and possibly subsequent notebooks, are lost). It covers the five-month period from August 1942 to January 1943, overlapping in time with Lazerson's surviving second notebook. In addition to expressing small but buoyant successes at defeating circumstances arrayed against them, Lazerson and Gerber share a broad awareness of the surrounding world and offer rare insight into youthful strategies of remaking their lives during the ghetto's period of relative calm.

Unlike most of Kovno's prewar Jewish youths, Lazerson, born in 1929, attended Lithuanian instead of Jewish schools. Her family seemed determined to assimilate into the national culture. They spoke Russian at home, neglecting Jewish holidays in favor of a secular observance of Christian holidays. Lazerson's father, Wolf (Vladimir in Russian), a senior lecturer in psychology at the University of Lithuania in Kovno, belonged to a Lithuanian defense group. His membership probably saved his life during the nationalist Lithuanian pogroms in June 1941, when he was arrested but only briefly detained; it could not, however, save his eldest son Rudolph when he, too, was seized. Rudolph was killed, a fact not known to the family for two more years.

Of course it did not matter to the Germans if the Lazersons had rejected ties to the Jewish community or if the professor, remembering German acquaintances from his student years, believed he could adjust to the German takeover. With her brother Victor, her mother Regina, and her father, Tamara was forced into the ghetto during the summer. Though young enough to avoid forced labor, she began working in the city brigades in 1942.

Lazerson wrote expressively in her diary about the rank misery of forced labor and the need to smuggle food into the ghetto. She seethed about the German regime, but also occasionally disparaged the ghetto police. She complained frequently about her spiritual

Tamara Lazerson, with her brother Victor in the uniform of the Soviet Army, after liberation

starvation as well. Lazerson was a young girl with yearnings for renewed purpose. Lamenting her boredom in a world where books were forbidden, she jumped at the chance to enroll in agricultural classes at the ghetto's vocational school. There she not only discovered a more accessible source of food for her family, but she also drew unexpected inspiration from the school's illegal Jewish education and cultural programs. She affectingly described her sheer joy in learning Yiddish and some Hebrew and, having made new friends at the school, in joining and taking an active part in underground youth movements. "You wouldn't recognize me now, because I am studying and working for the cause of my fatherland: The Land of Israel!"

Ilya Gerber, born in 1922, exercised a keen, observing eye for detail, commenting in his diary on events as well as on his friends' large and small preoccupations.

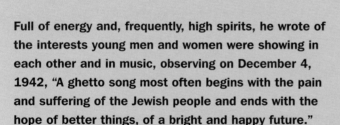

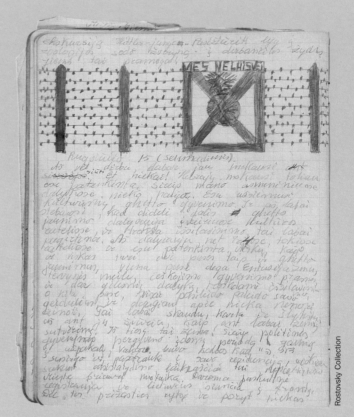

The title page of Tamara Lazerson's ghetto diary. Rudolph, her brother shown in the photograph, was caught and killed during the Lithuanian nationalist pogroms in the days after the German invasion.

A page of Tamara Lazerson's diary

Full of energy and, frequently, high spirits, he wrote of the interests young men and women were showing in each other and in music, observing on December 4, 1942, "A ghetto song most often begins with the pain and suffering of the Jewish people and ends with the hope of better things, of a bright and happy future."

After a brief stint at the vocational school (which his well-connected father arranged to save him from serving in the notorious airfield labor brigade), Gerber was ordered into a city brigade. For someone who expressed satisfaction at foiling the authorities, whether German or Jewish, the assignment, giving him an opportunity to participate in secret trading, was a source of momentary jubilation. But he did not miss the ominous signs or the gloom that engulfed the ghetto. In fact, his surviving diary opens with a long description of the panic over the impending resumption of the ban on bringing food into the ghetto. He devoted many pages to describing the German deportation in October 1942 of 369 Jews and their families to the Riga (Latvia) Ghetto, adding a sketch in the shape of a tombstone. In at least two of the many sketches punctuating his diary entries, he also recalled

the first anniversary of the "Great Action." A month later, he wrote about the terrified reactions to the Meck hanging. Nothing in the diary suggests what happened to Gerber after the last extant entry of January 23, 1943.

Lazerson started thinking about escape in December 1943. Following the "Children's Action" in March 1944, her parents inquired into possible places their daughter could hide outside the ghetto. Lazerson fled on April 7, 1944, finding shelter in the city of Kovno with her former teacher before moving to the teacher's sister's farm for the remainder of the war.

Lazerson's parents were among the thousands of ghetto inmates deported to German concentration camps during July 1944. Her father perished at Dachau, her mother at Stutthof. Tamara and Victor, her family's sole survivors, returned to the site of the ghetto after the war and succeeded in retrieving one of her note-books from a box she had buried beneath her window. In 1976, five years after leaving Kovno with her husband and two daughters for Haifa, Israel, she published the diary in Hebrew.

Ilya Gerber's drawing of a headstone, dated October 13, 1942, reads "Date of taking people to Riga," referring to the Germans' demand for 300 workers to labor at the Riga, Latvia, military airfield.

Drawing in Ilya Gerber's diary to mark "October 28, 1942—exactly one year after the 'Great Action'!"

Map from the diary of Ilya Gerber, September 27, 1942, showing how the carpentry vocational school *(blue square circled in red)*, though in a district to be excluded from the ghetto *(see yearbook map, p. 154)*, would be fenced in to remain part of the ghetto.

Notebook of Anti-Fascist Organization acts of sabotage, undated

The role of our members is not only to destroy the German industry and war machine, but also to encourage every such attempt and every colleague who will participate. Various small things and details have upset the Germans more than the big train wrecks. If their schnapps is not on time, if the clock is wrong by hours, or if the truck overturns because of tampering, or if the lunch is not ready, or the potatoes are too hard—the Germans call out curses on the leader of their unit and their land.

The slogan "Sabotage at the work place" has been useful. Everywhere you work, you can sabotage and can encourage your coworkers to do the same. . . . An Organization member brings reports from various work places where sabotage was carried out. There are cases of sabotage where hundreds of liters of benzene were destroyed during transport. As workers in factories and various undertakings, and as those working in military offices everywhere, in all areas of economic and public life, wherever an Organization member shows up, he carries out sabotage and convinces another to do the same.

Guide for "Encounter Actions" by the Anti-Fascist Organization

In an encounter action, the leader is required to show boldness, initiative, and determination; to easily comprehend the existing situation; to begin to appropriate operations; and to take the initiative. . . .

The chief goal of an encounter action must be: To break the enemy into pieces and to hit the pieces separately.

In an encounter action you will surely find opportunities to fight the enemy with technology that the enemy has lost or left behind in the attack. And we know not to be afraid of tanks, but to make the effort to blow up the infantry division that goes behind the tank and the tank itself.

The Anti-Fascist Organization's tactics guide to "encounter actions"

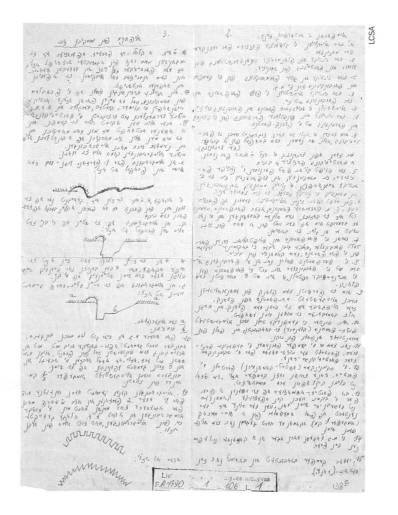

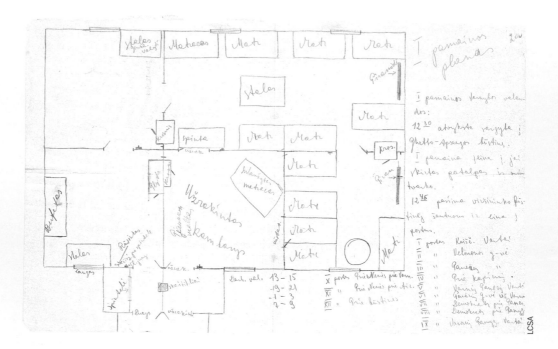

The Anti-Fascist Organization plan to attack the German
Ghetto Guard included this diagram of the guardhouse
cellar. The plan was never implemented.

The pledge of the Anti-Fascist Organization, handwritten
by Chaim Yelin and signed by its leadership in code

CHAIM YELIN

Pledge of the Anti-Fascist Organization, ca. 1941

Recognizing the struggle against fascism in all its forms, I hereby stress that it is my will to stand up as an active fighter in the ranks of the Red Partisans. I promise to fight without reservation against the fascist occupiers, to threaten their stations; disrupt their transports; set fires and blow up bridges; destroy railroads; organize and help to carry out acts of sabotage at every opportunity and situation. Not considering any personal circumstances, not concerning myself with my health, and if necessary sacrificing my own life, I promise to fight until the final victory by the Red Army.

Chaim Yelin was well-known among Kovno's Jews both as a promising Yiddish writer and as leader of the ghetto's underground resistance movement against the Germans. During the German occupation, he led the Communist underground until his capture and murder in spring 1944.

Yelin, born in 1912 in Vikija, a small Lithuanian town near Kovno, grew up in a home filled with intellectual discussion. His father, Eliezer (Lazar), a Hebraist (as was his mother Esther-Riebel), founded in 1921 and directed a library in Kovno for the Culture League, which was later called "Lovers of Knowledge." Chaim and his brother Meir helped run the library and participated in discussions about Jewish and secular literature and politics.

In 1932 Yelin completed his studies at Kovno's Reali Hebrew Gymnasium, receiving a few years later a degree in economics at the city's University of Lithuania. As a student he became interested in drama and participated in student theatricals. He also established a literary reputation as a result of stories, articles, and dramas he published in the daily *Folksblat* and in other Yiddish journals. He represented Lithuania in 1937 at an international conference in Paris on Jewish culture.

Exhibiting left-wing tendencies, Yelin was eager to support the Soviet regime when it occupied Lithuania in 1940–41. But his employment in the new government's printing office and his activity in Communist Party councils and institutions exposed him as a double target, as a Jew and as a Communist sympathizer, when the Germans occupied Lithuania and ghettoized Jews in the summer of 1941. Eventually the Germans captured him and forced him into the ghetto.

Yelin continued to write in the ghetto, mainly during 1941, developing ironic and semi-humorous vignettes about work brigades, German plunder, and other aspects of ghetto despoliation. His main concern, however, was

Chaim Yelin

Tory Collection

Partisans from the Kovno Ghetto pose for a photograph after their liberation by the Soviet Army

With the conversion of the ghetto into a concentration camp and news of the liquidation of the Vilna Ghetto in September and October 1943, membership in resistance groups increased. Already during the summer, members of *Matzok*, the ghetto's largest Zionist resistance organization, approached Yelin about the possibilities of joining forces. Accelerating underground activity led to the consolidation of Zionists, who were committed to Jewish self-defense, and Communists into one group called "The Organization" or the "Jewish General Fighting Organization" *(Yidishe Algemeyne Kamfs Organizatsie)*. Yelin's charisma, organizational skills, and outside contacts with the non-Jewish underground movements earned him widespread support and popularity across ideological lines as the de facto leader of "The Organization." The Zionists concentrated on getting help from ghetto authorities; the Communists concentrated on getting help from without, contacting partisans and obtaining arms for fighting within and without the ghetto.

In early fall 1943, Yelin received a mysterious note addressed to "the Jewish author Chaim Yelin" and signed "G." The note came from Gessia Glezer, alias Albina, a Soviet Jewish paratrooper who often visited Kovno and stayed with Kutorgiene. She came this time with a proposal to send Jewish partisans to join Soviet partisan units in the Augustow [Augustavas] Forest south of Kovno. The Augustow Plan proved to be a disaster. Traveling by foot, almost all of the 100-plus Jewish fighters were captured; the two who arrived safely learned that there had been no partisan activity there. Yelin quickly established new contacts and sent more than 300 Jewish youths, many by truck, to the Soviet partisan bases of the Rudniki Forest.

On April 6, 1944, while Yelin was in central Kovno trying to arrange another transport of Jewish partisans, the Gestapo captured him following an exchange of gunfire on the city's main road. He was confined, interrogated, and tortured. Concerned about the ghetto's possible collective punishment on his account, he insisted that he was a Russian paratrooper named Garmen. Yelin was killed sometime in early May. With the loss of his leadership after his arrest and disappearance, armed resistance in the Kovno Ghetto eventually fell apart.

political. Assuming a new identity, complete with mustache and pseudonym (Kadison), he became the leader of the ghetto's Communist resistance movement. Shortly after the mass executions of Jews in the summer and fall of 1941, Yelin, together with a number of close friends, formed the Activists Union (*Aktivistn Farband* in Yiddish), also known as the Anti-Fascist Organization.

Believing that the ghetto's survival was dependent on the defeat of Germany by the Soviet army and partisans outside the ghetto's perimeter, Yelin found ways to evade gate guards to meet with members of the Communist underground in the city and in the Rudniki [Rudninkai] Forest, the closest partisan base to Kovno. He also met with sympathetic Lithuanians, including the physician Elena Kutorgiene. Yelin used these contacts to smuggle ammunition and arms into the ghetto and gather information. Kutorgiene also offered sanctuary for Yelin's ghetto writings.

The German order of June 21, 1943, to transform the eastern European Jewish ghettos into concentration camps foreboded steady deterioration for the Kovno Ghetto. The SS took charge of the ghetto from German civil authorities on September 15, increasing German control over the Jews' daily lives and eroding even further the *Ältestenrat*'s narrow latitude of influence. As fall became winter, nearly 2,000 Jewish workers were dispersed to small labor camps outside the ghetto. Still, the Jews of Kovno, now inmates in Concentration Camp Kauen, endured their daily humiliations with the desperate hope that because the Soviet armies were approaching, they would outlast the German occupation.

Fears overshadowed hope in the fall of 1943 when news came about the two other major ghettos in Lithuania: the liquidation of the nearby Vilna Ghetto in late September, and in early November, the German murder of all Jewish children in the Shavli Ghetto. As the Soviet Army drew nearer, intensifying the atmosphere of crisis, the search for ways to escape grew more urgent. Small groups from the underground managed to escape to join pro-Soviet partisan units in the Rudniki Forest. Under the pretense of reporting for work assignments, more than 300 Jewish fighters reached their freedom over a period of six months, weapons replacing their humiliating yellow stars, to take part in guerrilla warfare against German troops.

Fort IX continued to be the scene of carnage. Throughout the fall, in the face of the Red Army's steady advance in Kovno's direction, the Germans implemented plans to erase evidence of their crimes at the killing center. Imprisoned Jews and Soviet prisoners of war were forced to exhume and burn the tens of thousands of corpses. On December 25, 1943, 64 prisoners took advantage of the guards' festive Christmas spirit and escaped through a tunnel to the fort's outer ramparts. A band of 21 set off to create their own partisan base, 20 went to join the partisans already in the forest, and 10 sought safety separately in nearby villages. The remaining 13 sneaked into the ghetto. The next day, 11 of them described in writing the final stages of Fort IX's hellish deeds, detailing the aggressive elimination of every last trace of the murdered Jews' existence.

Throughout the ghetto's history, individual Lithuanians risked their own lives to help their Jewish friends and former neighbors. The number of such exceptional saving gestures increased markedly during the winter and spring of 1943–44. By smuggling food packages through the ghetto fence, providing forged birth certificates, or offering shelter on remote farms, Lithuanians rescued up to 500 Jews, many of them children.

In the end, mere hundreds of Kovno's Jews reached sanctuary outside the ghetto. Others sought refuge within the ghetto in secret underground bunkers. For the vast majority of those still confined to the Kovno concentration camp in spring 1944, there was no escaping the last deportations and the ghetto's liquidation.

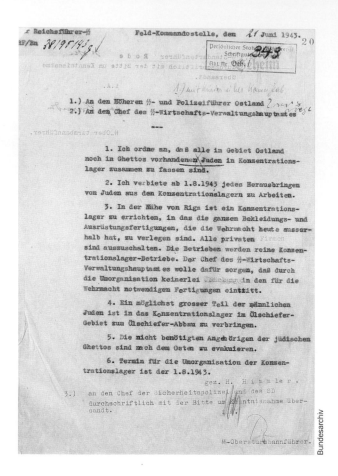

Order from *Reichsführer-SS* Heinrich Himmler, June 21, 1943 *(above)*

1. I order that all Jews still in ghettos in the *Ostland* [occupied Baltic States and Belorussia] are to be brought together in concentration camps.

2. As of August 1, 1943, I forbid any Jews to leave the concentration camp for work. . . .

5. The Jewish ghetto dependents that are not needed are to be evacuated to the East [i.e., to their deaths].

6. The date for reorganization is set for August 1, 1943.

One of Kovno's Jewish Ghetto Police looks at a sign pointing the way to the concentration camp (*Konzentratsionslager, K.L.*) workshops administration.

Postscript to Letter from Elkhanan Elkes to his children, November 11, 1943

It has been weeks since we were transferred from authority to authority. Our name has been changed now; instead of the ghetto, we are called Concentration Camp Kauen No. 4. We also have new officials and orderlies. Our vessel of tears is not yet full.

Work card (*Arbeitskarte*) issued June 1, 1944, to Fruma Rabinavičiene, an embroiderer, for the Concentration Camp Kauen workshops. Instructions on the use of the card (*left page*) came from Camp Commandant Wilhelm Goecke, captain of the *Waffen-SS*.

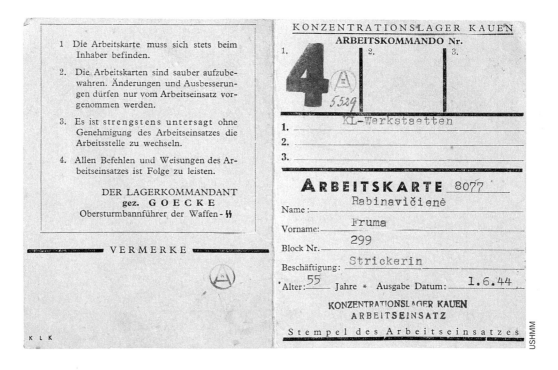

Diary of Tamara Lazerson, November 30, 1943

Today the [labor] brigades did not go downtown. The first "train" left [for the Aleksotas satellite labor camp]. I was at the station. A horrible sight. Krisčiukaičio Street was full of people, parcels, and small children. The people kept their composure, with stony expressions on their faces. There are no more tears. A truck arrives. The people mount the back of the truck, haul their belongings aboard, look over the ghetto one last time, and the truck begins to move. They begin waving their hats, handkerchiefs, anything they have. The tears of parting appear in the eyes of some, and some break down and cry. And that's all. . . .

Farewell note from Masha Musel to her brother, January 9, 1944

Meyshe, I just wanted to bid you farewell. . . . Be a Jew, be a good Jew—without Jewishness you cannot become anything. May God protect you on all your paths. Your sister, Masha

False identification papers for Kovno partisan Nehemiah Endlin to hide his identity for escape to the Rudniki Forest

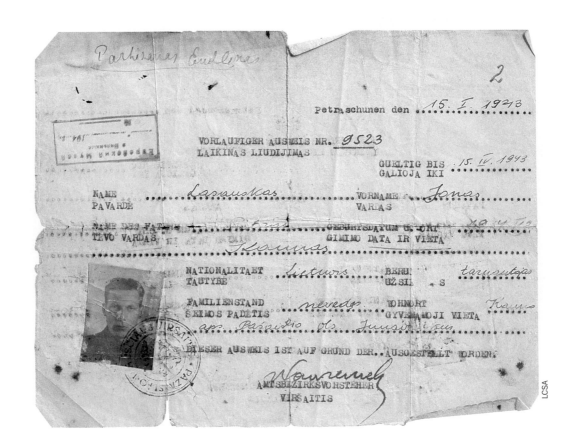

LCSA

Sara Ginaite, a partisan, with her rifle

Partisan Eliezer Zilber after the war

Key for deciphering coded partisan
messages

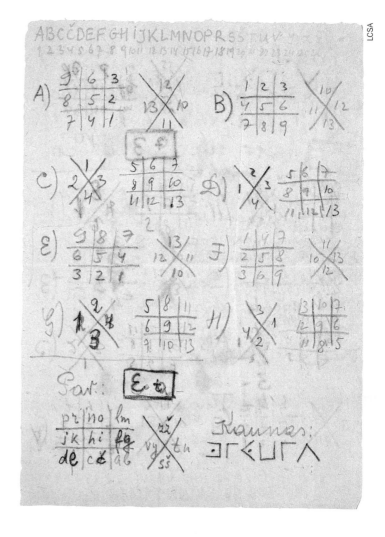

207

Postscript to Letter from Elkhanan Elkes to his children, November 11, 1943

We've learned with certainty that the Germans are now busy erasing and eradicating all shreds of their own murderous acts. The bones of our martyrs are going to be burnt now out of existence at Fort IX, and in all other pertinent places, by specialists for that kind of job.

A drawing by Soviet prisoner of war Anatoli Garnik illustrating the exhumation and burning of corpses at Fort IX

Kaunas 9th Fort Museum

Testimony of Escapees from Fort IX, December 26, 1943

We, the undersigned, a group of prisoners from the Ninth Fort, who escaped from there during the night from the 25th to the 26th of December of this year, consisting of J. L. Vaslenitski, A. Diskant, A. Faitelson, M. Gelbtrunk, P. Krakinowski, M. Daitz, A. Wilenczuk, T. Pilownik, Gempel, She. Idelson and A. Menaiski have put together this protocol regarding the following:

1. In the period of the years 1941–1942, the area of the Ninth Fort was used by the German Command to carry out mass shootings.

2. In order to conceal this crime, the German Command, in the person of the Commander of the Kovno Gestapo, arranged the re-opening of all the graves where the victims of the executions had been buried and set about the burning of the bodies. . . .

Diary of Elena Kutorgiene, October 12, 1942

The Jewish woman I hid last year has been released by the Germans into the custody of her Lithuanian husband, but on the condition that she be sterilized. Naturally, the couple is not in a rush to have the operation performed. In the meantime, they have got their child back from a shelter where he had been taken in under a different name by a woman doctor. Many Jews—seeing death standing in wait around them—are acquiring Christian passports for themselves and giving their children up to shelters or to private families. Rumors that children will be taken away and killed are becoming more and more persistent.

Elena Kutorgiene, a Russian-trained physician in Kovno, assisted many Jews from the ghetto to escape into hiding and maintained active ties with the partisan underground. She kept a diary of the German occupation of Kovno in which she agonized for the Jews.

Yad Vashem

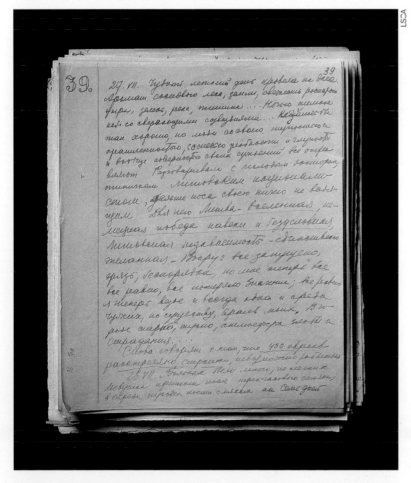

LSCA

A page from the diary of Elena Kutorgiene. The entry shown, dated July 27, 1941, concludes: "They are again saying that *400 Jews have been shot to death;* it's horrible, I can't work."

Father Bronius Paukštys, the Roman Catholic priest
who hid Avraham Tory after his escape from the
ghetto in March 1944

Tory Collection

USHMM

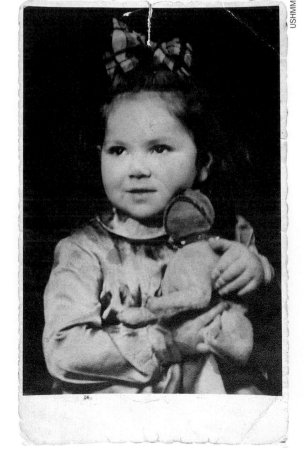

Henia Lewin was one of the estimated 200
children who survived the war because
they were hidden with Lithuanians in Kovno
and the surrounding countryside.

On October 26, 1943, in the first move to destroy the ghetto, the Germans deported more than 2,700 Jews to work camps in Estonia, a Baltic state north of Lithuania also under German occupation. It was devastating enough that the deportation uprooted more than 20 percent of the remnant ghetto. Worse were the deportees' destinies: almost no one bound for Estonia survived; children and the elderly, separated from the others, were sent straight to the gas chambers at Auschwitz.

On March 27, 1944, the SS ordered the 130 men of the Jewish Ghetto Police to assemble in full uniform for their usual work assignments. This time they were taken to Fort IX, where they were interrogated under torture about their connections with the underground and the whereabouts of the ghetto's hiding places. The Germans executed the police chief, Moshe Levin, and 35 others, including most of the leadership. That same day and the next, German soldiers conducted a house-to-house search to round up the ghetto's remaining children under the age of 12 and adults over age 55—more than 1,300 people in all—and sent them to their deaths at Fort IX.

As the Soviets neared Kovno in early July, the Germans commenced the transport of all remaining Jews, about 6,100 over a six-day period beginning July 8, to concentration camps in Germany—the women to Stutthof and the men to Dachau. Just three weeks before the Soviet liberation of Kovno, the Germans proceeded to raze the Kovno concentration camp. Total in its destructiveness, it is almost incomprehensible that any documentation survived: the *Ältestenrat*'s secret archives, police and underground reports, fragments of religious *responsa*, an adolescent's diary—all were buried beneath the ghetto's wasteland surface. The order to destroy arose from the suspicion that Jews might still be in hiding in underground bunkers. The SS ordered German troops to blow up every house with grenades and dynamite. They then poured gasoline over much of the former ghetto and incinerated it.

After one week, the fire burned out, leaving a charred landscape of rubble and stone chimneys.

From October 13 to 26, 1943, the ghetto was
panicked by the German order for laborers. The result
was the deportation to Estonian labor camps.

Kadish/GK

Esther Lurie, *Deportation near the Main Gate*, **1943**
(pen and ink, 11 x 14 in.)

Esther Lurie, Israel

A tearful farewell at the main gate

This woman betrays the fear that accompanied the order to transfer Jews from Kovno to labor camps in Estonia.

Letter from Elkhanan Elkes to his children, October 19, 1943

My beloved son and daughter!

I am writing to you, my beloved children, after we have been here, in the Valley of Tears, the Kovno Vilijampole Ghetto, for more than two years. We have learned that in the very near future our fate is to be decided: the ghetto in which we find ourselves will be cut to pieces. Only God knows whether all of us will be destroyed or whether a few will survive. We fear that only the slaves capable of working will be spared while the rest are probably doomed to die.

Kadish/BH

The final roll call of the Jewish Ghetto Police on the morning of March 27, 1944, prior to their forced march to Fort IX for interrogation and torture about the ghetto's hiding places. Thirty-six of the policeman were killed.

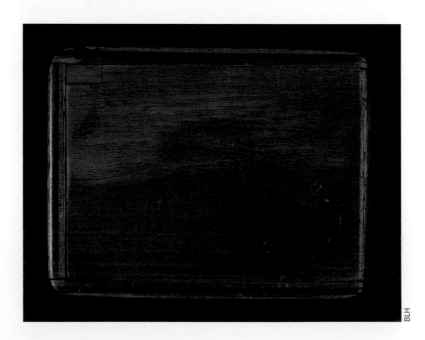

BLH

A wooden box marked with the date of the "Children's Action" and the name of one of its victims

Diary of Tamara Lazerson, March 27, 1944

"Action.". . . The entire young generation, everyone up to the age of 12, perished. So have all the elderly. We will also die! But the mothers, the mothers! A mother cat claws and bites, refusing to give up her kittens. The hen will protect her baby chicks with her body, defending them to the last drop of blood. But the Jewish mother is forced to give away her child and watch as he is tossed like a puppy into the truck. . . .

Kadish/BH

On July 8, 1944, the SS began the liquidation of the remaining sections of the ghetto, systematically setting fire to house after house in order to force the Jews from their hiding places. Many died in the conflagration; many more were caught and deported to concentration camps in Germany. Fewer than 100 emerged alive from their bunkers at Kovno's liberation.

Letter from Shulamith Rabinowitz, June 27, 1944

My dear fortunate sons:

I perceive our end. This will not last much longer and they will make an end to us. . . . I hope that just a few will be saved and will be able to tell you of our suffering and death. The fourth year is already under way and the end draws near. It is not worthwhile to have lived through such torment and not to survive. . . . We have learned so much and suffered so much in these years, and would be able to teach others so much; it is a shame that it will all come to nothing with us. If we could be saved we would be able to build whole worlds, not only drain swamps but even oceans. And show how little a person can manage with! . . .

We resent that we cannot give over to you all that we have experienced. You will probably know, but whatever you know and hear, the reality is a thousand times more terrible and painful. There are no words to relate this, there are no colors which convey it. . . .

Escapes and Deportations from the Kovno Ghetto, 1943–1944

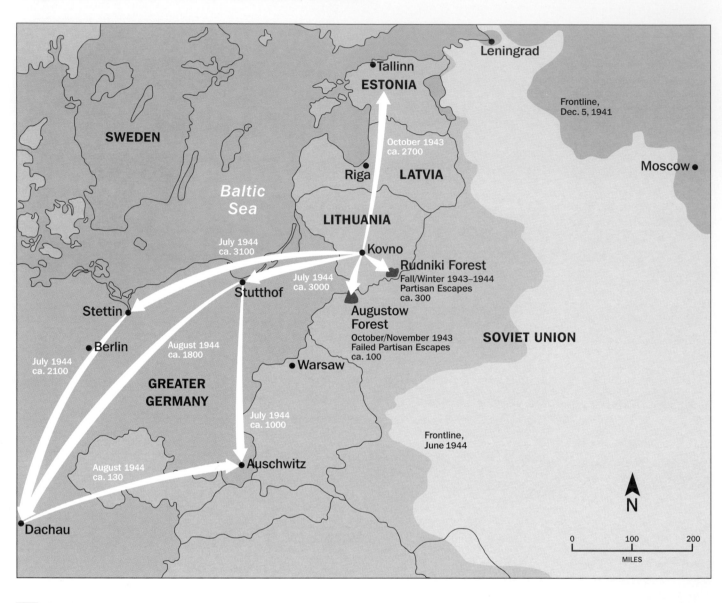

Leningrad

Tallinn

ESTONIA

Frontline,
Dec. 5, 1941

October 1943
ca. 2700

Riga

LATVIA

Moscow

*Baltic
Sea*

SWEDEN

LITHUANIA

July 1944
ca. 3100

Kovno

Rudniki Forest
Fall/Winter 1943–1944
Partisan Escapes
ca. 300

July 1944
ca. 3000

Stutthof

Augustow
Forest

October/November 1943
Failed Partisan Escapes
ca. 100

SOVIET UNION

Stettin

Berlin

August 1944
ca. 1800

July 1944
ca. 2100

**GREATER
GERMANY**

Warsaw

July 1944
ca. 1000

Frontline,
June 1944

August 1944
ca. 130

Auschwitz

N

Dachau

0   100   200

MILES

Greater Germany

Soviet Union

Territory liberated from German control, December 1941–June 1944

Territory under German control, June 1944

On the eve of the Holocaust there were 37,000 Jews in Kovno. At the end of the Holocaust an estimated 500 survived in forests, in hiding, or in bunkers, and some 2,500 survived the concentration camps in Germany.

In liberated Lithuania, only 8,000 to 9,000 Jews remained from the prewar population of 235,000. More than 95 percent of Lithuanian Jewry had been destroyed.

Kadish/GK

Diary of Tamara Lazerson, October 12, 1944 (10 weeks after liberation)
The ghetto left terrifying footprints as it was swallowed by the flames. Where proud homes had once stood, not a single house is left. Just gloomy naked chimneys reach for the heavens, testifying that this is a graveyard. They reach to the heavens praying for vengeance for the injustice that was done them.

Part III
A Half Century Later

Survivors among the ghetto's ruins after liberation by the Soviet army, August 1, 1944

Dov Levin

At the beginning of August 1944, when I returned with other partisans to Kovno—the ghetto had just been liberated by Soviet troops from Nazi occupation—I experienced a crushing disappointment. On the day of my arrival I wrote in my diary: "Everyone approached his home with awe and reverence. We went to our home at Mildos 7. . . heaps of dust and burnt bricks—all that remained was an enamel-covered plaque with the number 7 inscribed on it. . . . Most of us cannot walk on this blood-stained earth." Once again, as I had done before the abyss of war but did now with a vengeance, I could think about only one goal: I would go to a Jewish homeland.

I grew up when Lithuania was still independent, in a home imbued with a Zionist spirit. My mother Bluma (née Wigoder) and father Zvi-Hirsh made sure to give me and my twin sister Basia a Jewish national education and decided that after I finished high school, I would study engineering at the Technion in Haifa, Palestine. This pleasant dream began to fade with the Soviet occupation of Lithuania and the closing of its borders on June 15, 1940. Deeply suspicious of competing national loyalties, the Soviets prohibited all

Zionist activities and even an education conducted in Hebrew, which the Soviets associated with Zionism. Now, in the same building where for years I had studied in Hebrew (the famous Shwabes Gymnasium) I had to study in a different language—in Yiddish, a language still acceptable to the Soviets because, among other things, they could exploit it as a propaganda vehicle. Those of us who were involved in the Zionist socialist youth movement *Hashomer Hatzair* continued our Zionist activities underground.

Like most Jewish families, mine experienced additional setbacks under Soviet rule. Because my parents, like other workers, were now compelled to work on the Sabbath (as well as on other Jewish holidays), we had to abandon the custom of a family Sabbath meal filled with songs and discussions on various topics. The new regime, which was to last for just one year, confiscated my grandfather Rabbi David Levin's well-known store in the city as well as the businesses of most of my uncles and relatives. Unemployed and labeled as "capitalist exploiters" or simply as "enemies of the Soviet people," they feared the same fate as the one experienced by my Jewish history

Celebrating liberation in Kovno, August 1944

Kadish/BH

Essay author Dov Levin *(second row, in white shirt)* with classmates from the Shwabes Gymnasium **(high school) before the war**

teacher, Meir Kantorovitz—exile in Siberia. My illegal Zionist activities became extremely dangerous and had to remain as secret as ever.

Our Lithuanian neighbors, on the other hand, did not conceal their glances of hatred. Although we were terrified of the Soviets, accepting their regime only when we would compare it to a German occupation of Lithuania—we referred to the Soviets as the "lesser of two evils"—Lithuanian nationalists believed we actually welcomed the Soviets. Feeling betrayed, they went so far as to hold Jews responsible for the Soviet occupation and the Sovietization of their state. Like others, I dreaded the possibility that the Soviets would leave Lithuania, giving free rein to nationalist rage.

When I went to school on Sunday morning, June 22, 1941, to receive my graduation certificate, I was surprised by the sound of bombs from German planes. This was the start of the war between Germany and the Soviet Union. I recall that, within days, when it became clear that the Red Army was retreating, the phone rang in our apartment. It was my friend and classmate Avraham Jashpan. He suggested that we escape to the Soviet interior along with the retreating Soviet Army. I answered, "I will stay with my parents and sister!" He: "Do you want our [Lithuanian] neighbors to slaughter us?!" And then I heard his mother in the background berating him: "Your friend is a more loyal son than you are." In the course of time, we learned that Avraham in fact succeeded in escaping, and like many of the escapees he volunteered for the Soviet Army. He was wounded a number of times in battles against the Germans.

I knew that trouble lay ahead for those of us who remained when I heard over the radio the threatening announcement by Lithuanian nationalist Colonel Jurgis Bobelis that for every German

killed, one hundred Jews would be murdered. Our immediate concern was gangs of armed Lithuanians who savagely butchered their Jewish neighbors, including many rabbis. They broke into our apartment with accusations that we had fired shots from our windows on columns of Germans. One of them turned to me with a loaded weapon; we were terrified that he surely would shoot me. However, they satisfied themselves with stealing valuables. In the adjacent apartments, they killed Jewish males and raped young women. In my grandfather Levin's apartment, an armed Lithuanian boasted about how many Jews he had killed, and to prove it he showed us their blood-stained passports.

Although crowds of Lithuanians in the streets greeted the Germans with flowers, it was no surprise that we closed our shutters, lowered our curtains, and locked ourselves up in our homes. Apparently my curiosity was greater than my fear: I peered out a corner of the shutter and saw German soldiers entering the city on the same road that the Soviet tanks had triumphantly tramped on only a year before. However, unlike the Soviet troops whose appearance was poor and forsaken, I had a clear impression of the Germans shining and glowing with health and confidence. For a few minutes I felt that no one would ever be able to stand up to such an army. I sensed that, without a doubt, such a military force would eventually succeed in conquering the entire world.

As soon as the Germans appeared on the streets, they mounted large posters to the walls that declared *"Wer plündert wird erschossen"* (whoever steals will be shot to death). I found at least a little comfort in this warning, but it quickly became clear to me that this announcement was not meant to restrain Lithuanians from harming Jews. On the contrary, Lithuanians, who called themselves "partisans," continued to kill and humiliate Jews, particularly in the Jewish quarters of Slobodka.

During an ebb in the wave of this terror, we met frequently with our friends to find out how they were faring. Ela Volpe, a friend and former classmate who was freed from the notorious Fort VII, told us nightmarish stories of wanton rape and murder. She reported on how adult women mixed water and sand and spread it on their faces so they would look ugly, handicapped, or elderly so that no one would lust after them or attack them. She was one of the few who was freed from that hellhole. It is no wonder that we welcomed rumors about the establishment of a ghetto in the neighborhoods of Slobodka: "It would be better if they already built the ghetto where the Lithuanians can't get to us," we said. "At least we will be living among Jews!"

Like many of Kovno's more than 25,000 Jews who were compelled to move into the ghetto by August 15, my family moved into an area called the Small Ghetto. Food and housing were, or course, our most urgent concerns, but I soon realized that even these necessities would not be the most important thing. I remember overhearing a well-to-do man say to his friend, "I really want to get a bag of flour for the house." I found out that this man got what he wanted, and yet he and all of his family wound up in Fort IX, the main killing site in Kovno. Most of the Jews, in fact, who moved into the Small Ghetto were killed about six weeks after they entered in one of the successive mass murders that had come to characterize our lives in the ghetto. Only a small handful, including my family, succeeded in escaping this "action." We now found ourselves living in the main part of the ghetto.

It is no wonder, then, that during fall 1941 none of us knew what would await us even for the next few hours. Without letup we were burdened with this terrible anxiety as well as with incredible hardship. The persistence of our fears had reminded me of a passage from the Torah: "In the morning you will say, 'If only it were evening,' and in the evening you will say, 'If only it were morning'" (Deuteronomy 28:67). It was therefore natural for me to assume that all Jews would comply immediately with German orders, including the order to hand over money and jewelry. I learned later, however, that this wasn't always true. After my wealthy uncle Moses Levin was taken to Fort IX during the Small Ghetto "action," I went to his abandoned house to collect some Hebrew books. Upon examining them I discovered some pages that had been glued together, and inside them

Dov Levin's family before the war, including the author *(front right)*; his grandfather, Rabbi David Levin *(second row, third from right)*; his father Zvi-Hirsh *(second row, second from left)*; his mother Bluma *(back row, second from left)*; and his uncle, Moses Levin *(back row, second from right)*

—paper money! Afterwards, this money served to alleviate the great hunger that prevailed in the ghetto during the winter of 1941.

Though I was not yet seventeen and therefore not obligated to work (the minimum age dropped to sixteen in December 1941), I saw and experienced the severity of slave labor. On several occasions I agreed to be a *mal'akh,* an "angel," in exchange for a loaf of bread. In other words, I agreed to work in place of someone else at various work sites, including the dreadful *Flugplatz* (airfield). This workplace was both the largest and most difficult of all. Thousands of Jews and Soviet prisoners of war worked there from early in the morning to late at night, exposed to the elements, in all sorts of weather. They were beaten and treated with sadistic ruthlessness. During the day they were given only one slice of bread and some thin broth. In addition to this, the workers had to walk four hours to and from this work site.

On October 27, 1941, the day before the "Great Action," they kept us at our slave labor for 24 hours! Upon returning home at daybreak the next day, October 28, I barely managed to join my parents and sister who were hurrying to assemble in Demokratu Square. Despite the fact that I was exhausted, I remember several episodes that fateful day: hysterical cries from family members looking for each other, someone holding an umbrella up high as a sign for his family to find him, and so much more. All of a sudden an old man stood by us—it was my grandfather Levin. He had trimmed his beard in the style of the nineteenth-century Austrian emperor Franz Josef in order to look younger. This was the first and the last time I saw him looking like this—as if he were naked! On this day, that old man, along with more 9,200 Jews "unfit for work," were imprisoned in the Small Ghetto and taken the next day to Fort IX. We knew the next day that he had been killed, but many of us, including my father, refused to believe it. Though our material needs were desperate, we refused for a long time to wear Grandfather's clothes.

Even when the "actions" abated, none of us completely fooled ourselves into thinking that the killing would end. But the ensuing period of relative calm allowed me to take stock of what was going on. I made note, for example, of who was suffering from hunger. I noticed that the Jewish Ghetto Police and other *Ältestenrat* functionaries seemed satiated and self-satisfied. Thus I completely identified with those who criticized high-ranking officials and other Jewish leaders—the *yales* (big shots), as they were called. I joined in the folksongs that sprang up in the ghetto. One, called "No Such Luck," scathed the Labor Office for routinely rejecting requests for leave from work at the airport:

> No such luck, you get no leave.
> Off to work, and no reprieve.
> Don't deceive yourself, you fool,
> We've got to fill our labor pool.

We believed that the higher-ups had forgotten that their "elevated" status, as compared to that of the "simple" people, depended entirely on the whim of murderous German rulers and in fact furthered their interests. The rest of us continued to be afflicted with the constant feeling of hunger. If we were lucky, we ate two or three watered-down bowls of soup, called *yushnik,* each day. It resembled animal food. Bread was by necessity a rarity. Once, my parents sent me to the food distribution site, the so-called Parama, to bring home the family's weekly bread ration—a loaf and a half. On the way home I began, without thinking, to chew on the half loaf and then on the whole loaf; when I came home there was not even a crumb of bread left. To this day, I feel ashamed of this!

Among the more than 2,700 Jews deported to Estonian labor camps in October 1943 were Dov Levin's parents and twin sister. They did not survive the war.

Kadish/BH

Even during those difficult days, some of us went out into the ghetto streets in the cleanest clothing possible. We would greet acquaintances by tipping our hats like free people, not like prisoners, in order to prove to ourselves that we still had at least some control over our lives. For that reason, even during the period of greatest famine, we ate our meager food whenever possible with forks and knives and continued to use a toothbrush. There even were more than a few Jews who fabricated aesthetic "yellow stars" for their chests and backs. Whenever I was required to remove my hat on my way past the gate guards upon my return from forced labor, I tried do so with my head held high.

But deep within me, I constantly suffered from the strangulation of living behind barbed wire. How envious I felt whenever I saw a cat that could go through the ghetto fence with such remarkable ease! More than once I wondered, "Is there anyone in the world who knows anything about us?" I talked to many others about this. I would ask, "What will happen to us?" To this equally unanswerable question, what I usually heard was, "Things will be good—but only for the Jews in America."

We were strictly forbidden from bringing food, fuel, and of course arms into the ghetto. We were also absolutely forbidden from bringing in any printed material. Yet, because of our constant feeling of hunger and the cold of our house, I took several risks to smuggle food and charcoal through the gate and the closely guarded fence. From time to time, I succeeded in smuggling in a newspaper in order to learn exactly what was happening outside the ghetto—especially on the battlefronts.

One day I got hold of a German newspaper with a picture of a man identified as *"Bandenführer* (gang leader) Tito," who was leading the fight in Yugoslavia against the Germans. How I yearned to meet a man like that in Kovno! With time I heard thrilling stories about the activities of anti-Nazi partisans operating in the forests of eastern Lithuania. But how could we get to them? When I revealed my ambitions to my friends from *Hashomer Hatzair,* it became clear to me that many of them already belonged to an underground cell dedicated to the same anti-Nazi goals. Naturally I joined them.

The head of my three-person cell was a young woman, Gita Pogir. A strange feeling grabbed hold of us when, on one summer evening in 1943, Gita brought us a rifle wrapped up in a German newspaper. We already knew that there were arms in the ghetto, and the stories of owning weapons had passed from one to another. However, this was the first time we felt the cold iron in our hands. We knew that we quickly had to learn how to unload the rifle and assemble it in order to pass it along to another cell. Gita tested our knowledge, even though it seemed she herself had learned how to use the gun only the day before. I was forbidden from telling even my parents and sister about my association with the underground. They probably sensed I was involved in something serious and important, but they never talked to me about it.

During the fall of 1943, rumors circulated that the *Ältestenrat,* on orders from German authorities, was preparing lists of Jews for deportation to work camps outside the ghetto. Afterwards it became clear that they were referring to Estonia, the northernmost Baltic state. Members of the underground believed that its members and

Dov Levin, Israel

Dov Levin's parents, Bluma and Zvi-Hirsh, before the war

their families would likely not be on the lists of deportees. The deportation began on the morning of October 26, 1943, when a group of German and Lithuanian policemen, escorted by members of the Jewish police, scattered to every house in the ghetto to round up people. The underground mobilized its members, including me, and placed them in predetermined gathering places in case we would be needed or required to hide.

That noon I was sent to do a chore at the three-story building called Block C, which, according to rumor, had an elaborate hiding place (or in the ghetto slang, a *maline*) in its basement. On my way, as I passed by my house, I was shocked to see Jewish policemen and Germans forcibly evicting my family. Seeing my sister bitterly crying and my father looking desperate, I thought that I should join them. But at that same moment, my mother made a sign that I never will forget for my entire life. She gave me a firm glance whose meaning was clear: "Get away from here immediately!" And that is what I did without ever looking back. I never saw them alive again. After the war I learned that my father perished just before the Germans were expelled from Estonia in fall 1944, and that my mother and sister were deported to the Stutthof concentration camp, where they died from disease (my mother, on November 25, 1944). Seeing their helpless looks gave me, in addition to deep pain, a burning anger that the underground movement failed to guarantee the safety of my family as I had hoped it could.

When I arrived at Block C, desolate and ashamed, a Jewish policeman met me at the entrance. I gave him the necessary password: "Can I sleep here tonight?" Someone lifted a floor covering and shifted some stones underneath. All of a sudden I felt myself sliding down to the bottom until several pairs of hands grabbed me and brought me to a dark room, where I could make out only some cigarette sparks. After a short while, someone handed me a sandwich.

During the many hours that I sat there, my eyes grew used to the darkness. I realized that besides me, dozens of other friends from the underground were here in the basement of Block C. Some had weapons and were ready to defend themselves with force against deportation. Indeed, a few times we heard the voices of Germans outside looking for people to deport, but luckily they never discovered us. Later our connections from the outside told us that the danger had passed: the Germans had succeeded in locating and deporting some 2,700 people they needed for work in Estonia.

We were permitted to leave our hiding place. On our way out, we were told, "You are free for the moment, but in a short while you will have to gather in an apartment at 8 Broliu Street. It is possible that you will leave the ghetto tonight." The thought of escaping to the partisan forests gave me some consolation after this long black day in which I had lost, apparently forever, my parents and my only sister without a word of separation worthy of the name.

I decided to say good-bye to the green wooden house at 56 Linkuvos Street, where my family and I had lived almost from the moment we entered the ghetto. When I arrived, it looked like a

pogrom had swept through: the doors, windows, and cupboards had been burst open, and all the household possessions, clothing, and scraps of food lay in disorder all over the floor. I got the impression that someone had dug through all of this looking for something useful. Perhaps the neighbors did this? After all, they greeted me as much with surprise as with kind expressions. They must have felt sure that I had been deported with my family that morning to Estonia. At that same moment, I resolved that no matter what happened, I would never go back to that house! I made sure the neighbors understood that as well, but naturally I did not even hint to them that there was a possibility that I was about to leave the ghetto. I agreed to take a few sandwiches from them and ran with all my might to 8 Broliu Street.

We received a very disappointing announcement. Because the ghetto was still surrounded by large police forces, it would not be possible to break out; we would have to wait patiently for the next opportunity. Though we were all eager to escape to the forests, there were those among us, myself included, who were especially disappointed because we no longer had a family and felt utterly bereft. As brothers with a shared fate, we were determined to stay together from then on. Therefore, after that critical night, some of my closest friends and I continued to live in the same place.

With the passing of time, other friends from *Hashomer Hatzair* (and from *Hechalutz Hatzair,* another Zionist socialist youth movement) joined us in larger quarters located in house number 7 on Mildos Street. We called it "Kibbutz Mildos 7" because we based

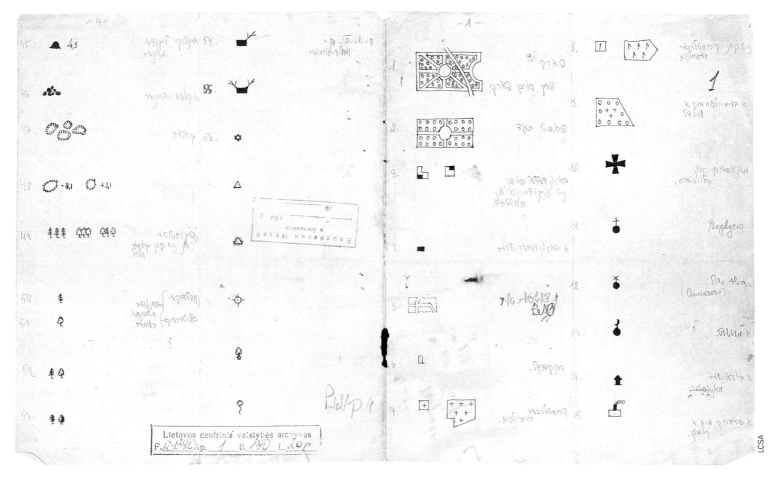

Topographic symbols used on military maps by partisans from the Kovno Ghetto

Partisans from the Kovno Ghetto in the Rudniki Forest after the war

the house's administration and its collective and cultural activities on the example of kibbutzim in Palestine. We engaged in ideological and political discussions and joined together in communal song. One of our popular songs was "Hey, Accordion, Play for Me"; we often danced a "Hora" to it with our many visitors. One of those who joined us was a policeman, Hirsh Friedman, who had participated in deporting my family to Estonia. When I reminded him of that terrible incident, he tried to explain that no one had told him that they were related to a member of the underground. I was perfectly aware that underground members who were in the police were compelled to act like other policemen by following orders, but once the matter affected me personally, it became difficult for me to make peace with their double role. My regard for the ghetto establishment grew even more negative.

The three months I spent in the kibbutz was like life in a warm spring within the ghetto's dark existence. The warm and loving relations with members of the kibbutz grew stronger the more we planned our escape to the forests and the partisans. Finally my turn to leave arrived. I had to figure out how to get a rifle. Without hesitation I decided to sell my Swiss watch, a bar mitzvah gift from my uncle Moses Levin. For several weeks we trained and supplied ourselves with proper clothing and weapons. The day of our escape was postponed several times; we began to worry that this dream might never materialize. Still, I placed my trust in the underground organization the way a pious believer trusts God.

We were finally given the long-awaited order to mount the trucks parked outside the ghetto gate. I was shocked when I saw two armed German soldiers in uniform on the truck's cargo bed. I realized only after a few minutes that these two belonged to our group. All of a

sudden the electricity above the gate was cut. Again it took me a few moments to realize that this was a maneuver by our group intended to conceal us from the gate guards. I was overcome with admiration for the leadership of our underground organization—they seemed so clever and sophisticated. I was full of hope that, from now on, everything would go as planned. Then, crowded together in the truck, we heard somebody near the gate (a policeman or someone else) ask, "Where are you going?" Another voice answered that we were going to join a work brigade. In fact, we were headed toward the overgrown forests of eastern Lithuania in the Rudniki region.

Not far from the ghetto we were stopped. We had made certain not to take anything with us that would identify us as Jews. I left behind pictures of my family. Not a single written word in Yiddish or Hebrew could be found among our possessions. Soon enough, when we resumed our journey, our commander told us to remove our yellow stars: "From now on we are partisans!"

Traveling by night, we eventually reached our partisan unit, "Death to the Occupiers." We felt free, proud, happy. There are no words that can express the joy we felt in the kingdom of the partisans. I was so trusting. Our partisan leaders provided an extraordinary example of authority for me. When we arrived at our base, we kissed everybody. It was difficult to adjust to the conditions of partisan life in the forest and the reality of our friends falling almost daily in battles with Germans and their Lithuanian helpers. But I was happy that at long last I was able to defend myself with a weapon in hand.

On July 8, 1944, we received an order to join up with groups of Soviet troops who were approaching our area. Though our anticipation of returning to liberated Kovno heightened our anxiety and

The photograph of Dov Levin saved from the ghetto by his friend Rifkale

graph, at extraordinary risk to her life, by hiding it in the sole of her shoe while she was in a concentration camp. Seeing her again reminded me of the words I wrote in early August 1944, upon seeing the ghetto's destruction:

> We have been freed from the [Nazi] regime and from its terrors. . . . But who will ever release us from the pain in our hearts, from the loneliness, from our memories of orphans gazing out from every street corner, from the echoes of cries that call out to us from every piece of earth?

> —*Translated from the Hebrew by Judith Cohen*

Dov Levin, a survivor of the Kovno Ghetto, is Chairman of the Oral History Division of the Institute of Contemporary Jewry at the Hebrew University of Jerusalem. He is author of several books on Lithuania's Jews during the Holocaust.

fears, we had no idea at the time that, on that very day, Jews were being hurriedly evacuated from the ghetto to concentration camps in Germany.

Like many others in the ghetto, it was important for me to keep a private diary. Almost from the first day, I wrote in it about what happened to the ghetto and to me. I recorded fleeting words, folklore, and jokes from those days, as well as news from the war fronts and rumors that I culled from various sources. Just before I left the ghetto to join the partisans, I decided to give this diary to one of my closest friends. But I soon learned she was deported to a concentration camp. Assuming that my diary was lost (it was), I immediately started a second diary.

Early in the morning of July 9, 1944, Ruzcka Korzcak, a prominent partisan from the Jewish Vilna Detachment with whom we had secret underground and Zionist contacts, came to see us with a secret mission. She told us to go to Vilna, in order to set up an organization, the aim of which was to go to Palestine immediately upon leaving the forests by any possible means.

My dream of going to Palestine, which had faded when the war started, came back to me. I decided that day in July to go, but the real journey didn't began until January 19, 1945. For ten months I traveled from Vilna through Belorussia, Poland, Romania, Hungary, Austria, and Italy, where we boarded a small boat that took us to sea. I reached Palestine on October 23, 1945, and began to build my new life.

One day in 1984, a messenger arrived at my home in Israel with my boyhood photograph, which I had given as a keepsake to another friend, Rifkale, back in the ghetto. A short while after this startling discovery, Rifkale herself (whose name was now Rose Kurland), visited me and explained how she had saved this photo-

Lawrence L. Langer

Kadish/BH

A major temptation facing anyone trying to enter the unfamiliar milieu of the Kovno Ghetto under German rule is to view it through the lens of values that governs our own daily lives. Even though everyone does not always follow them, normal society has clear-cut rules about what comprises acceptable and unacceptable behavior: honesty is preferable to lying, sharing to greed, and theft violates both law and the principles of decent behavior. But the ordeal of the Jews in the Kovno Ghetto did not reflect "normal society," so any effort to ease our discomfort by supporting it with the props of our own less threatened existence is bound to distort the truth of their situation. We need to imagine a community whose members were hungry, exhausted, plagued by memories of the murder of friends and family, and haunted by the possibility of a similar fate for themselves.

In the ghetto, smuggling and stealing from and lying to the Germans became necessary strategies for remaining alive, as human beings struggled to stay afloat amid the twin currents of hope and despair. The atmosphere resembled what Primo Levi called a "gray zone," that uncertain moral realm where a flexible behavior was shaped more by external circumstance than by inner conviction. Neither hope nor despair reigned for long, because ghetto residents could not control their lives in any meaningful way. Although fewer than ten percent of its prewar inhabitants outlived the disaster of the Kovno Ghetto, the voices of those who experienced it help us to gain a sense of the diverse and often contradictory attitudes that prevailed there. Any effort to assemble a consensus, however, must be doomed from the start.

Unfortunately, no reassuring vocabulary emerges to describe life in a ghetto ringed by the threat of death. Many commentators speak of a "relatively quiet period" of nearly two years in the Kovno Ghetto, following the initial slaughter by Lithuanians and Germans after the German invasion of the Soviet Union in June 1941. But we should not be beguiled, as some Jews desperately seeking solace may have been at the time, by this interlude in the unrelenting process of mass murder. Today, it is difficult to imagine how anyone who

Along the Neris River separating the ghetto from the city of Kovno

A child's shoes left behind

experienced the "Great Action" of October 28, 1941, when more than nine thousand Jews were selected to be killed at Fort IX the next day, could erase from memory the unsettling legacy of that event. There was hardly anyone who did not lose a relative to that explosion of violence. Immediately afterward, we are told,

> A deep mourning descended on the ghetto. In every house there were now empty rooms, unoccupied beds, and the belongings of those who had not returned from the selection. One-third of the ghetto population had been cut down. The sick people who had remained in their homes in the morning had all disappeared. They had been transferred to the Ninth Fort during the day.[1]

To assume that mere time could ease the pain of this ordeal is to misjudge the power of such atrocity to capsize the tranquil vessel of the mind. As one survivor of the Kovno Ghetto reported many years later, "It stays for you, till today. You never forget it. You dream about it. You can't sleep. You are nervous like a dog."[2]

Ghetto inhabitants thus faced the constant problem of searching for equilibrium by balancing loss against gain, but did not always solve it successfully. For example, after the Germans burned down the hospital for contagious diseases with patients, doctors, and nurses still inside, what ghetto occupant could ever again believe that he or she was safe from the cruelty of such a regime? Yet the head of the Jewish *Ältestenrat*, Dr. Elkhanan Elkes, repeatedly sought pledges from German officials that the most recent "action" would be the last one, and that the future was relatively secure for the remaining Jews provided they worked diligently and did not openly violate current German laws. In so doing, he expressed a common psychological need for inner assurance that most human beings depend on in moments of stress. A decent and intelligent man with no interest in advancing his personal needs before those of the community, Elkes could not repress the impulse to seek in

his oppressors some faint ember of the honor that warmed his own life. Today we may deem this a fatal error, but at the time Elkes's behavior only proved how impossible it was for the human consciousness, Jewish or otherwise, to accept as a non-negotiable finality the doom of an entire people. Hampered by an inadequate knowledge of German intention—a limitation that would have been shared by any other leader in his place—he strove to hold back a flood with a finger in a dike that was bound to collapse eventually in spite of his strenuous efforts.

In his Kovno Ghetto diary, Avraham Tory relates that when the news spread on October 27, 1941, of an order for all Jews in the ghetto to assemble the following morning in Demokratu Square, panic mounted among the residents. Roll calls of such magnitude raised a strong possibility of large-scale selections and mass executions. To allay his people's anxiety, Elkes asked for a meeting with Sergeant Rauca, at which he "pleaded with 'Mr. Master Sergeant' to reveal the whole truth behind the roll call." Today we may regard with wonder and dismay the guileless assumption that a Gestapo official would be moved by an appeal to his honesty from a Jew, an appeal based on the belief that beneath the surface of German contempt lay a bedrock of integrity still joining one human being to another. How else can we explain Elkes's language, as recorded by Tory:

> Dr. Elkes attempted to appeal to the "conscience" of the Gestapo officer, hinting casually that every war, including the present one, was bound to end sooner or later, and that if Rauca would answer his questions openly, without concealing anything, the Jews would know how to repay him.[3]

Addressing the conscience of a Gestapo official or offering him a kind of postwar "bribe" of support may seem like an absurd idea today (especially when we reflect that in October 1941 the German juggernaut throughout Europe seemed invincible); but a far more complex issue at the time was finding a strategy for facing the crisis

Elkhanan Elkes, chairman of the
Ältestenrat

without abandoning to total disaster the people whose leadership Elkes had reluctantly accepted.

Tory considered Elkes's conversation with Rauca a daring maneuver; others might call it foolish or naive. Trust may be a laudable virtue in ordinary times, but when the threat is mass murder, it proves a vulnerable defense indeed. This was certainly the opinion of some other survivors of the Kovno Ghetto like Dr. Lazar Goldstein, who spoke of the Germans' use of a Jewish council as a plan to "rake hot coals with Jewish hands." His view cannot be dismissed simply as mere retroactive resentment. His charge that "step by step the Elders Council became more and more involved in helping Nazis, even if unwittingly, to carry out their diabolical plans," must be addressed.[4]

Large ghettos like Kovno had a public life and a private life, and unfortunately the interests of the two did not always coincide. For example, in their capacity as "public" officials, members of the *Ältestenrat* had to assign individual Jews to different work squads, some of them, like the airport brigade, requiring exhausting daily labor after a long march from the site of the ghetto. It was natural for some individuals to resent the decisions of the council, seeing in its cooperation a form of collaboration. But in order to prevent the swift and chaotic dissolution of the community, someone had to take responsibility for finding and assigning living space, distributing food, organizing work details, meeting sanitary and medical needs, and handling the dozens of other matters that would make day-to-day subsistence minimally possible. The *intention* of those who finally agreed to accept custody of the ghetto's welfare under the constraints of the German occupation was to wrest some control of the community's fate from a seemingly hopeless situation. At first, this proved to be a herculean task, and finally, because of the

ruthless German determination to destroy all of Kovno Jewry, an insuperable one.

In normal times, public life is designed to bolster private expectations, but in the Kovno Ghetto so often did one prove an obstacle to the other that a seamless interaction between the two became impossible. On February 4, 1943, immediately after their defeat at Stalingrad, almost as a petty and spiteful act of revenge for their humiliating loss, the Germans rounded up forty-four ghetto inmates and sent them to Fort IX for execution. This was right in the middle of the so-called relative calm between the initial executions and the final liquidation. The effect, Tory says, was a temporary paralysis of Jewish existence at every level:

> There was no work at the Jewish institutions in the ghetto. It was simply not possible to conduct any public activity under the conditions of the prevailing mood of depression. The life of no person is secure any longer. Anyone may stumble all of a sudden. All the same, our will to go on living is as strong as ever— to go on living and to leave the horrors behind.[5]

Tory's concluding words in this passage sound paradoxical, since depression rarely coexists with hope. Yet precisely this paradox characterized much of Jewish life during the ordeal of the ghetto, not as a form of denial but as a desperate effort to ignite amid the gloom of daily despair some spark that might enable the individual and the community to go on.

Today we realize what the Jews of Kovno should have known from the first moment of the ghetto's creation, and from the mass executions preceding it—that, as Tory admitted, the life of no person was secure anymore. But such a perception at the time must have been psychologically and emotionally intolerable. Ironically,

Kadish/BH

though the Germans despised the Jews as a species incapable of moral vision, they exploited both the private and the public need to believe in a bond between diligence and endurance, survival and hope. They took advantage of Elkes's devotion to the idea of a common human allegiance to truth, just as they cynically abused each inmate's desperate faith (and even perhaps relief, terrible as it may sound) that if some Jews were expendable to the Germans, others were not.

Even more difficult for us to understand today is the impact of the brutal principle of "collective responsibility" that the Germans imposed on the ghetto residents. This perversion of the idea of moral conduct left the Jews deprived of a sound basis for ethical behavior. As reported by Tory, the Gestapo issued the following order:

> Labor brigade leaders would be answerable for unauthorized trading and absenteeism from the place of work. If anyone is caught committing these offenses, his brigade leader and the members of his family will be arrested and executed. In more serious cases, several labor brigade leaders will be executed, together with their families. The guiding principle behind this order is: all are responsible for everyone and everyone responsible for all.[6]

Ironically, a similar sentiment in Dostoyevsky's fiction makes each man an indispensable partner to the spiritual life of all others; the Germans twisted this principle to make each Jew in the Kovno Ghetto a potential indirect accomplice to the physical murder of any other member of the community.

In spite of the German edict, ghetto inhabitants "lucky" enough to work in brigades within the precincts of Kovno city itself continued to trade their remaining possessions with Lithuanians for food in order to keep themselves and their families alive. According to Leib Garfunkel, vice-chairman of the *Ältestenrat,*

Kadish/GK

Hunger was one of the severest problems that faced the Kovno Ghetto. It was impossible to survive on the daily food rations that the Germans gave to the ghetto residents. In actuality, these were starvation rations. The rations given to the Jews represented one-third of the minimum calories required for daily survival.[7]

Avoiding death and courting death thus became simultaneous rules of personal existence, though after the German edict the perimeters of risk expanded to include the lives of others. The psychological effect of this tension on those who continued the smuggling we can only surmise, but it must have been overwhelming. Tory himself sees it as a deliberate consequence of German malevolence, though he will not allow even this extreme form of malice to dampen his spirits.

His comments betray the irrepressible human instinct to see some light even in the blackest tunnels, as he mingles his private vision of hope with an acknowledgment of the life of desperate

Ghetto gardens

confusion that the Jews' oppressors forced them to lead. He begins with a clear-sighted statement of German intentions:

> This is always the way with the Germans. They do not tell you things clearly, except when they curse you and scream at you. It is therefore imperative to assess their mood properly before they open their mouths. We must understand that, from their point of view, our situation must always remain unclear. . . . We are to remain always in a state of anticipation, without understanding what is going on around us.

But he follows this with a counter-view that gives us a glimpse into how a strangulating people managed to go on breathing:

> However, it is impossible for us to live in a state of permanent nervous tension. Despite the eleven chambers of hell that the Jews—as individuals and as a community—have gone through, our spirit has not been crushed. Our eyes are wide open and we are attuned to what is going on around us. We do not forget for one moment the hallowed purposes of our people.[8]

Other commentators would greet with dismay Tory's conviction that "our eyes are wide open and we are attuned to what is going on around us." What was going on around them by 1943 was the unhallowed purposes of the Germans to destroy not only Lithuanian but all of European Jewry, and the members of the *Ältestenrat* were decidedly *not* attuned to this reality.

Indeed, survivors like Lazar Goldstein argued that rhetoric from council members about keeping the spirit from being crushed *blinded* them to the true nature of German intentions from the beginning.

He criticized the members of the council for cooperating with Nazi authorities in the "mistaken belief that in this way they would be able to *help* Jews," and even suggested that Elkes's basic decency made him the *wrong* man to "have been in a position of leadership in such a terribly cruel and critical time."[9] He may have been correct; but who would have been the "right" man, and how was he to be recognized, not to say recruited? Rumkowski in Lodz and Gens in Vilna fared no better: all these council heads may have been instrumental in postponing, but not in preventing, the liquidation of their ghetto communities. Who knows what qualities of mind or character were necessary to anticipate the German plan to murder all the Jews of Europe, and given that power of insight, what strategies were adequate to greet this gruesome design?

In the absence of a cogent answer—though there is much to deplore in the limited foresight of those responsible for guiding the Kovno Ghetto through its hopeless years, and much to admire in the tenacity with which these leaders tried to make the best of an impossible situation—we must conclude that all policies would have led to the same finale, some sooner, some later. A few concessions to special pleading, like temporarily increasing the allotment of food or firewood, fooled the leadership into believing that their powers of persuasion had some impact on the more "reasonable" German minds; in fact, in the end, they could do nothing to halt the doom of the Kovno Ghetto.

Many individual Jews in the ghetto had a clearer sense of their ordeal than did their leaders, though for most of them this made little difference after the Germans had decided to kill them all. One survivor wrote later of the period of relative calm in the ghetto:

For us normal meant the absence of mass executions or deportations. It meant having just enough food to exist. . . . It meant survival of the community while individuals were shot. It meant life behind barbed wires, like criminals, like slave laborers without rest or relaxation. This was normal in the ghetto.[10]

This is a much bleaker view than Tory's, who, in addition to the surges of optimism that seemed native to his temperament, as a public official was excused from slave labor, had greater access to food, and was free to leave the ghetto for the city several times weekly. That is why we need to weigh various voices before we reach even tentative conclusions about life in the ghetto before its liquidation.

Although there were resistance groups in the Kovno Ghetto (supported by both the Jewish police and the *Ältestenrat*), they were neither numerous enough nor sufficiently armed to mount any meaningful opposition to the Germans. Toward the end of the ghetto's existence, some units of young Jews tried to escape to the forests to join with partisans, but most of them were caught and killed.[11] Resistance was not uppermost in the mind of the average ghetto inhabitant, and one witness who spent three years there offers a possible explanation why. His testimony also sheds light on both the public and private impact of the constant German endeavor to deceive:

> There was always the little carrot that the Germans did, saying, "Now this is the last 'action.' You don't have to be afraid to go to work," saying "Now, you see, nothing's going to happen to

you anymore, because this is the last time.". . . And of course that was all nonsense. Psychologically, of course, we were very glad to be fooled. If maybe they would be very blunt, it would be a natural reaction to fight, but this way we were just lured into . . . even though we knew that this was not so. But still everybody figured maybe . . . maybe they're telling the truth.[12]

Few analyses capture so succinctly the inner consciousness of a trapped community, their will to action paralyzed by simultaneously affirming and denying their utter vulnerability at the hands of the Germans.

Some have celebrated the fact that in Kovno (as in Vilna) concerts and other forms of cultural activity sustained the spirit of the physically oppressed Jews, but here too there is no unanimity. Just as in Vilna the librarian Hermann Kruk protested with the famous slogan "No theater in a cemetery," so in Kovno, as one survivor writes, comparing the concert he attended with earlier times,

> Most of the people were hungry, tired from slave labor, and the mood was subdued. Everybody had the same feeling: was it really right to have a concert, when the blood of our murdered people was still warm?[13]

One thing is clear to anyone who listens patiently to the voices of those who outlived the catastrophe of the Holocaust. For every "yes" there was a "no," just as here whatever pleasure one derived from listening to familiar music was shadowed if not contaminated by an aura of pain and loss. This does not negate the role of positive feelings in the midst of despair; but it complicates them, and cer-

**Violinists of the Jewish
Ghetto Police orchestra**

Kadish/GK

tainly limits the strength of their appeal. When Avraham Tory applauds "the will of our people to live under any conditions and situations,"[14] he does so by temporarily suppressing any mention of the oppressive details of those conditions and situations.

For a commentator much younger than Tory, those "conditions and situations" could blight the hope for a brighter future. Tamara Lazerson kept a diary in the ghetto for almost three years, beginning when she was twelve and ending after her fifteenth birthday. The earliest notebook is lost, but the remaining one offers a remarkably mature portrait of ghetto existence from the pen of one of the youngest survivors of the ordeal. Not yet fifteen, she describes the end of a working day:

> The spattering mud, wading through puddles, the cursing, and the groans of an exhausted existence. Finally, the gates. We are at the ghetto. We are finally home. You would think I would be happy about that, but no. Because tomorrow it will be the same all over again. The days run on one into the other without change. It is the day of a manual laborer, a day of exhaustion. The shout for bread and light! Only darkness and hunger are around.[15]

We delude ourselves if we believe we can enter into the daily existence of the Kovno Ghetto without first confronting the physical reality of melancholy visions like this one. Both of Tamara's parents were killed, and after her liberation she described herself in her diary as "an orphan, alone, like a single finger in the world."[16] Views like hers may not be the whole truth, but they are the basis on which all other reconstructions must build. If the resultant edifice is morally and spiritually precarious, this is only a testament to the brutal legacy that ended the lives of more than ninety percent of Lithuanian Jewry. Those who survived, like Tamara Lazerson herself, may have resolved to create for themselves a brighter future, but this does not mean that either they or we could ever escape entirely from the memory of their darker past.

Lawrence L. Langer is Professor Emeritus of English at Simmons College. Among his several books on Holocaust topics is Holocaust Testimonies: The Ruins of Memory, *winner of the 1991 National Book Critics Circle Award for Criticism.*

Notes

1. Avraham Tory, *Surviving the Holocaust: The Kovno Ghetto Diary,* ed. Martin Gilbert (Cambridge, Mass., 1990), 55.
2. "Testimomy of Paula G.," tape T-984, Fortunoff Video Archive for Holocaust Testimonies, Yale University, New Haven, Conn.
3. Tory, *Surviving the Holocaust,* 45.
4. Dr. Lazar Goldstein-Golden, *From Ghetto Kovno to Dachau,* trans. Max Rosenfeld, ed. Berl Kagan (New York, 1985), 55. Goldstein had planned a five-volume work on "The Doom of Lithuanian Jewry," but died, leaving, according to his editor, only "a heap of brief notes on many subjects." His editor arranged some of them into a "sequential manuscript," taking responsibility for some of the style but insisting that "the thoughts expressed in this book are Dr. Goldstein's completely."
5. Tory, *Surviving the Holocaust,* 195.
6. Ibid, 207.
7. Leib Garfunkel, "The Destruction of Kovno's Jewry," trans. and paraphrased by Alfred Katz (United States Holocaust Memorial Museum, Washington, D.C., 1995), 41.
8. Tory, *Surviving the Holocaust,* 209–10.
9. Goldstein-Golden, *From Ghetto Kovno to Dachau,* 57–58.
10. William W. Mishell, *Kaddish for Kovno: Life and Death in a Lithuanian Ghetto, 1941–1945* (Chicago, 1988), 129.
11. See Dov Levin, *Fighting Back: Lithuanian Jewry's Armed Resistance to the Nazis, 1941–1945,* trans. Moshe Kohn and Dina Cohen (New York, 1986).
12. "Testimony of Shalom S.," tape T-190, Fortunoff Video Archive for Holocaust Testimonies.
13. Mishell, *Kaddish for Kovno,* 132.
14. Tory, *Surviving the Holocaust,* 210.
15. Tamara Lazerson, "Diary of Tamara Lazerson," trans. Andrew Eitavicius (United States Holocaust Memorial Museum, Washington, D.C., 1995), 40.
16. Ibid, 43.

Kadish/BH

Ghetto remnants, August 1944

NOTES

Page   **Chapter 3**

47   "Order No. 15," July 10, 1941 (in Lithuanian), Lithuanian Central State Archives, Vilnius, Registry R-1444, inventory 1, file 1, document 5, trans. Andrew Eitavicius.

48   "Operation Situation Report USSR No. 19," July 11, 1941 (in German), Bundesarchiv, Germany, document R-58214, p. 3, trans. Linda Bixby.

49   "Order No. 1" (in Lithuanian and German), *I Laisve* [To freedom], July 28, 1941, Lithuanian Central State Archives, Vilnius, Registry R-1390, inventory 1, file 160, trans. from the German by Linda Bixby.

49   "Public Announcement No. 2," July 31, 1941, *Official Gazette of the Kaunas Commissar General* (in German) (Kaunas, November 1, 1941), National Archive of the Republic of Belarus, Minsk, document 370-4-3, trans. Linda Bixby.

50   Elena Kutorgiene, "Diary" (in Russian), August 1, 1941, Lithuanian Central State Archives, Vilnius, Registry R-1390, inventory 1, file 137, p. 42, trans. Martha Wexler.

50   Ibid., p. 46.

51   Instructions to implement "Order No. 15," July 25, 1941 (in Lithuanian), Lithuanian Central State Archives, Vilnius, Registry R-1444, inventory 1, file 6, pp. 3–4, trans. Andrew Eitavicius.

54   Meir Yelin, ed., *Khaym yelin, geto kemfer un schrayber* [Chaim Yelin, ghetto fighter and writer] (Tel Aviv: Association of Lithuanian Jews, 1975), 162; excerpt trans. from the Yiddish by Tina Lunson.

59   Ibid., 161.

60   "Committee for the Transfer of Jews" to *Stadtkommissar* Hans Cramer, July 10, 1941 (in German), Yad Vashem, Archives Department, Jerusalem, Document 048 B/12-4, trans. Linda Bixby.

62   Yelin, *Khaym yelin,* 161, 163.

62   Ibid., 164.

63   "Health Institutions in the Ghetto," mid-1943 (in Yiddish), Avraham and Pnina Tory, Israel, trans. Tina Lunson.

63   Avraham Tory, "Diary," September 15, 1941 (in Yiddish), Avraham and Pnina Tory, Israel, trans. Tina Lunson.

64   Order from the Commander of the SD, October 3, 1941 (in German), "And These Are the Laws—German Style" compilation, Avraham and Pnina Tory, Israel, trans. Linda Bixby.

64   "Health Institutions in the Ghetto."

65   Order from the Commander of the SD, October 27, 1941 (in German), "And These Are the Laws—German Style" compilation.

67   Tory, "Diary," October 28, 1941.

68   Kutorgiene, "Diary," October 30, 1941, pp. 86b–87.

69   Tory, "Diary," October 28, 1941.

70   Kutorgiene, "Diary," December 4, 1941, p. 91.

Page

70   Deposition of Ignas Velavicius-Vilius, December 20, 1945 and January 12, 1946 (in German), Zentrale Stelle der Landesjustizverwaltungen, Ludwigsburg, document 207 AR-Z 14/58, pp. 4171–73, trans. Jürgen Matthäus.

74   Tory, "Diary," June 12, 1942.

75   Tamara Lazerson, "Diary" (in Lithuanian), September 18, 1943, courtesy of Tamara Lazerson Rostovsky in memory of her family who perished in the Holocaust, trans. Andrew Eitavicius.

76   K. L. Yemo [Moshe Klein], "Nightmares" (in Hebrew), Lithuanian Central State Archives, Vilnius, Registry R-1390, inventory 1, file 150, trans. Moshe Dor.

Chapter 4

78   Tory, "Diary," June 5, 1943.

80   "Slobodka Ghetto 1942" yearbook (in Yiddish), Avraham and Pnina Tory, Israel, trans. Tina Lunson.

81   Avrom Akselrod, "Ghetto-Jew, Answer Me This," in *Lider fun getos un lagern* [Songs from ghettos and concentration camps], text and melodies compiled by Shmerke Kaczerginski, edited by H. Leivik, music arranged by M. Gelbart (New York, 1948), 161, trans. from the Yiddish by Tina Lunson.

83   Elkhanan Elkes to his children Joel and Sarah, October 19, 1943 (in Hebrew), Dr. Joel Elkes, Florida, trans. Moshe Dor and Judith Cohen.

86   "History of the Vilijampole Jewish Ghetto Police," 1942–43 (in Yiddish), YIVO Institute for Jewish Research, New York, Territorial Collection, Baltic: 3.0 Lita, pp. 121–22; trans. Solon Beinfeld.

90   "Oath," November 1, 1942 (in Hebrew and Yiddish), Lithuanian Central State Archives, Vilnius, Registry R-973, inventory 2, file 23, trans. from the Yiddish by Tina Lunson.

91   "Brief Descriptions of the *Ältestenrat* and Its Offices," before August 1943 (in Yiddish), Avraham and Pnina Tory, Israel, trans. Tina Lunson.

91   "Slobodka Ghetto 1942" yearbook.

93   "Brief Descriptions of the *Ältestenrat* and Its Offices."

96   "Health Institutions in the Ghetto."

97   "Slobodka Ghetto 1942" yearbook.

97   "Health Institutions in the Ghetto."

98   Dr. Jacob Nochimowski, "The Effect of Work on Illnesses and of Illnesses on Work in the Ghetto," May 9, 1943 (in German), Avraham and Pnina Tory, Israel, trans. Gerald Liebenau.

99   Memorandum from *Reichskommissar* Hinrich Lohse, August 13, 1941, National Archives, Washington, D.C., National Archives Collection of World War II War Crimes Records, Record Group 238, Office of the U.S. Chief of Counsel for War Crimes, document USA2841138-PS.

99   "Order No. 1," August 25, 1942 (in German), "And These Are the Laws—German Style" compilation.

102   Nochimowski, "The Effect of Work on Illnesses."

Page

102 Tory, "Diary," March 30, 1943.

104 Ibid., May 4, 1943.

105 "Brief Descriptions of the *Ältestenrat* and Its Offices."

106 Ibid.

106 Tory, "Diary," July 17, 1943.

107 "Brief Descriptions of the *Ältestenrat* and Its Offices."

108 Lazerson, "Diary," November 1, 1942.

109 Chaim Nachman Shapiro, "Report No. 1," July 15, 1942 (in Hebrew), Avraham and Pnina Tory, Israel, trans. Judith Cohen.

114 "History of the Vilijampole Jewish Ghetto Police," pp. 7–8.

114 Order from SA-Captain Fritz Jordan, October 1, 1941 (in German), "And These Are the Laws—German Style" compilation.

115 Tory, "Diary," October 13, 1943.

117 "Decision no. 21," May 3, 1943, "Vilijampole Jewish Ghetto, Council of Elders: Proceedings Book" (in Lithuanian and Yiddish), Lithuanian Central State Archives, Vilnius, Registry R-973, inventory 3, file 4, trans. from the Yiddish by Alfred Katz.

117 Tory, "Diary," June 5, 1943.

Chapter 5

126 Order from the Labor Office, October 29, 1941 (in German), USHMM, 1995.89.322, trans. Jürgen Matthäus.

126 "Complete inventory of executions carried out in the *Einsatzkommando 3* zone up to 1 December 1941," December 1, 1941 (in German), CPHDC, *fond* 500, *opis* 1, file 25; copy at USHMM, Archives, RG 11.001M, Selected records from the "Osobyi" Archive [Moscow], reel 1, trans. Jürgen Matthäus.

126 Tory, "Diary," March 16, 1943.

127 Yelin, *Khaym yelin*, 176.

127 Lazerson, "Diary," January 23, 1944.

129 Yelin, *Khaym yelin,* 180.

129 Tory, "Diary," March 23, 1943.

130 Avrom Akselrod, "Jewish Brigades," in *Umkum fun yidisher kovne* [The destruction of Jewish Kovno], ed. Josef Gar (Munich, 1948), 404, trans. from the Yiddish by Solon Beinfeld.

134 Yelin, *Khaym yelin,* 182.

135 Shaul Shenker, "Rise Up to the Airfield," in *Lider fun getos un lagern*, 149, trans. from the Yiddish by Solon Beinfeld.

135 "The Population and the Labor Force according to the Tables from the Statistics Office, May 31, 1942 (in Yiddish), Avraham and Pnina Tory, Israel, trans. Solon Beinfeld.

136 "Order No. 15," July 10, 1941.

136 Lazerson, "Diary," September 14, 1942.

136 "History of the Vilijampole Jewish Ghetto Police," 94; excerpt trans. Solon Beinfeld.

137 Order from the Commander of the SD, March 11, 1942 (in German), "And These Are the Laws—German Style" compilation.

138 Avrom Akselrod, "By the Ghetto Gate," in *Umkum fun yidisher kovne,* 406, trans. from the Yiddish by Tina Lunson.

139 Tory, "Diary," February 5, 1943.

Page

139 "By the Gate," in *Lider fun getos un lagern*, 135, trans. from the Yiddish by Tina Lunson.

140 "Report on the Workshops in the Jewish Ghetto Community in Vilijampole for the period to April 25, 1942" (in German), Avraham and Pnina Tory, Israel, trans. Gerald Liebenau.

142 Tory, "Diary," February 10, 1943.

142 Ibid., March 28, 1943.

143 K. Brenner, "Life," in *Lider fun getos un lagern*, 40, trans. from the Yiddish by Solon Beinfeld.

144 Lazerson, "Diary," February 26, 1944.

148 Tory, "Diary," June 5, 1943.

Chapter 6

151 Avraham Tory, "Last Testament," December 1942 (in Yiddish), Avraham and Pnina Tory, Israel, trans. Tina Lunson.

161 Ibid.

164 Tory, "Diary," July 25, 1943.

165 Jacob Lifschitz, "Dying Confession," July 5–6, 1944 (in Yiddish), Lithuanian Central State Archives, Vilnius, Registry R-1390, inventory 1, file 134, trans. Tina Lunson.

167 "Slobodka Ghetto 1942" yearbook, January 11, 1942.

172 Lazerson, "Diary," December 11, 1942.

172 Ilya Gerber, "Diary," December 28, 1942 (in Yiddish), Lithuanian Central State Archives, Vilnius, Registry R-1390, inventory 1, file 144, p. 569, trans. Solon Beinfeld.

173 K. L. Yemo [Moshe Klein], "Lullaby" (in Hebrew), Lithuanian Central State Archives, Vilnius, Registry R-1390, inventory 1, file 150, pp. 31–31b, trans. Moshe Dor.

175 "Slobodka Ghetto 1942" yearbook, January 3, 1942.

176 "History of the Vilijampole Jewish Ghetto Police," pp. 252–53, trans. Tina Lunson.

176 Moshe Diskant, "In the Yeshiva," in *Lider fun getos un lagern,* 24, trans. from the Yiddish by Tina Lunson.

177 "Slobodka Ghetto 1942" yearbook, November 15, 1942.

177 Orders from Commander of the SD, November 17–19, 1942 (in German), "And These Are the Laws—German Style" compilation.

178 "Slobodka Ghetto 1942" yearbook, November 15, 1942.

179 Gerber, "Diary," November 18, 1942.

179 Lazerson, "Diary," November 18, 1942.

179 Ibid., November 19, 1942.

180 Tory, "Diary," February 25, 1943.

181 *Ältestenrat* announcement, September 8, 1942 (in German and Yiddish), Lithuanian Central State Archives, Vilnius, Registry 1390, inventory 3, file 14, document 7; trans. from the Yiddish by Tina Lunson.

181 "Health Institutions in the Ghetto."

182 Tory, "Diary," February 18, 1943.

183 Ibid., June 5, 1943.

183 Gerber, "Diary," December 4, 1942.

184 Order from *Einsatzstab Rosenberg,* February 27, 1942 (in German), "And These Are the Laws—German Style" compilation.

185 "History of the Vilijampole Jewish Ghetto Police," pp. 173–74.

186 Tory, "Diary," June 5, 1943.

188 Rabbi Ephraim Oshry, *Responsa from the Holocaust* (New York, 1983), 9–10.

189 Ibid., 113–14.

190 Ibid., 39.

191 "Decree No. 1," August 25, 1942 (in German), "And These Are the Laws—German Style" compilation.

191 Tory, "Diary," March 28, 1943.

191 "Ghetto Child" (in Hebrew), in "Slobodka Ghetto 1942" yearbook, trans. Judith Cohen.

192 "Slobodka Ghetto 1942" yearbook, September 13, 1942.

192 Tory, "Diary," April 26, 1943.

192 Lazerson, "Diary," April 4, 1943.

194 *HaMapilim* unit of the Organization of the Covenant of Zion, "Ten Commandments" (in Hebrew), Yad Vashem, Archives Department, Jerusalem, document 0-48/12-5, trans. Judith Cohen.

199 Sabotage journal (in Yiddish), Jewish State Museum of Lithuania, Vilnius, document 22/26/50/JM3 VZM 1294, trans. Tina Lunson.

199 Anti-Fascist Organization, "Encounter Actions" (in Yiddish), Lithuanian Central State Archives, Vilnius, Registry R-1390, inventory 1, file 106, p. 1, trans. Tina Lunson.

201 Anti-Fascist Organization, "Solemn Oath" (in Yiddish), Lithuanian Central State Archives, Vilnius, Registry R-1390, inventory 1, file 107, p. 2, trans. Tina Lunson.

Epilogue

204 Order from *Reichsführer-SS* Heinrich Himmler, June 21, 1943 (in German), Bundesarchiv, Germany, signature no. NS19/1740, pp. 20–21, trans. Linda Bixby.

205 Elkhanan Elkes to his children, November 11, 1943 (in Hebrew), Dr. Joel Elkes, Florida, trans. Moshe Dor.

205 Lazerson, "Diary," November 30, 1943.

206 Masha Musel to her brother, January 9, 1944 (in Yiddish), The Musel Family, Israel, trans. Tina Lunson.

208 Elkhanan Elkes to his children, November 11, 1943.

208 "Evidence of Jewish Escapees from the Ninth Fort in Kovno on the Burning of Bodies," December 26, 1943, reprinted in *Documents on the Holocaust: Selected Sources on the Destruction of the Jews of Germany and Austria, Poland, and the Soviet Union,* ed. Yitzhak Arad, Yisrael Gutman, and Abraham Margaliot (Jerusalem, 1981), 473–75.

209 Kutorgiene, "Diary," October 12, 1942.

213 Elkhanan Elkes to his children, October 19, 1943.

214 Lazerson, "Diary," March 27, 1944.

215 Shulamith Rabinowitz to her sons in Israel, June 27, 1944 (in Yiddish), Shmuel Elhanan, Israel, trans. Tina Lunson.

217 Lazerson, "Diary," October 12, 1944.

CHRONOLOGY

WAR AND HOLOCAUST

KOVNO GHETTO

1939

August 23
Molotov-Ribbentrop Non-Aggression Pact, amended September 28, divides Poland between Germany and the Soviet Union and cedes the Baltic States—Lithuania, Estonia, Latvia—to the Soviet sphere of influence.

September 1
German forces invade Poland; World War II begins.

November 23
Nazis introduce Jewish star of David as identifying badge throughout occupied Poland.

1940

April 30
First major Jewish ghetto, in Polish city of Lodz, is sealed.

June 15
Soviet army occupies independent Lithuania.

November 15
Warsaw Ghetto is sealed.

1941

June 22
"Operation Barbarossa" begins: German troops, violating the 1939 Molotov-Ribbentrop Pact, attack Soviet Union, crossing into Lithuania at 3:05 A.M.

June 23
The four *Einsatzgruppen* units, mobile task forces attached to major German army units, begin their killings in the USSR. SS-Brigadier General Walther Stahlecker leads *Einsatzgruppe A* in the Baltic States and parts of Belorussia. In Lithuania, SS-Colonel Karl Jäger commands *Einsatzkommando 3,* a subdivision of *Einsatzgruppe A.*

June 24
German armed forces occupy Vilna, Lithuania, 57 miles southeast of Kovno. Jewish population numbers 55,000.

June 26
German armed forces occupy Shavli, Lithuania, 70 miles northwest of Kovno, where 5,300 Jews reside.

June 23
Soviet armed forces, having occupied Lithuania since June 1940, retreat from Kovno. Lithuanian pro-Nazi partisans begin terrorizing Jews in the city.

June 24
German forces enter Kovno at night.

June 25–26
Encouraged by the SS, ultra-nationalist Lithuanian "partisans" accelerate pogrom against Kovno's Jews, attacking rabbis and their followers in suburb of Vilijampole, known to local Jews as Slobodka. The partisans set fire to several synagogues and burn down some 60 houses. Between 800 and 1,000 Jews are killed.

June 27
While crowds of jeering spectators and many German soldiers look on, Lithuanian "partisans" kill 60 Jews at the Lietukis garage in central Kovno, battering most of them to death, one by one, with iron bars.

June 28
Germans abolish Lithuanian "partisans" and begin forming Lithuanian auxiliary police.

July 1
German armed forces occupy Riga, Latvia.

July 4
Jewish council (*Judenrat*) is formed in Vilna.

July 31
Nazi leader Hermann Göring authorizes Reinhard Heydrich, head of Reich Security Main Office (RSHA), with organizing a "total solution" to the "Jewish question."

July 4–6
Lithuanian auxiliary police, acting under orders of SS-Colonel Karl Jäger, commander of mobile killing unit *Einsatzkommando 3,* kill 2,977 Jews in mass shootings at Fort VII, one of several Imperial Russian fortifications surrounding Kovno used as prisons and execution sites during the war.

July 7
Germans inform prominent members of Kovno's Jewish community that ghetto is to be established for Kovno's Jews in Vilijampole/ Slobodka. This neighborhood is characterized by old, wooden, single-story houses without running water. To coordinate the move, a "Committee for the Transfer of the Jews to Vilijampole" is formed from among the Jewish community.

July 10
Jurgis Bobelis, Lithuanian military commander of Kovno, and Kazys Palciauskas, mayor of Kovno, order Jews moved into Slobodka ghetto by August 15. Lithuanians residing in Slobodka are to be evacuated, and Jews from neighborhoods across the city, the vast majority of Kovno's more than 30,000 Jews, are to join those already living in Slobodka. Jews, regardless of sex and age, are ordered to wear a yellow star of David sewn to clothing and observe a 6 A.M. to 8 P.M. curfew. Kovno's Jewish leaders appeal to city authorities to cancel measure establishing ghetto, arguing that crowding Kovno's Jews into Slobodka will produce intolerable living conditions and lead to spread of contagious diseases, but the effort fails.

July 24
Kovno municipal authorities order Jews to erect fence around ghetto.

July 28
The German civil administration takes over affairs in Kovno from the German military. Newly appointed *Stadtkommissar* (city commissioner) of Kovno, SA-Colonel Hans Cramer, issues his first orders, including forbidding Jews to walk on sidewalks, to enter public parks, to sit on public benches, or to use public transportation.

August 2
Einsatzkommandos lead mass shootings by Lithuanian auxiliaries of more than 200 Jewish men and women at Fort IV. Most of the women held at the fort endure rape and other forms of abuse; some are released.

August 4
Acting on German orders, surviving leaders of Kovno's prewar Jewish community form Jewish council—*Ältestenrat*—for purposes of carrying out German decrees and administering ghetto affairs. Leaders elect as chairman Dr. Elkhanan Elkes, a physician and one of Kovno's most prominent Jewish citizens.

August 7–8
One thousand Jews are arrested and shot at Fort IV.

August 15
Ghetto is closed under police guard, with some 29,700 Jews crammed into a Large Ghetto and a Small Ghetto, the two sections separated by Paneriu Street, a main artery outside ghetto limits. A small bridge will later be built between the two. Jews are prohibited from freely leaving ghetto.

August 17
Ältestenrat announces the creation of Jewish Ghetto Police "to protect public order and to supervise implementation of orders from authorities and *Ältestenrat*."

August 18
"Intellectuals Action," the first of the German operations to reduce the ghetto population: 534 Jews, including many professionals lured by offer of clerical work in city archives, are removed from ghetto, taken to Fort IV, and killed. (German sources report killing 711 Jews in this "action.")

August 29
Germans forbid transport of food and other items into ghetto.

WAR AND HOLOCAUST

August 31
Shavli Ghetto is established.

August 31
Vilna Ghetto is formed.

September 2
Ten members of the Vilna Jewish Council are executed by the Gestapo.

September 3
First gassing experiments with Zyklon B at Auschwitz; 600 Soviet prisoners of war and 250 ill Polish prisoners are killed.

September 28–29
SS *Einsatzgruppe C* kills more than 33,000 Jews at Babi Yar, outside Kiev, Ukraine.

October 15
Deportations of Austrian and German Jews to Lodz, Poland; Minsk, Belorussia; Riga, Latvia; and Kovno begin.

October 29
Vilna's "small ghetto" is liquidated; 33,500 Jews are killed between June and December.

November 24
Theresienstadt Ghetto opens near Prague, in German-controlled Protectorate of Bohemia and Moravia.

KOVNO GHETTO

September 3
Germans order ghetto inhabitants to hand over money and valuables, including jewelry, paintings, furs, livestock, and stamp collections.

September 7
Germans prohibit Jews from buying in the city. Illegal purchases nevertheless continue.

September 8
First brigade of workers is marched out of ghetto to Aleksotas military airfield, three-and-a-half miles from ghetto.

September 15
Ältestenrat issues 5,000 craftsmen certificates provided by German specialist on Jewish affairs in Kovno, SA-Captain Fritz Jordan. These *Jordan-Scheine,* also known as "life certificates," would later protect holders from certain German "actions" by ensuring them work.

September 26
Some 1,000 ghetto inhabitants are taken from the neighborhood of the Slobodka Yeshiva to Fort IV and shot in retaliation for an alleged shooting at Commander Kozlovski of the German Ghetto Guard.

October 4
Germans liquidate the Small Ghetto: After burning the contagious diseases hospital with patients and staff inside, hundreds of Jews, mostly women and children who do not hold "Jordan certificates," are taken to Fort IX. Some 1,800 people are killed.

October 28
The "Great Action": SA-Captain Fritz Jordan and Gestapo Sergeant Helmut Rauca preside over massive, day-long "selection" in ghetto's Demokratu Square, where all ghetto Jews assembled upon penalty of death. By evening, 9,200 men, women, and children, more than 30 percent of the ghetto population, have been sent "to the right," i.e., chosen to be killed. They are shot the next day at Fort IX. Those sent "to the left" return home. The 22-month-long "period of relative calm" begins.

November 25
Education Office is established in ghetto under direction of cultural leader Chaim Nachman Shapiro, who begins secret archival project. Shapiro encourages artists such as Esther Lurie and writers to begin documentary efforts. Avraham Tory of the *Ältestenrat* collects ghetto and German documents for the archives.

November 29
2,000 Jews (including 1,155 women and 152 children) from Vienna and Breslau are shot at Fort IX; 19 Jews from the ghetto are also shot.

December 1

SS-Colonel Karl Jäger reports that "our objective, to solve the Jewish problem for Lithuania, has been achieved." He claims a total of 136,442 Jews killed by *Einsatzkommando 3* and Lithuanian auxiliaries. He reports that there remain 15,000 Jews in the Kovno Ghetto, 15,000 in the Vilna Ghetto, and 4,500 in Shavli Ghetto. (A census report prepared by Kovno *Ältestenrat* in November shows a slightly higher ghetto population of 17,237 men, women, and children.)

December 7

Japanese bomb Pearl Harbor, Hawaii.

December 8

Chelmno killing center, northwest of Lodz, Poland, begins gassing operations. United States declares war on Japan.

December 11

Germany declares war on the United States.

December 12

Acting on German demands for more workers, the *Ältestenrat* orders individuals previously exempted from work (men ages 16 to 17 and 55 to 60, women ages 45 to 50, and women with children up to age 8) to register with the ghetto Labor Office on December 17. All persons who fail to register are to "be handed over to the ghetto court as shirkers and . . . severely punished."

December 31

The several Communist resistance groups merge to form the Anti-Fascist Organization under Chaim Yelin.

1942

January 5

German ghetto guard chief prohibits demolishing houses or parts of houses or fences. Ghetto inmates, desperate for fuel during one of the coldest winters on record in Kovno, defy the prohibition.

January 12

Ghetto workshops, employing prisoners unable to endure forced labor conditions, begin operations, mending uniforms and manufacturing gloves for the German military.

January 14

Germans shoot cats and dogs in small synagogue on Veliuonos Street; the remains are left to rot, desecrating the place of worship.

January 20

At the Wannsee Conference, RSHA head Reinhard Heydrich presides over meeting of key German government leaders to discuss implementation of "Final Solution."

January 26

Area within three meters of either side of ghetto fence is declared "death zone." Anyone inside this area is to be shot without warning. This order is meant to deter Jews smuggling food into ghetto or Lithuanians entering ghetto to plunder Jewish homes.

February 6

Gestapo deports 359 Jews, including 137 women, from the ghetto for forced labor in the Riga Ghetto (Latvia), 140 miles north of Kovno.

February 16

Ghetto laundry workshop, employing mostly women, begins work washing clothes of German police and civil administrators.

February 27

Germans order confiscation of all books in the ghetto for recycling into paper. Ghetto inmates hide many books and Torah scrolls brought to the ghetto from city's synagogues.

March 2

Some 3,000 Jews from Minsk Ghetto (Belorussia) are killed; following this "action," flight of thousands of Minsk Jews to forests begins.

WAR AND HOLOCAUST

March 17
Belzec killing center in occupied Poland begins operations.

May
Sobibor killing center in occupied Poland begins operations.

July 15
Deportations begin of Jews from Netherlands to Auschwitz and Sobibor.

July 22–September 21
Mass deportations from Warsaw Ghetto; approximately 265,000 Jews are killed at Treblinka.

July 23
Treblinka killing center in occupied Poland begins operation.

July 28–31
At least 10,000 Jews from Minsk Ghetto (Belorussia) are killed by Germans using mobile gas vans and mass shootings.

August 10–23
50,000 Jews from Lvov Ghetto (Poland) are deported to Belzec killing center.

August 15
Births are forbidden in the Shavli Ghetto.

August 16–18
Radom Ghetto (Poland) is liquidated; 20,000 Jews are killed, most of them at Treblinka.

KOVNO GHETTO

March 10
A group of 24 Jews from the ghetto are shot for selling goods on black market and not wearing Star of David badges.
Ghetto workshop is set up for manufacture of toys for children.

March 12
Ghetto shoemaking workshop begins repairing military boots and other footwear.

April 26
Ältestenrat issues regulations regarding the planting and protection of vegetable gardens and the operation of a communal soup kitchen.

May 1
Germans again reduce area of ghetto by redrawing boundaries. Crowding worsens.

May 12
Germans arrest four members of *Ältestenrat* staff, including the head of the administrative Secretariat, for participating in illegal mail service with the Vilna Ghetto. Avraham Tory named head of Secretariat.

June 2
Acting on German orders, *Ältestenrat* sends 73 people to dig peat in Palemonas, six miles from Kovno. Some escape on way to camp. Forty additional workers are sent two days later. Work conditions and regime at this camp are so harsh that many Jews are killed there or die of hunger or exhaustion.

June 16
Germans order transfer of the ghetto workshops from *Ältestenrat* to German control.

June 28
The Jewish Ghetto Police orchestra of well-known musicians plays for schoolchildren in former yeshiva. Organizers asked audience to refrain from applauding out of respect for dead.

July 2
Ältestenrat transmits German order requiring work for all men older than 15 and all women aged 17 to 47 with no children under 6.

July 4
Germans order dissolution of ghetto court.

July 7
German ghetto commander issues regulation for fencing off section of Vilija River for bathing.

July 24
Germans issue order prohibiting pregnancies and births in ghetto: "Pregnancies have to be terminated. Pregnant women will be shot."

August 26
Germans prohibit all religious observances in ghetto and order closing of schools. Prisoners clandestinely continue religious and educational activities and expand curriculum of still-legal vocational school to include regular school subjects.

August 31
Ältestenrat announces German order to end the ghetto's cash economy and the smuggling of food into the ghetto.

September 8
In fulfillment of earlier German orders, the *Ältestenrat* prohibits births and offers abortions in ghetto hospital.

September 11
Germans order the *Ältestenrat* to provide 150 workers for the Palemonas peat bogs.

September 12
Battle of Stalingrad begins.

October 19
German army encounters tenacious Soviet defense at Stalingrad.

October 23
Germans deport 369 Jews from Kovno to the Riga Ghetto (Latvia). Jewish Ghetto Police help round up those unwilling to leave.

November 7
Allied forces invade North Africa.

November 15
Ghetto prisoner Nahum Meck allegedly shoots at German sentry during attempt to escape from ghetto. Germans arrest Meck and hold the *Ältestenrat* and other Jews as hostages.

November 18
Meck is hanged publicly in the ghetto by Jewish Ghetto Police. The next day, his mother and sister are shot at Fort IX.

November 19
Soviet armed forces begin a counterattack near Stalingrad.

1943

January 5
Lvov Ghetto (Poland) is transformed into labor camp; 10,000 Jews are killed.

February 2
Final surrender of German forces at Stalingrad.

February 4
"Stalingrad Action": following surrender by German forces at Stalingrad, Germans shoot 44 ghetto Jews at Fort IX. Pretext is illegal smuggling activities. Shortly thereafter, cultural leader Chaim Nachman Shapiro asks artist Esther Lurie to encourage other artists to speed up documentation efforts.

February 5–12
Some 10,000 Jews from Bialystok Ghetto (Poland) are deported to Treblinka; an additional 2,000 are killed on the spot.

February 28
Burial of Rabbi Avraham Duber Shapiro, chief rabbi of Kovno and Lithuania, who dies after long illness.

March 15
Deportations begin of Jews from Greece to Auschwitz.

April 19–May 16
Warsaw Ghetto revolt; ends with the destruction of the ghetto.

May 12
Axis forces surrender in North Africa.

WAR AND HOLOCAUST

June 1–6
Some 10,000 Jews are deported to Auschwitz from Sonsowiec Ghetto (Poland).

June 11
Reichsführer-SS Heinrich Himmler orders liquidation of all ghettos in occupied Poland. This results in mass deportations to Treblinka and other killing centers.

June 21
Himmler orders all ghettos in the *Ostland* liquidated and reorganized into concentration camps.

July 10
Allies invade Sicily.

August 2
Armed prisoner revolt at the Treblinka killing center.

August 16–20
Liquidation of Bialystok Ghetto (Poland); 25,000 Jews are deported to their deaths.

August 4–September 4
About 7,000 Jews are deported from Vilna Ghetto to Estonia for forced labor.

September 1
Vilna Ghetto fighters clash with German forces.

September 8
Italy signs armistice with Allies.

September 23–24
Final liquidation of Vilna Ghetto: 3,700 Jews are sent to Estonian and Latvian labor camps, and 4,000 are deported to their immediate deaths at killing centers in occupied Poland.

October 14
Armed prisoner revolt at the Sobibor killing center.

KOVNO GHETTO

June–July
Zionist and pro-Soviet leftists in ghetto unite to form Jewish General Fighting Organization under the leadership of Chaim Yelin. The two groups agree that "each side will recruit its own men" but will join in a "united program for training and activity until departure to the forests." At its peak, the Jewish General Fighting Organization has close to 600 members.

July 24
Exhibition of ghetto artist Esther Lurie's drawings is held for small circle of friends.

September–December
Seeking to hide crimes in anticipation of forced retreat, Germans use Jewish prisoners and Soviet prisoners of war to exhume and burn corpses from mass graves at Fort IX.

September
Jewish Soviet partisan Gessia Glezer enters ghetto for discussions with activists, including Chaim Yelin, central figure in the Jewish General Fighting Organization. Plans are developed to send armed groups into Augustow Forest, 80 miles south of Kovno.

September 15
SS-Captain Wilhelm Goecke of Gestapo announces takeover of Kovno ghetto administration and workshops by SS from German civilian authorities. Move begins the transformation of the ghetto into a concentration camp and signals end to more than 22 months of relative calm in ghetto.

October 13
Germans order *Ältestenrat* to collect 3,000 Jewish workers for deportation to labor camps beyond the Kovno area.

October 26
Russian and Ukrainian auxiliaries assist Germans in deportation of at least 2,700 Jews from Kovno. Those of working age are transported to labor camps in Vaivara and Klooga, Estonia, while very young and old are deported to their deaths at Auschwitz. (German documents record a deportation of 2,800 Kovno Jews.)

October 28
At least 43 partisans leave ghetto for Augustow Forest. Only two men succeed in reaching the forest; most are killed or captured, and eleven return safely to the ghetto after imprisonment. This is one of several attempted escapes to forest in October and November involving a total of nearly 100 partisans. Most were arrested and killed.

November 1
SS-Captain Wilhelm Goecke officially reclassifies the Kovno Ghetto as a concentration camp.

November 2

Final liquidation of Riga Ghetto (Latvia); more than 2,000 Jews are sent to Auschwitz.

November 5

Germans murder all Jewish children in the Shavli Ghetto.

November 24

Ten armed partisans leave the ghetto on foot for Rudniki Forest, 94 miles away; six reach their destination. During the following weeks, nine groups of partisans, totaling 180 people, are driven to the forest in trucks; not all arrive safely.

November 30

Some 1,000 ghetto inhabitants are taken to satellite camp in the suburb of Aleksotas. The 7,000 to 8,000 Jews remaining in the ghetto are confined to small area.

December 2

Chaim Nachman Shapiro, the leader of the ghetto's cultural affairs, his wife, son, and mother (the widow of Chief Rabbi Avraham Duber Shapiro) are taken to Fort IX after being led to believe they were to have safe passage to Switzerland.

December 16

Some 900 Jews are taken from Kovno camp to satellite labor camp in the suburb of Sanciai. Later, Jews are taken to Palemonas, Keidan, and Koshedar.

1944

March 19

German forces occupy Hungary.

March 27

Forty Jewish policemen shot at Riga.

March 27

In an effort to obtain information about the ghetto underground, Gestapo agents arrest and torture some 130 Jewish ghetto policemen at Fort IX. Thirty-six men are killed after refusing to cooperate, including Police Chief Moshe Levin and his assistants, Joshua Greenberg and Yehuda Zupowitz.

March 27–28

"Children's Action": Gestapo and Ukrainian auxiliaries round up 1,300 Jews, most of whom were children under 12 and adults over 55. Dragged from their homes, the victims are taken to Fort IX and killed. A few women in the ghetto resistance manage to hide 60 children during the "action."

April 3

Final meeting of the *Ältestenrat*. Chairman Elkhanan Elkes recommends that they flee or go into hiding, although he states he will remain until end.

April 4

Germans liquidate all remaining ghetto institutions, including the *Ältestenrat*, whose members are taken to Fort IX but released.

April 6

Ghetto underground leader Chaim Yelin is arrested in central Kovno after an exchange of gunfire with police. He is executed in early May after being tortured.

April 16

The forced ghettoization of Hungarian Jews begins.

May 15

Mass deportations of Jews from Hungary to Auschwitz begins. By July 9, 437,402 Jews have been deported; most of them are gassed immediately upon arrival at Auschwitz.

June 6

D-Day: Allied invasion of western Europe begins.

July 8

As the Soviet army nears, the Germans begin six-day liquidation of Concentration Camp Kauen, evacuating the former ghetto's remaining population by train and by barge for deportation to the Stutthof and Dachau concentration camps in Germany. The camp is set aflame to smoke out those still hiding in underground bunkers.

July 13

Soviet armed forces liberate Vilna.

July 20

German officers' attempt to assassinate Hitler fails.

July 22

Final deportation of Jews from the Shavli Ghetto, mostly to Stutthof in Germany; some 500 survive to see liberation.

July 24

Soviet troops liberate Majdanek concentration camp and killing center in Poland.

August 1

Soviet Army enters Kovno. A few Jews who survived hiding in bunkers are liberated.

August 30

Last transport of Jews from Lodz Ghetto, bringing to 74,000 the number of persons deported to Auschwitz in August.

October 2

After 63 days of fighting, Warsaw uprising organized by Polish underground Home Army is quashed by Germans; acting on Hitler's orders, German army razes the city.

October 7

Prisoners blow up one crematorium in revolt at Auschwitz.

October 13

Soviet forces liberate Riga.

October 17

Dr. Elkhanan Elkes dies in Dachau.

1945

January 25

The evacuation of approximately 50,000 Jews from Stutthof concentration camp and its subcamps in Germany begins; some 26,000 perish by war's end.

January 27

Soviet troops liberate Auschwitz.

April 11

Prisoners and U.S. troops liberate the Buchenwald concentration camp.

April 29

U.S. troops liberate the Dachau concentration camp.

April 30

Hitler commits suicide.

May 7

Germany surrenders to Allies; war ends in Europe.

May 8

V-E-Day: the war in Europe officially concludes.

FURTHER READING

Part I: Kovno and the Holocaust

Chapter 1: Assault and Destruction

Arad, Yitzhak, Shmuel Krakowski and Shmuel Spector, eds. *The Einsatzgruppen Reports*. New York: Holocaust Library, 1989.

This books presents translated extracts from reports compiled by the *Einsatzgruppen* regarding the murder of Jews in the German-occupied parts of the Soviet Union. A brief introduction summarizes the tasks and deployment of these killing units.

Bartov, Omer. *The Eastern Front, 1941–1945: German Troops and the Barbarization of Warfare*. New York: St. Martin's Press, 1985.

Based on the incisive perception that the German army was massively involved in criminal activities during the war against the Soviet Union, this book reconstructs the conditions facing German soldiers at the front, their background, and their susceptibility to propaganda. According to Bartov, "the barbarization of warfare" resulted from political indoctrination in conjunction with the brutality emanating from the war itself.

Breitman, Richard. *Architect of Genocide: Himmler and the Final Solution*. New York: Knopf, 1991.

Focusing on the role of *Reichsführer-SS* Heinrich Himmler, Breitman reconstructs the events surrounding the implementation of the "Final Solution." Based on extensive research, Breitman argues that the decision to kill all Jews had already been made in spring 1941, just months before the German army started to invade the Soviet Union.

Dallin, Alexander. *German Rule in Russia, 1941–1945: A Study of Occupation Policies*. London: Macmillan, 1988.

First published in 1957, Dallin's massive study still provides important information on German political planning and actual occupation practice.

Ehrenberg, Ilya, and Vasily Grossman, eds. *The Black Book*. New York: Holocaust Publications, 1981.

A collection of eyewitness testimonies, letters, diary entries, and assembled histories of towns or ghettos, including accounts by rescued Jews, collected for an extraordinary commission to investigate what had happened to Soviet Jews. The table of contents lists the Lithuanian accounts according to the manuscript, although they are not reproduced here.

Headland, Ronald. *Messages of Murder: A Study of the Reports of the Einsatzgruppen of the Security Police and the Security Service, 1941–1943*. Rutherford N.J.: Fairleigh Dickinson University, 1992.

A historical analysis of the reports compiled by the *Einsatzgruppen* in the occupied parts of the Soviet Union. While the book by Arad *et al. (above)* presents a selection of the reports, Headland investigates their significance for the understanding of key issues like the killing operations or the attitude of the local population.

Hilberg, Raul. *Documents of Destruction*. Chicago: Quadrangle Books, 1971.

The first comprehensive collection of contemporaneous German documents illuminating the overall structure of the "Final Solution" and key aspects of German policy.

Kaslas, Bronis J., ed. *The USSR-German Aggression against Lithuania*. New York: Robert Speller & Sons, 1973.

Klee, Ernst, ed. *The Good Old Days. The Holocaust as Seen through Its Perpetrators and Bystanders*. New York: Free Press, 1991.

A collection of eyewitness testimonies, diary accounts, letters, confidential reports, and photographs written and compiled by executioners, supporters, and witnesses of acts of atrocities during the Second World War.

Matthäus, Jürgen. "What about the 'Ordinary Men'? The German Order Police and the Holocaust in the Occupied Soviet Union." *Holocaust and Genocide Studies* 10 (Spring 1996): 134–50.

Mulligan, Timothy P. *The Politics of Illusion and Empire: German Occupation Policy in the Soviet Union, 1942–1943*. New York: Praeger, 1988.

Covering a wide variety of aspects involved in the topic, this book provides insight into the mechanisms and discrepancies of German occupation policy. The perception of how the German apparatus worked is essential for the understanding of the murderous events in the Soviet Union.

Porat, Dina. "The Holocaust in Lithuania: Some Unique Aspects." In *The Final Solution: Origins and Implementation,* ed. David Cesarani, 159–174. London: Routledge, 1994.

Porat identifies several elements in connection with the timing, scope, and setting of the murder that contribute to the "uniqueness" of the Holocaust in Lithuania. In doing so, she elaborates on some of the crucial aspects of the policy adopted by the Germans as well as the reaction of Lithuanian Jews and Gentiles.

Reitlinger, Gerald. *The House Built on Sand: The Conflicts of German Policy in Russia, 1939–1945*. New York: Viking Press, 1960.

Already immediately after the Nuremberg trials massive documentation was available on German occupation policy in the Soviet Union. Thus, Reitlinger's study is still useful, especially in regard to German political planning and occupation practice.

Chapter 2: Life and Survival

Dubnow, Simon M. *History of the Jews in Russia and Poland from the Earliest Times until the Present Day*. Translated by Israel Friedlaender. New York: Ktav, 1975.

Gitelman, Zvi. *Century of Ambivalence: The Jews of Russia, 1881 to the Present*. New York: YIVO Institute for Jewish Research, 1988.

Gitelman provides an extraordinary survey of cultural, political, and intellectual thought among Jews from the age of emancipation in Russia to the present, in an essay for a volume of photographs from YIVO.

Greenbaum, Masha. *The Jews of Lithuania: A History of a Remarkable Community, 1316–1945*. Jerusalem: Gefen Publishing House, 1995.

Written by an inmate of the Kovno Ghetto, this concise survey provides English-language readers with an overview of the history of Lithuania and the course of Jewish settlement there. At issue in this work is the gradual destruction of the Jewish presence at the hands of both Lithuanians and Germans.

Levin, Dov. *Baltic Jews under the Soviets, 1940–1941*. Jerusalem: Hebrew University, 1994.

A collection of essays on the effects of Sovietization on the Jewish populations in the Baltic States during the period of annexation. Several studies on Jews in the Soviet army during World War II and Jews in the immediate postwar period form a comprehensive view of the racial, economic, and political position of Jews under Soviet rule.

Levin, Dov. *The Lesser of Two Evils. Eastern European Jewry under Soviet Rule, 1939–1941*. Philadelphia: The Jewish Publication Society, 1995.

This recent study builds an Levin's earlier work and focuses on issues facing the Jewish population following the Molotov-Ribbentrop pact. The role of Jews in the Soviet army is treated extensively.

Levine, Hillel. *In Search of Sugihara: The Elusive Japanese Diplomat Who Risked His Life to Rescue 10,000 Jews from the Holocaust*. New York: The Free Press, 1996.

A biography devoted to the Japanese deputy consul, Chiune Sugihara, in Lithuania prior to Soviet annexation. The author offers historical and eyewitness accounts in the attempt to discover the underlying motives of Sugihara's rescue of Jews in summer 1940.

Lewin, Isaac. *Remember the Days of Old*. New York: Research Institute of Religious Jewry, Inc., 1994.

A personal memoir by this distinguished historian who, together with his family, escaped from Lithuania with Dutch visas for Curaçao and a Japanese transit visa.

Mendelsohn, Ezra. *The Jews of East Central Europe Between the World Wars*. Bloomington: Indiana University Press, 1983.

Lithuania is considered in depth in one chapter in Mendelsohn's comprehensive book on the political situation of Jews in east central Europe. The author studies the composition of Jewish political and economic groups in Lithuania and their interaction with the Lithuanian government during the prewar period.

Shochat, Azriel. "Jews, Lithuanians, and Russians, 1939–1941." In *Jews and Non-Jews in Eastern Europe 1918–1945,* ed. Bela Vago and George L. Mosse, 301–14. New York and Toronto: John Wiley Press, 1974.

Warhaftig, Zorach. *Refugee and Survivor: Rescue Attempts during the Holocaust*. Jerusalem: Yad Vashem, 1988.

Serving with the Palestine Commission, the author details his efforts to engage international support for refugees from Poland via Lithuania, the Soviet Union, and Japan.

Part II: Inside the Kovno Ghetto

Historical Studies

Arad, Yitzhak. "The *Judenräte* in the Lithuanian Ghettos of Kovno and Vilna." In *Patterns of Jewish Leadership in Nazi Europe 1933–1945,* ed. Yisrael Gutman and Cynthia J. Haft. Jerusalem: Yad Vashem, 1979.

Beinfeld, Solon. "Life in the Ghettos of Eastern Europe." In *Genocide: Critical Issues of the Holocaust,* ed. Alex Grobman and Daniel Landes, 173–189. Los Angeles: Simon Wiesenthal Center, 1983.

An excellent overview of the hardship and ordeals of ghetto life across eastern Europe with emphasis on the cultural life that emerged. The author treats the Kovno and Vilna ghettos in substantial detail.

Hilberg, Raul. "The Ghetto as a Form of Government." *The Annals of The American Academy of Political and Social Science* 450 (July 1980): 98–112.

Expanding on the findings of Isaiah Trunk *(below),* Hilberg identifies the characteristics and structural similarities of ghetto bureaucracies established by the Germans in Eastern Europe. In its summary of the dilemmas facing the Jewish councils, this article is crucial for the understanding of the pressures created by German anti-Jewish policy.

Porat, Dina. "The Jewish Councils of the Main Ghettos of Lithuania: A Comparison." *Modern Judaism* 13 (May 1993): 149–163.

Porat compares the ghetto leaderships in Shavli, Vilna, and Kovno and tries to determine the reasons why, among the three, the Kovno Ghetto remained in existence until summer 1944.

Trunk, Isaiah. *Judenrat: The Jewish Councils in Eastern Europe under Nazi Occupation*. New York: Stein and Day, 1977.

Authoritative and still unsurpassed study on the *Judenräte*, especially in Poland and Lithuania, and their struggle to facilitate Jewish survival in the face of German extermination policy. The focus is on the structure and behavior of the Jewish Councils and their subordinated agencies, e.g., police and welfare institutions, as well as on the strategies adopted towards the Germans and the attitude towards physical resistance.

Cultural Life

Blatter, Janet, and Sybil Milton. *Art of the Holocaust*. New York: The Rutledge Press, 1981.

Costanza, Mary S. *The Living Witness: Art in the Concentration Camps and Ghettos*. New York, 1982.

Roskies, David, ed. *The Literature of Destruction. Jewish Responses to Catastrophe*. Philadelphia: The Jewish Publication Society, 1988.

Religious Life

Oshry, Ephraim. *The Annihilation of Lithuanian Jewry*. 1958. Reprint, New York: Judaica Press, 1996.

An account by one of the few surviving rabbis of events in Kovno from before the establishment of the ghetto through its liquidation, with emphasis on the continuation of religious observance and education. The second half of the book treats 44 other towns in Lithuania with significant Jewish populations.

———. *Responsa from the Holocaust*. Translated from the Hebrew by Y. Leiman. New York: Judaica Press, 1983.

An edited, English-language version of Rabbi Oshry's monumental five-volume work *Sefer Sheilot u-Tshovot min ha-Maamakim* [Questions and responses from out of the depths (New York: Gross Brothers, 1959–79; in Hebrew). A collection of questions and Rabbi Oshry's learned, precedent-based responses, concerning how to adapt—or not to adapt—religious observance in the circumstances of ghetto life.

Rosenbaum, Rabbi Irving J. *The Holocaust and Halakhah*. New York: Ktav Publishing House, 1976.

This work describes the observance of Jewish religious law and its application during the Holocaust. Rabbi Rosenbaum discusses in depth the *responsa* of Rabbi Oshry from the Kovno Ghetto.

Resistance

Eckman, Lester, and Chaim Lazar. *The Jewish Resistance to the Partisans in Lithuania and White Russia during the Nazi Occupation, 1940–1945*. New York: Shengold, 1977.

Levin, Dov. *Fighting Back: Lithuanian Jewry's Struggle Against the Nazis 1941–1945*. Translated by Moshe Kohn and Dina Cohen. New York: Holmes and Meier, 1985.

Based on Levin's earlier monumental study in Hebrew (with Zvie A. Brown, *Toldotehah shel Mahteret. Ha-irgun ha-lohem shel Yehudei Kovnah be-Milhemet ha-Olam ha-Sheniyah* [The story of an underground. The resistance of Jews of Kovno (Lithuania) in the Second World War], Jerusalem: Yad Vashem, 1962), this revised volume offers to English-language readers an excellent survey of resistance and partisan activities in Lithuania.

Rescue

Paldiel, Mordecai. *The Path of the Righteous: Gentile Rescuers of Jews during the Holocaust*. Hoboken, NJ: Ktav Publishing House, 1993.

A collection of stories of rescue in all parts of occupied Europe, gleaned from the files in the registry at Yad Vashem, Israel's Holocaust memorial and museum.

Diaries and Memoirs

Birger, Trudi. *A Daughter's Gift of Love. A Holocaust Memoir.* Philadelphia: Jewish Publication Society, 1992.

    A survivor describes her ordeals as a young woman in the Kovno Ghetto and at the Stutthof concentration camp.

Faitelson, Alex. *Heroism and Bravery in Lithuania, 1941–1945.* Jerusalem: Gefen Publishing House, 1996.

    The story of resistance in the Kovno Ghetto, including an account of the escape from Fort IX.

Frome, Frieda. *Some Dare to Dream: Frieda Frome's Escape from Lithuania.* Ames: Iowa State University Press, 1988.

    A fifteen-year-old girl's story of escape from the Kovno Ghetto and her attempt to reconstruct her life in postwar Lithuania.

Ganor, Solly. *Light One Candle. A Survivor's Tale from Lithuania to Jerusalem.* New York: Kodansha International, 1995.

    A moving account of a young boy who survived the Kovno Ghetto and the Dachau concentration camp. Ganor's memoirs also include his meeting of the Japanese deputy consul, Chiune Sugihara.

Gordon, Harry. *The Shadow of Death: The Holocaust of Lithuanian Jewry.* Lexington: University of Kentucky Press, 1992.

    The candid ordeals of a young teen-ager who struggles to keep his family intact.

Mishell, William. *Kaddish for Kovno: Life and Death in a Lithuanian Ghetto, 1941–1945.* Chicago: Chicago Review Press, 1988.

    In a strikingly personal way, Mishell presents the well-written account of the ordeals of the ghetto and the fate of his colleagues in the Paint and Sign Workshop, the ghetto's graphics office.

Tory, Avraham. *Surviving the Holocaust: The Kovno Ghetto Diary.* Translated from Hebrew by Jerzy Michalowicz. Martin Gilbert, ed. With textual and historical notes by Dina Porat. Cambridge: Harvard University Press, 1990.

Part III: A Half-Century Later

Langer, Lawrence. *Holocaust Testimonies: The Ruins of Memory.* New Haven: Yale University Press, 1991.

Langer, Lawrence, ed. *Art from the Ashes: A Holocaust Anthology.* New York: Oxford University Press, 1995.

Littman, Sol. *War Criminal on Trial: The Rauca Case.* Toronto: Lester and Orpen Limited, 1983.

    The investigation and prosecution by the Canadian Department of Justice of Gestapo Sergeant Helmut Rauca, a central figure in the "Great Action" of October 28, 1941, in which some 9,200 Kovno Jews were "selected" for death.

For Young Readers

Neshamit, Sarah. *The Children on Mapu Street.* Translated from the Hebrew by David S. Segal. Philadelphia: Jewish Publication Society of America, 1970.

    A novel about how the war disrupted the lives of four children, once residents of Mapu Street in Kovno.

INDEX